TREES &
SHRUBS

HEARST
GARDEN
GUIDES

TREES &
SHRUBS

R. William Thomas, Editor

Principal Photography by

Andrew Lawson

HEARST BOOKS
New York

Library of Congress Cataloging-Publication Data

Thomas, R. William (Roger William)
    Trees and Shrubs / compiled from the Good Housekeeping illustrated
    encyclopedia of gardening; completely rev. by R. William Thomas;
    photography by Andrew Lawson.—1st U.S. ed.
       p.   cm.—(Hearst garden guides)
    Includes index.
    ISBN 0-688-10015-5
    1. Ornamental trees.   2. Ornamental shrubs.   3. Landscape
gardening.   4. Ornamental trees—United States.   5. Ornamental
shrubs—United States.   6. Fruit trees—United States.
I. Title.   II. Title: Good Housekeeping illustrated encyclopedia of
gardening.   III. Series.
SB435.T465   1992
635.9'77—dc20   92-5227 CIP

Printed in Singapore
First U.S. Edition
1 2 3 4 5 6 7 8 9 10

Produced by Smallwood and Stewart, Inc.
New York City

Editors: Charles A. de Kay and Ruth Lively
Designer: Michelle Wiener
Illustrator: Lisa Zador
Managing Editor: Robin Haywood

HEARST

GARDEN

GUIDES

CONTENTS

INTRODUCTION

This volume of the Hearst Garden Guides presents a selected list of the trees and shrubs best suited for home landscape and garden use. It combines the most commonly available species and cultivars with other interesting and unusual varieties that are well worth the extra effort to find.

PLANT CLASSIFICATION

Over the ages, plants have been classified in various ways. The ancient Roman writer Pliny the Elder, who used size and form as his criteria, set up three major groupings: trees, shrubs and herbs. In the Middle Ages, plants were classified according to whether they were medicinal, edible or poisonous. Later the great 18th-century Swedish botanist, Carl Linnaeus (1707–1778), used the number of stamens in plants as his basis for classification.

Such arbitrary systems are considered artificial today; and even though most gardeners continue to classify plants much as Pliny did, modern taxonomists have moved to a so-called natural system of classification in which plants are grouped according to their generic and evolutionary relationships. Under this system, related species of plants make up a genus. Related genera make up a family. Related families make up an order. Related orders make up a class. Related classes make up a subdivision (or subphylum). Related subdivisions make up a division (or phylum). Related divisions make up a subkingdom.

And the two subkingdoms make up the plant kingdom.

The following outline of the positions of the white oak and the white pine illustrate this method of classifying plants.

WHITE OAK	WHITE PINE
Kingdom *Plantae*	Kingdom *Plantae*
Division *Tracheophyta*	Division *Tracheophyta*
Subdivision *Pteropsida*	Subdivision *Pteropsida*
Class *Angiospermae*	Class *Gymnospermae*
Order *Fagales*	Order *Coniferales*
Family *Fagaceae*	Family *Pinaceae*
Genus *Quercus*	Genus *Pinus*
Species *alba*	Species *strobus*

Note that, in both examples, the names on the same line (except at the genus and species levels) have the same endings. This helps to identify the classification level of which a person may be speaking. Generally, division names end in "-phyta;" subdivision names in "-opsida;" class names in "-ae;" order names in "-ales;" and family names in "-aceae."

Nomenclature

Most familiar garden plants have a common name (or names) and a scientific name. Because the common names are in English, they are easier to pronounce—which is probably why most gardeners prefer them. Unfortunately, using only common names leads to much confusion. First of all, many plants have not one but several common names. For example, *Nyssa sylvatica* is called black

LEAF SHAPES

Simple

Simple

Secondary veins extend out from pronounced central midrib.

Pinnate

Secondary veins are fewer and fuller than those of simple leaf, forming distinct lobes.

Palmate

Several major ribs, including central midrib, flare out from tip of leafstalk.

Compound

Pinnate

In compound form, leaflets occur in pairs or staggered along a long central leafstalk.

Bipinnate

Double compound form on which pairs of pinnate leaves extend out from a central leafstalk.

Serrate

Leaf margin is finely-toothed.

LEAF SHAPES

Leaf Margins

Smooth

Leaf margin is smooth and regular.

Palmate

*In compound form, leaflets flare out from
a single point at end of leafstalk.*

Dentate

*Margin is more deeply-toothed than that
of serrate leaf.*

Conifers

Needle-like

*Long, thin, stiff leaves grow bunched (on pine
or larch tree) or in double rows (on spruce,
fir or hemlock).*

Awl-like

*Small, stiff leaves grow in tight points out
of twig; usually found on juvenile trees.*

Scale-like

Small, flat leaves lie flush to twig.

gum, pepperidge and sour gum. Frequently, two or more totally different plants have the same common name: ironwood identifies both *Carpinus caroliniana* and *Ostrya virginiana*. Occasionally, closely related plants have such different common names that their relationship is obscured: almond, peach, plum and cherry are all closely related members of the genus *Prunus*.

Because these problems made it difficult for people to communicate clearly about plants, 200 years ago botanists adopted a binomial system devised by Linnaeus, which identifies each plant more accurately by using two names—the genus followed by the species.

Both the generic and specific names are for the most part derived from Latin or Greek rendered into Latin. Both names are italicized or underlined when written; and the first (generic) name is always capitalized. Thus, the scientific name of the white oak is *Quercus alba* (which may be abbreviated *Q. alba* once the generic name has been spelled out in reasonably close context).

If a species of plant includes varieties or cultivars (defined below), that name is added directly after the specific name—in Latin for varieties or in English or Latin for cultivars. Thus, the naturally occurring variety of concolor fir is known as *Abies concolor* var. *lowiana*, but the nursery-selected cultivar is *Abies concolor* 'Compacta'.

Genus

In the classifications in the plant kingdom, a genus lies between a family and a species. A family may contain one or several genera; a genus may include one or several species. The genus *Cotoneaster*, for example, includes deciduous and evergreen shrubs, which are featured here, and a number of ground covers. All flower in shades of white or pink and have opposite, simple and entire leaves. All *Cotoneaster* species are members of the Rose Family.

Species

A species is the specific plants within a genus. All of the species within a given genus will be different but have one or more characteristic in common. In plant classification, a species (the word is both singular and plural) lies between a genus and a variety.

A genus may contain anywhere from one to over a thousand species. In turn, a species may encompass a number of varieties. Species, in contrast with most varieties, cultivars and hybrids, may reproduce themselves from seeds and may often be interbred; interbreeding among species of the same genus sometimes occurs naturally.

To the gardener, species are significant because they are specific types of plants. If one wants a fir tree, for instance, he or she would not order *Abies* (the generic name for fir trees), because there are about 40 different kinds of firs. Instead, gardeners must order a distinct species—an *Abies concolor* (a white fir), for example, or an *Abies lasiocarpa* (Rocky Mountain fir) for gardens further south. To be absolutely precise, varietal or cultivar names may be required as well. There is a very important variety of *Abies lasiocarpa*, for example, that survives better in the East than the species.

According to the accepted binomial system of plant nomenclature, the species name follows the name of the genus. In *Abies lasiocarpa*, *Abies* is the generic name, *lasiocarpa* the specific name. The varietal name, which might be, for example, *arizonica*—would be the third name.

Many specific names are descriptive of some feature of the plant; some, however, are derived from the names of the geographical regions where they were found or the names of individuals.

Variety

The lowest, or final classification of plants found in nature is the variety. Not all species have natural varieties, but most species have several. A

LEAF STRUCTURES

Alternate
*Arranged on a twig or shoot by only one leaf
per node.*

Opposite
*Arranged along a twig or shoot by pairs, with
the leaves of a pair on opposite sides.*

Whorled
*Arranged along a twig or shoot by groups of
three or more per node.*

variety retains the basic character of the species, but has one or more distinctive characteristics of its own. Varieties occur naturally, usually in populations, and exist whether or not people notice them. The flowers of the cucumber tree (*Magnolia acuminata*), for instance, are green, but there are a significant number in the wild that have yellow flowers. These are classified as *Magnolia acuminata* var. *subcordata* (yellow cucumber tree).

Cultivar

A new plant selected in cultivation, propagated (usually as a clone) and named is a cultivar. It exists only because people work to propagate it. For example, a nursery worker discovered that in a field of white pines (*Pinus strobus*), one individual was narrower in form than the rest. It was propagated through graftings (seedlings would have reverted to the normal form), and named *Pinus strobus* 'Fastigiata', thereby inventing a new cultivar.

Cultivars are noted by the abbreviation cv. or by single quotation marks (*Pinus strobus* 'Fastigiata' or *Pinus strobus* cv. Fastigiata), are always capitalized, and never appear in italics.

Hybrid

A hybrid is a plant resulting from the crossing of two specific plants. The process of hybridization is unusual in nature; most are developed as the result of human actions, either accidental or on purpose. A famous example of an accidental hybridization is the Leyland cypress (× *Cupressocyparis leylandii*). When Monterey cypress (*Cupressus macrocarpa*) from California and Nootka false cypress (*Chamaecyparis nootkatensis*) from Oregon were planted next to each other in a garden in England, the pollen from one fertilized the seed of the other, a seedling grew, and it became a hybrid genus. One of the seedlings of Leyland cypress was found to be more blue than the others. It was propagated (in this case by cuttings, since it rooted easily), named, and so became × *Cupressocyparis leylandii* cv. Naylor's Blue.

Hybrids are noted with a multiplication sign or "×." The symbol precedes the genus when the genus itself is a hybrid. It is written between the generic and specific names if the species is a hybrid. Cultivars *can* be (but are not always) selected from hybrids.

2

GARDEN DESIGN

By common definition, a tree is a woody plant with a single or several trunks, usually over 15 ft. in height and a shrub is usually multi-stemmed and under 15 ft. in height. These are very broad definitions and it is often impossible to clearly define the difference between a small tree and a large shrub. Maples, for instance, are usually considered trees. However, *Acer grinnala* (Amur maple), which can grow to 20 ft. with a single trunk, is often multi-stemmed and can be grown as a shrub. Conversely, most viburnums are thought of as shrubs, but *Viburnum sieboldii* (Siebold viburnum) can be trained to a single trunk and will grow over 20 ft. tall.

LANDSCAPING WITH TREES

Cultivation requirements aside, form is the first consideration in landscaping with any plant. Trees vary in form, ranging from narrow upright shapes, such as Italian cypress or Irish yew to rounded globes, such as ash or sugar maples. They also vary in size from tall and wide to narrow and relatively short. The entries in the encyclopedia (Chapter 4) list the average ultimate heights and widths expected in American gar-

dens. Depending on the conditions in the garden—soil, climate and so forth—a particular tree may grow much larger or smaller.

As the largest plants in a garden, trees have the greatest visual impact. They define spaces, screen and frame views, and form the ceiling of the garden. So, the locations of trees should be selected before designing for the shrubs and smaller plants.

Trees can be used in masses and as specimens. When designs call for an individual specimen, make sure it is allowed to stand out and that no other tree is planted within the tree's potential crown spread. Flowering trees make good specimens but ideally a specimen tree should have a very distinct form, such as the weeping varieties that can be enjoyed all year round.

In a mass planting, young trees may be planted much more closely together. As the trees grow older, their branches will grow together. Trees to consider include those that are often seen growing together in the wild, *Acer saccharum* (sugar maple) and *Pinus strobus* (Eastern white pine), for example. While some of these trees may have forms graceful enough to warrant planting as a specimen (such as the sugar maple), they are so popular in the region that it is unnecessary to single them out. Sugar maples are also useful in mass plantings because of their brilliant fall foliage, which is set off particularly well against a backdrop of evergreens. Other trees to consider are those that lack a distinctive form, but have ornamental qualities, such as fall color, to offer. For best results, stay with simple designs using only three (or fewer) species of trees. Too many different types can lead to an unsettled feeling in the garden.

Choosing the Best Sized Trees

When selecting trees for a garden, notice the relationship between the size of the total area of the garden, the size of the house (which is an essential part of the garden) and the size of the trees at maturity. Suppose the house seems too large for its setting. Large trees will dominate the scene, reduce the apparent size of the house and soften the overall feeling.

With smaller homes, large trees can lend a cottage feeling. Smaller trees, conversely, may help the house look more impressive and larger. Trees that are too small, however, may make the house look even smaller and out of scale.

If there is a fine old specimen shade tree on the property, such as a large oak, let it determine the scale of the garden. A huge tree demands a large-scale plan. The trick in this case is to design the garden as though it were a small part of a very much larger property. To achieve this effect, first screen off all boundary lines with boldly curved banks of shrubs; they will help enclose the garden. If possible, allow the lawn area to flow visually into the lawn area of a neighbor's property at some point. One way to achieve this is to let the open lawn meet the neighbor's open lawn, without dividing lines of hedges, fences, or even different heights of the lawn. This technique visually borrows from the neighbor's property so that the garden seems larger than it really is.

Other Criteria for Selecting Trees

Deciduous trees are fundamentally different from evergreens in their form, seasonal behavior and life cycle. Because they do not lose their leaves, evergreens remain essentially one color and retain their form year round. They are particularly effective as hedges, boundary markers, windbreaks and sound barriers. They block light as well as view, wind and sound. But as well as creating a sense of privacy, they cast shade year round. Avoid planting evergreen trees or shrubs where they will grow to cast too much shade on flower beds.

Always consider the tree's height and width at maturity when determining the area it will shade. This is much less of a problem with specimen plantings than with mass plantings or hedge plantings. *Cedrus* (cedar) and the varieties of *Picea pungens* form *glauca* (Colorado blue spruce) are among the many favorite evergreen trees for specimen plantings. *Tsuga* (hemlock) and *Pinus strobus* (Eastern white pine) are often used in mass plantings.

Deciduous trees, on the other hand, visually open up an area after the leaves turn in fall, so that the view changes with the season. Deciduous trees change color—from the first leaves in early spring to bursts of brilliant red, orange and yellow in fall—and form—from skeletal winter shapes to the full bushy shapes of midsummer. Many deciduous trees have showy flowers and fruits, so that they are preferred for the variety of color they bring to the garden.

Some ornamental fruit trees can be messy, so careful consideration should be given to the planting site. Avoid planting them where dropping fruits or nuts will create problems, such as near a patio, swimming pool or parking area. Other trees, such as *Salix babylonica* (weeping willow) are invasive and can damage underground septic systems.

TREE SHAPES

Broad Cone

Fagus *(beech)*, Ilex aquifolium *(English holly)*, Pseudotsuga menziesii *(Douglas fir)*.

Vase

Ulmus americana *(American elm)*, Lagerstroemia indica *(crape myrtle)*, Amelanchier *(serviceberry)*.

Open Head

Populus *(poplar)*, Quercus alba *(white oak)*, Platanus occidentalis *(sycamore)*, Celtis *(hackberry)*.

Column

Ilex opaca *(American holly)*, Liquidambar styraciflua *(sweet gum)*.

Globe

Fraxinus *(ash)*, Acer saccharum *(sugar maple)*, Magnolia grandiflora *(southern magnolia)*.

Fastigiate

Cupressus sempervirens *(Italian cypress)*, Carpinus betulus *(European hornbeam)*.

Weeping

Betula pendula *(European white birch)*, Salix babylonica *(weeping willow)*.

Horizontal

Malus *(crabapple)*, Cercis *(redbud)*, Gleditsia *(honey locust)*, Cornus *(dogwood)*.

Flowering Trees

The shimmer, blaze and dazzle of a tree in full flower is a beautiful sight in any garden. Even when the blossoms are gone, the tree remains in all its leafy glory and some, like the crabapple and hawthorn, also have handsome fruit following the flowers. (Keep in mind also that fruit display can last much longer than a floral display.) Some, like *Oxydendrum* (sourwood) and *Crataegus phaenopyrum* (Washington hawthorn), have spectacular foliage in the fall. And there are those, like *Cornus* (dogwood), that have all three—marvelous flowers, fruit and fall color.

No matter where they are located, trees in flower will dominate the landscape. But to dramatize the impact of early blooming trees, plant them in front of evergreens, which will provide a dark green contrast.

A flowering tree, if planted to be seen through a window, will brighten the whole room, and, on the street, will do the same for a neighborhood.

Ornamental Fruits & Berries

Late summer and fall berry and fruit displays are also important aspects of good garden design. While most trees and shrubs are selected for their flowers, fruit should actually be considered as the most important feature because berries usually are showy for several months, while flowers usually last less than two weeks. With some species that bear inconspicuous or not-too-showy flowers, the fruit is the only consideration. The cotoneasters, pyracanthas and some of the hawthorns are examples of this. Mountain ashes and crab apples are examples of trees with important fruit displays.

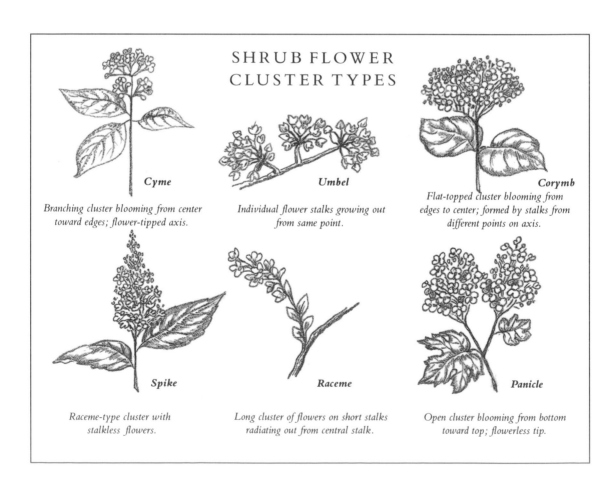

SHRUB FLOWER CLUSTER TYPES

Cyme

Branching cluster blooming from center toward edges; flower-tipped axis.

Umbel

Individual flower stalks growing out from same point.

Corymb

Flat-topped cluster blooming from edges to center; formed by stalks from different points on axis.

Spike

Raceme-type cluster with stalkless flowers.

Raceme

Long cluster of flowers on short stalks radiating out from central stalk.

Panicle

Open cluster blooming from bottom toward top; flowerless tip.

FLOWERING TREES

Spring

Amelanchier (shadbush). Billowy clusters of white flowers in early spring followed by great fall color.

Cercis (redbud). Rose-pink or white clusters of bloom.

Cornus (dogwood). These trees have it all—form, flower, fruit, foliage, fall color.

Crataegus (hawthorn). Showy white flowers, attractive fruits, and good fall color.

Halesia (silver-bell). Pendant bells of creamy white hang in clusters on slim, graceful branches.

Laburnum (golden-chain tree). Dramatic drooping clusters of yellow flowers.

Magnolia (magnolia). Provide a magnificent show of pink or white flowers (also, atypically, dark wine or yellow). Among these are the earliest of flowering trees.

Malus (flowering crabapple). Healthy cultivars of this genus are the cold-hardy rivals of dogwood for form, flowers, and fruits.

Prunus (flowering cherry and plum). Flowers pink or white; shapes varying from wide-spreading to weeping.

Summer

Albizia julibrissin (silk-tree). Fernlike foliage and powderpuff flowers of pure pink.

Cornus kousa (Japanese dogwood). White flowers (bracts) are much like *C. florida*, but produced a month later; also display attractive fruits and fall color.

Koelreuteria paniculata (golden-rain tree). Bright yellow flowers in upright clusters on a relatively small tree.

Magnolia grandiflora and *M. virginiana* (magnolia). Fragrant, showy white flowers throughout most of the summer.

Oxydendrum (sourwood). Flowers like lily-of-the-valley on a small tree. Superb red fall color.

Sophora japonica (Japanese pagoda tree). Flowers of creamy yellow festoon branch ends and are followed by pale green seed pods.

Stewartia (stewartia). Showy white flowers. Often with attractive bark and fall color.

Styrax (snowbell tree). The fragrant white bell-like flowers are carried beneath graceful limbs.

Syringa reticulata (Japanese tree lilac). Showy groups of cream-colored flowers on a shapely small tree.

Late Summer and Fall

Franklinia alatamaha (Franklin tree). Small upright tree with cup-shaped bright, white flowers.

Lagerstroemia indica (crape myrtle). Colorful (white, pink, purple and red) clustered flowers.

Fall Color

It is as important to select plants that will give foliage color in the fall as to select them for their flowers. The glory of dogwood leaves, the burning flame of the sugar maple and the brilliance of a euonymus highlight the garden long after flowers have gone. This bright display of scarlet, orange and yellow is nature's annual parting gift to the garden. Evergreens mixed with the flashes of brilliant color tend to make the colors even more effective.

What causes fall color in deciduous plants? The following is an extremely simplified explanation. A substance called chlorophyll, continually produced in leaves, makes them green. This green pigment masks all other pigments present in the leaves. In fall, as the plant goes dormant, chloro-

phyll begins to break down. Then the yellow or red pigments have a chance to assert themselves.

Yellow pigments need nothing extra to be produced. Certain trees are genetically bound to turn more yellow than others while some have the genetic ability to produce red pigments. However, these pigments require sugars in order to form. Sugars are produced through photosynthesis, which requires light and water. Trees growing in the shade, therefore, rarely produce red fall color. Likewise, a drought in fall can result in a yellow display. The best weather for red pigments is cool, sunny days and cold evenings that barely dip below freezing. Temperatures that are too low will kill the leaves. Cool temperatures reduce the rate of respiration, allowing the sugars to last longer.

TREES FOR FALL COLOR

Yellow

Cercidiphyllum japonicum (Katsura tree)
Cercis canadensis (Eastern redbud)
Cladrastis lutea (American yellowwood)
Firmiana simplex (Chinese parasol tree)
Ginkgo biloba (maidenhair tree)

Gleditsia triacanthos var. *inermis* (thornless honey locust)
Halesia (silver-bell)
Larix (larch)
Liriodendron tulipifera (tulip tree)

Red or Orange

Acer griseum (paperbark maple)
Acer saccharum (sugar maple)
Amelanchier (shadbush)
Cornus florida (flowering dogwood)
Cornus kousa (Japanese dogwood)
Crataegus (hawthorn)
Franklinia alatamaha (Franklin tree)

Liquidambar styraciflua (Sweet gum)
Metasequoia glyptostroboides (dawn redwood)
Nyssa sylvatica (sour gum)
Quercus alba (white oak)
Quercus coccinea (scarlet oak)
Sorbus (mountain ash)
Taxodium distichum (bald cypress)

STREET TREES

Trees planted along streets and boulevards need to be given generous root space because root area is diminished by the roadway and sidewalks. The better the soil and the greater space given to roots, the healthier (and thus more beautiful and safe) the trees will be. Recent research indicates that planting trees in clusters or groves in a large planting bed, rather than as individuals in small beds, is a way of giving more root space to the trees.

Where buildings are set well back and there is no obstruction, large, spreading trees may be used. Where buildings are close to the roadway, tall, narrow trees are more useful. Overhead wires or other obstructions call for low-growing trees that are high enough for pedestrian headroom below, yet low enough to not interfere with the wires. Some good trees that remain low are: *Acer buergeranum, A. campestre, A. ginnala, A. griseum, A. palmatum, Amelianchier, Chionanthus, Cornus kousa, Halesia diptera, Ilex opaca, Juniperus virginiana, Malus* and *Syringa reticulata*. Today an important consideration is tolerance of city conditions, such as soil compaction, air pollution, salt spray in winter and reflected heat and light from buildings and pavement. Freedom from insect pests and diseases is another desirable characteristic. Nonfruiting trees may be more desirable than those that drop seeds,

berries or other fruits on sidewalks and roadways. Not all fruiting trees have to be avoided, however. For instance, many of the small-fruited crabapples (*Malus* spp.) are successful street trees because birds eat the fruits, keeping them from becoming litter problems.

Large trees
Some successful, large street trees include *Acer rubrum* (red maple), *Celtis* species (hackberry), *Fraxinus americana* (white ash), *Ginkgo biloba* (maidenhair tree), *Gleditsia triacanthos* cultivars (thornless honey-locust), *Gymnocladus dioica* (Kentucky coffee tree), *Liquidambar styraciflua* (sweet gum), *Magnolia grandiflora* (southern magnolia), *Tilia* species (linden), *Pinus* species (pine), *Platanus occidentalis* (sycamore) and many of the *Quercus* species (oaks) and *Cornus alternifolia* (pagoda dogwood).

Small & Moderate Trees
Some favored trees maturing at a relatively modest stature include *Acer campestre* (hedge maple), *Acer buergeranum* (trident maple), *Acer grinnala* (Amur maple); *Carpinus* (hornbeam); *Cornus* (dogwood); *Malus* (crabapple); *Syringa reticulata* (Japanese tree lilac); *Crataegus* (hawthorn); *Halesia carolina* (Carolina silverbell); *Koelreutia paniculata* (goldenrain tree); *Prunus* (cherries); *Pyrus* (pears).

SELECTING AND CULTIVATING CRABAPPLES

Malus species are versatile, small, ornamental, deciduous trees. In the spring they produce very showy flowers and then in the fall they delight with attractive red or yellow fruits. The crabapples bloom in the time between the early flowering cherries (*Prunus subhirtella* and *P. yedoensis*) and the late cherries (*P. serrulata*), filling an important void in the spring-flowering display. The fruit display, however, is even more important to some people because the fruits can be impressive from Sept. through March whereas the flowers only last about ten days. The fruits of many crabapples also attract birds to the garden.

The trees are often grown as individual specimens, but may be used in mass where there is sufficient room. Urban foresters are increasingly finding this genus useful for street trees, of value due to their small size, their wide range of forms and their ornamental flowers and fruits. Most are tolerant of city conditions.

Crabs are relatively easy to grow, especially if care is taken before planting to choose pest-resistant species and cultivars. They should be grown in full sun and well-drained soil. They are quite hardy and very important in northern landscapes. They are less useful in the South. University of Georgia Professor of Horticulture, Michael Dirr, rates *Malus floribunda*, *M. sargentii*, *M. sieboldii* var. *zumi* and *M. 'Callaway'* as the best crabapples for the South.

Crabapples are popular in most areas of the country in which winters are cold. Almost everyone who has studied crabs in any way has his or her own list of favorites. A good way to choose crabapples for your own garden is to visit public gardens and notice the best plants. When is the best time of the year to do this "shopping?" No, not in spring. Almost every crabapple is beautiful in flower, so bloom should be a secondary consideration.

September is a good time to visit. Look for trees that are attractive, still have clean, green leaves, and no sign of disease. Look also at fruit display. Fruits should be showy by this time. If you are really interested in studying the subject before determining the plants for your garden, return in December. The best trees will still have attractive fruits.

Also look at the ground around the trees. Avoid crabs that have a lot of fruit on the ground. The best trees for most landscapes have small fruits that are "bite-size" for birds. The fruits on these trees should stay colorful on the plant through much of the winter until they are finally consumed by birds. Large-fruited crabs are usually a mess in the winter. If the landscape where you will be using the treees must be as clean as possible, you may even want to choose a crab that is fruitless.

The very last step in the selection process is to view the plants in bloom. Take your list of favorite plants and look at them in mid-spring when the trees are in bloom. Make sure the flower color is acceptable for your garden. If you have not already checked the correct form, do that at this time.

Members of the genus transplant easily. Young trees can be transplanted bare root.

Care should be taken to not let the roots dry out. Never let bare root plants sit exposed in the sun. They should be kept in the dark, with moist sphagnum moss or soil around their roots. Soaking the roots in a bucket of water for up to eight hours is beneficial. However, do not soak for more than eight hours, because the roots will start dying due to the low oxygen level of the water.

Crabapples can also be transplanted balled-and-burlapped (B & B), with a ball of soil around the roots. This technique is used for any large treees, generally those with a basal diameter greater than 1¼ in. (this basal diameter is actually measured either 6 or 12 in. from the soil level and is called the tree's caliper.)

Malus are bothered by many pests. Some of the most severe insects and diseases include apple scab, fire blight, rust, aphids and wooly aphids. With crabapples, the fruits are small enough that one need not worry about the additional pests that attack the fruits, which are the biggest problem for commercial apple growers.

Thankfully, members of the genus vary greatly in their resistance to insects and diseases. There are sufficient numbers of pest-resistant cultivars that there is absolutely no need to plant one that has problems with pests. The local extension service can supply you with names of the best crabapples for your area. Some of the ones to avoid in any part of the country are the disease-susceptible cultivars 'Alney', 'Hopa', 'Eleyi', 'Bechtel', 'Strathmore' and 'Red Silver'.

Fertilizer and water can be used to increase the rate of growth. If the growth rate is sufficient, do not bother with fertilizer. Otherwise, use balanced or low-nitrogen fertilizers at dilute levels several times during the year.

The flowers of *Malus* species are perfect, a botanical term meaning that the individual flowers have functional pistils and stamens (the female and male parts of the flower). Theoretically, each flower could pollinate itself. In reality in-breeding is avoided because the flowers are self-sterile. More than one type of crabapple is needed to pollinate the flowers. Commercial, or eating apples, will generally pollinate crabapples.

If there are no other apples or crabapples nearby, it will be necessary to plant more than one cultivar. One could have a planting of 200 crabapples, all of one cultivar and have lovely flowers but no fruit set. But a planting of only two trees, of different names (and genetic makep), will result in wonderful fruit set. Crabapples are insect-pollinated.

The first rule of pruning crabapples is "don't" if you do not have to. The trees are lovely without any pruning (except for an occasional crossing branch) and one can often do more harm by pruning than by not pruning. The key here is to plant the correct form for the available space.

If you are dealing with an existing tree that has the wrong form, it may be best to remove that tree and plant a new one. Crabs grow quickly, and if you try to change the natural form of a crabapple, you will spend the rest of your gardening life modifying the form.

Further suggestions for cultivating varieties and detailed information on the diseases and pests that can plague these plants appears in the encyclopedia on pages 129–131.

RECOMMENDED CRABAPPLES

Round

Selection	Height	Flowers	Fruit	Disease Resistance	Zones
Malus 'Adams'	20 ft.	carmine fading to pink	small, red, through winter	high	4-7
Malus 'Beverly'	20 ft.	white	small, bright red	moderate to fire blight	4-7
Malus 'Donald Wyman'	20 ft.	white	small, bright red, shiny, through winter	high	4-7
Malus floribunda Japanese Flowering Crabapple	20 ft.	pale pink fading to white, red buds	small, not showy, amber turning brown, loved by birds	moderate to fire blight & scab	4-8
Malus 'Indian Summer'	20 ft.	red, fading to pale pink	small, bright glossy red, through winter	moderate to scab, rarely defoliates prematurely	4-7
Malus x robusta Cherry Crabapple	40 ft.	single or semidouble white	yellow or red, can be messy	high	4-7
Malus spectabilis Chinese Crabapple	30 ft.	single or double, blush pink	1 in., yellow	high to fire blight, sometimes bothered by scab	5-8

Spreading

Selection	Height	Flowers	Fruit	Disease Resistance	Zones
Malus baccata var. jackii	35 ft.	white, very fragrant	small, bright red	moderate to fire blight	3-7
Malus 'Dolgo'	40 ft.	white	large, egg-shaped, messy, bright red, excellent for jelly	high	3-7
Malus 'Molten Lava'®	15 ft.	white	small, bright red, liked by birds	moderate to scab & fire blight	4-7
Malus 'Ormiston Roy'	25 ft.	white, pale pink buds	small, yellow with red flush, through winter	moderate to fire blight	4-7
Malus 'Prairifire'	20 ft.	bright pinkish-red	small, maroon, through winter	high	4-7
Malus 'Professor Sprenger'	25 ft.	white, pink buds	small, orange-red, through winter	high	4-7
Malus 'Profusion'	27 ft.	deep purplish-pink	small, reddish purple	moderate to powdery mildew	4-7
Malus 'Red Jewel'®	18 ft.	white	small, bright glossy red, through winter	low to scab & fire blight	4-7

RECOMMENDED CRABAPPLES

Spreading *(continued)*

Selection	Height	Flowers	Fruit	Disease Resistance	Zones
Malus 'Sugar Tyme'®	15 ft.	white, pink buds	small, glossy, bright red, through winter	moderate to fire blight	4–7
Malus 'White Angel'	20 ft.	white	small, bright red, through winter	low to scab & fire blight	4–7
Malus x *zumi* 'Calocarpa' Redbud Crabapple	25 ft.	white, red in bud	small, dense clusters, bright red, through winter, liked by birds	moderate to fire blight	4–7

Columnar

Malus 'Centurion'	25 ft.	rose red	⅜ in., cherry red	high	4–7
Malus hupehensis Tea Crabapple	27 ft.	fragrant, pink, turning white	small, yellow with red tinge	low to fire blight	4–7
Malus 'Liset'	15 ft.	rose red	½ in., not showy, dark red	moderate to powdery mildew	4–7
Malus yunnanensis var. *veitchii*	20 ft.	white	small, purple	moderate to fire blight	5–8

Weeping

Malus 'Anne E.'	15 ft.	white	small, bright red	high	4–7
Malus 'Candied Apple'	15 ft.	pink, single	small, cherry red	low to scab	4–7
Malus 'Louisa'	15 ft.	pink	small, yellowish with a flush of red	high	4–7
Malus 'Red Jade'	12 ft.	single white, sometimes with pink flush	½ in., egg-shaped, red, through winter	moderate to scab, fire blight & powdery mildew	5–7

Shrub

Malus 'Coralburst'™	8 ft	coral pink in bud, opening to double rose-pink	orangy red, not found very often	moderate to scab	4–7
Malus 'Jewelberry'	8 ft.	white	½ in., glossy red	high	4–7
Malus sargentii Sargent Crabapple	10 ft.	white	tiny, deep red, through winter	high	4–8

LANDSCAPING WITH SHRUBS

Evergreen shrubs are important in the landscape because they provide color all year round. Many broad-leaved evergreen shrubs have spectacular periods of bloom as well as permanent foliage. Deciduous flowering shrubs lose their leaves in the winter, but often have attractive fall color and offer bursts of color in the garden through brilliant flowers and/or fruits. They also bloom with considerably less investment in labor than herbaceous flowering plants.

Deciduous Flowering Shrubs

Useful in flower beds and borders, deciduous flowering shrubs offer low maintenance and versatility. Once planted they require little attention beyond periodic pruning, and there is a deciduous shrub for every season. *Camellia, Corylopsis* (winter hazel), *Forsythia* and *Hamamelis* (witch hazel) bloom in early spring; *Chaenomeles* (flowering quince), *Philadelphus* (mock-orange) flower in spring; a wide range of deciduous shrubs, including *Buddleia* (butterfly bush), *Clethra* (sweet pepperbush) and *Potentilla*, produce summer flowers; *Hydrangea paniculata* 'Grandiflora' (the "PeeGee" hydrangea) and *Lagerstroemia indica* (crape myrtle), to name just two, have beautiful late summer blossoms; and *Erica arborea* (tree heather) and *Lonicera fragrantissima* (fragrant honeysuckle) will brighten any winter with their flowers.

Many deciduous flowering shrubs are also attractive when not in flower. Several, such as *Callicarpa* (beautyberry), have very ornamental fruit; while others like *Ilex decidua* (the deciduous holly) have fruit that persists for a display in the winter garden. *Cornus sericea* (red-osier dogwood), has colorful red bark during winter, *Euonymus elata* (winged euonymus) has attractive quirky wings on its branches and *Exochorda* (pearlbush) has bark that peels off in showy strips.

Broadleaf Evergreen Shrubs

For year-round beauty and usefulness, no other shrubs compare with the broadleaf evergreens. Well-known examples include species of *Berberis, Buxus, Cotoneaster, Daphne, Euonymus, Ilex, Leucothoe, Kalmia, Pieris* and *Rhododendron*. Most broadleaved evergreens do best in relatively mild, moist climates; they generally require an annual rainfall of 30 in. or better—such as is found in the eastern one-third of the country and along the west coast—and grow best with a permanent leaf mulch above their roots. Some of the major

---

S H R U B S   F O R   F A L L   C O L O R

Yellow

Hamamelis (witch hazel)

Parrotia persica (Persian parrotia)

Chionanthus virginicus (fringetree)

Clethra alnifolia (summer-sweet)

Red or Orange

Cotinus coggygria (smoke tree)

Enkianthus (enkianthus)

Euonymus alata (corkbush)

Euonymus alata 'Compacta' (corkbush)

Fothergilla (fothergilla)

Photinia villosa (photinia)

Rhododendron schlippenbachii (royal azalea)

Viburnum (viburnum)

broadleaf evergreens are:

BARBERRY (*Berberis*) is a large genus of thorny but boldly attractive shrubs. Their flowers are yellow; the fruit is blue or red. Barberries are tough barrier plants that can be unpopular because of their spiny stems and leaves. They thrive in full sun or shade and are quite adaptable to soils. They do need good drainage, however. When allowed to grow freely, they develop a rounded symmetrical shape. All of them tolerate shearing very well.

BOXWOOD (*Buxus*), when allowed to grow freely, makes a magnificent billowing display of soft green foliage, or it can be shaped through shearing to any form. This handsome evergreen takes well to the rigors of life in a city garden. It grows well from Florida to New England, but the less hardy forms may be damaged by a cold winter. Box grows best in rich, well-drained soil that is not too acid. It responds beautifully to shearing.

HOLLY (*Ilex*) has attractive glossy green leaves, black or red berries and distinctive texture. It makes an attractive contrast with other shrubs. All evergreen species of this genus are prized for their striking foliage, tolerance of shearing and, many, for their attractive red fruit. Most hollies tolerate sun or shade and a wide range of soils (although some have trouble with alkaline soils). *Ilex crenata* (Japanese holly) is often grown as a hedge or a foundation plant and it is used as a substitute for boxwood in some gardens. *Ilex glabra* is similar, but has larger leaves and is tolerant of wet conditions.

MOUNTAIN LAUREL (*Kalmia*) has striking clusters of buds and flowers in tints of white to pink. Well-grown mountain-laurels have extremely attractive foliage. The very best conditions for the mountain-laurel are not always to be found in the average garden. It prefers a well-drained, acid soil.

LEUCOTHOE (*Leucothoe*) has graceful, arching branches with long leathery leaves in shades of purple, bronze and green (the purple and bronze come in winter). Pinkish to white bell-shaped flowers are borne in fragrant clusters. *Leucothoe fontanesiana* (drooping leucothoe) does best in the shade but will tolerate full sun if the soil is adequately moist and the plant is protected from the wind. Winter sun brings out a rich bronzy-purple foliage. For optimum growth of flowers and foliage, plant it in slightly acid soil. It will grow to about five feet in height and width. With its spreading habit and arching stems, it is excellent for mass effects.

OREGON-GRAPE (*Mahonia aquifolium*) is distinguished for bright yellow flowers in spring. This beautiful upright shrub is a close relative to the barberries and adapts itself to acid or alkaline soil. It grows quite well in either sun or shade. In the northern parts of its range, it does best with wind and winter sun protection. It is especially effective in a mass planting, where the yellow flowers, shiny, compound foliage and blue berries make an impressive showing.

PIERIS (*Pieris*) has pendant clusters of light green buds that turn to waxy white flowers and new bronzy leaves that turn deep green. *Pieris japonica* (Japanese andromeda) is a showy and adaptable plant. Although it will take full sun, it does best in light shade and slightly acid, well-drained soil. When healthy, it is beautiful in every season. The graceful form of the mature plant is wonderful as a specimen or when used in groups as a mass planting.

FIRETHORN (*Pyracantha*) is tough, growing in sun or shade primarily for its dazzling display of orange-to-red berries in the fall. Grow on a wall or trellis or as an individual specimen. It will grow in slightly acid or slightly alkaline soil. It blooms and berries best in full sun, but will also tolerate shade. It can be trained as a tall climber or as a conventional shrub. The showy berries vary in size and color depending upon the species and cultivar. They range from yellow to orange-red to red.

RHODODENDRON and azalea (*Rhododendron*), which come in countless forms and shades of color, have extremely showy foliage and clusters of flowers. With hundreds of species and hybrids, this great genus is one of the most popular of all shrubs. Rhododendrons perform best in light shade, in soil that is moist but well drained and at least slightly acid. It is always best to give them some protection from the wind and hot sun. *Rhododendron catawbiense* (Catawba rhododendron), a native of Virginia and Georgia, is a handsome representative and grows in a wider range of conditions than most.

VIBURNUM (*Viburnum*) is a genus of spectacular deciduous and evergreen shrubs. The evergreens are most useful in Zones 6 southward and typically have bold, coarse leaves, white or pinkish flowers and strongly colored fruits. Viburnums are remarkably tough plants. *Viburnum rhytidophyllum*, the leatherleaf viburnum, is tall-growing and coarse-textured. Grow it in sun or shade with good drainage and a slightly acid soil. Prague viburnum (*V.* × *pragense*) is finer textured, with shiny green leaves. Both have showy flowers.

Shrubs and Trees for Hedges

A hedge is a living fence that in a garden will provide a background, screen out a view, keep out people or animals, break the wind, enclose part or all of a property, create privacy or border a walk, flower bed or terrace.

Many hedges are clipped, but often a very satisfactory effect is possible by choosing a shrub that is naturally the right shape and size and leaving it unclipped. Such informal hedges are much less costly in terms of maintenance.

Fothergilla major (large fothergilla), *Physocarpus opulifolius* 'Nana' (dwarf ninebark), *Syringa meyeri* (dwarf Korean lilac) and *Viburnum carlesii* 'Compactum' (dwarf Korean spice viburnum) all make good informal hedges without shearing.

Almost any shrub could be a formal clipped hedge, but some are better than others, depending on the desired effect. Some deciduous species, such as privet, are inexpensive, grow fast and are quite satisfactory. They obviously do not make a solid screen in winter, but the mass of twigs can be thick enough to lend a feeling of enclosure.

Slower growing, more expensive shrubs may seem like a disadvantage when faced with purchasing enough plants for a long hedge. However, slower growing plants may actually be less expensive in the long run because they require less shearing. *Euonymus alata* (winged euonymus) is one of the finest deciduous clipped hedges and has the added benefits of glorious fall color and interesting twigs.

All of the deciduous shrubs resprout on old wood. This means that if a mistake is made in shearing, such as too deep a cut, or a damaged hedge, proper pruning can restore it to its former beauty.

Evergreens, such as *Ilex* (holly), *Taxus* (yew), *Thuja* (arborvitae) and *Tsuga* (hemlock), have the advantage of providing year-round screening. Holly, yew and arborvitae will resprout on old wood, just as the deciduous shrubs will. Yew puts on two growth spurts each summer, requiring two prunings (in June and late July) for perfect form. It is often best to wait until after the second flush of growth in mid-summer for a once-a-year shearing.

Thorny plants, notably *Berberis* (barberry), *Crataegus* (hawthorn), *Pyracantha* and *Poncirus trifoliata* (hardy-orange) shear well and are used when the main goal is to keep out intruders.

Deciduous shrubs are usually sold with bare roots. To plant them, dig a trench at least 12 in. wide and no deeper than the spread of the roots of the plants. Set the plants at 1 to 2 ft. intervals. Spread the roots out in the trench and fill around them with good soil into which a generous quantity of organic matter has been incorporated. Firm the soil and water and cut all the stems back to 4 in. stubs. During the first season water especially well and control weeds through mulch or hand-pulling. Fertilizer will help increase the growth rate of a new hedge. Each time new growth is 4 to 6 in. long during the summer cut them back to half to encourage branching.

Evergreens for hedges should be purchased balled and burlapped. Although they, too, can be set into a trench, it is easier to dig individual holes about 2 to 3 ft. apart. This spacing may be wider if the plants are large to begin with or if the hedge will be a tall one. Plant at the same depth or higher than they previously grew and do not begin to clip them until they are making strong growth.

No matter what species of plants are used in a hedge, they should always be trimmed so they are wider at the bottom than at the top. This assures that the lower branches receive enough light to leaf out and grow. If a hedge is allowed to become wider at the top than at the bottom, growth at the base soon becomes sparse and then usually dies out altogether.

If the situation calls for a definite line and mass, choose something that can be clipped to the desired shape and kept that way. Fine-textured plants are usually better choices for formal hedges than are large-leaved, coarse-textured shrubs.

Flowering shrubs such as forsythia and azalea can be grown as clipped hedges and still bloom if the shearing is done soon after the shrubs bloom so that flower buds can form for the next season.

For all other hedges, prune, clip or shear in the spring, midsummer, late fall and winter, as is necessary to keep them in shape. To avoid the danger of winterkill of new, soft growth, do not prune between midsummer and mid-fall. Do not allow a young hedge to attain its desired height too quickly. Keep it compact by frequent pruning and allow only a small part of the new growth to remain on each time. This will result in a full hedge that is attractive and dense from top to bottom.

W I N D B R E A K S

A dense arrangement of woody plants will break the force of the wind on both sides of the planting. A windbreak can be used to protect other plants from heavy winds, to prevent blowing and drifting of snow, soil or sand, or to protect a living space such as a terrace or play area. Good windbreak plants must tolerate wind, be densely branched from bottom to top, and can be evergreen or deciduous. Genera for windbreaks include

Abies, Acanthopanax, Acer, Aesculus, Caragana, Castanea, Catalpa, Ceanothus, Celtis, Cercis, Chaenomeles, Cistus, Cornus, Crataegus, Elaeagnus, Euonymus, Fraxinus, Ginkgo, Gleditsia, Gymnocladus, Juniperus, Larix, Ligustrum, Lonicera, Maclura, Morus, Myrica, Picea, Pinus, Populus, Prunus, Pseudotsuga, Pyrus, Quercus, Rhus, Ribes, Robinia, Salix, Viburnum.

HOLLY IN THE GARDEN

Hollies have been valued for their evergreen foliage and red berries since prehistory. The druids of Britain and France worshipped holly trees. Romans gave cut branches as gifts of goodwill and the Chinese traditionally used holly for decorations at New Year's celebrations.

Today, hollies are grown as both ornamental landscape plants and as cutting plants for branches of foliage and berries. In gardens, both evergreen and deciduous species of *Ilex* are important as specimens, screens and hedges, while commercial nurseries and orchards are the primary growers for cut branches.

Another reason for the popularity of this genus is the relative ease with which the plants can be grown. One can find a species (or several) to thrive in most parts of the country, except the Midwest and the Southwest. If hardiness is a problem, sheltering plants from the wind and winter sun will usually increase the chances of survival. The number of useful species diminishes as one goes northward and southward. Two of the best for the South are *I. vomitaria* and *I. cornuta*. Hardiest in the north are *I. verticillata*, *I. rugosa*, *I. opaca* and some of the Meserve hybrids. Most hollies will tolerate sun or shade, and some species will even grow well where drainage is poor.

The two most popular evergreen species of holly are *I. aquifolium*, the English holly, and *I. opaca*, the American holly. These two have what is considered "perfect" holly leaves, edged with prickly spines. English holly is usually preferred because it has shiny foliage. American holly is hardier and has dull green leaves.

I. crenata, Japanese holly, has evergreen leaves that do not have spines, but almost unnoticeable teeth around the edge. Plants are quite similar to boxwood and are frequently used in the same way. The last of the most commonly seen hollies is a deciduous one, *I. verticillata*. This is certainly the most popular of the species that lose their leaves in the autumn. It is grown for its magnificent fruit display. *I. serrata* and *I. decidua* are very similar species.

This group is remarkably easy to prune. All shear well and can be used as formal hedges and even topiary. Great Britain is filled with holly hedges, including plantings of mixed colors (green-leaved with yellow-leaved cultivars). Light shearing can also be done with young plants to encourage fuller growth. All species have attractive natural forms and very satisfactory results are possible with very little pruning. The general rule is to cut back to a bud, branch or to the trunk (this is the basic concept for pruning almost anything).

Hollies will resprout on old wood, which means one can cut back very hard and the plant will recover. This is useful to know when renovating old plants and for repairing "holes" in hedges and topiaries. New growth usually occurs just below where the cut was made. Light is required for these new shoots, so the top should always be kept thinner than the bottom.

All hollies transplant best with as little disturbance to the roots as possible. This usually means with a ball of soil (known as "balled-and-burlapped" or "B & B") or using a container-grown plant. The deciduous species can be moved with bare roots while dormant and leafless, but even with these species success is better if moved with soil around the roots. Evergreen hollies can be moved in spring or early fall.

Pests do attack hollies, but the severity of attack is a judgment call. Most of the pests do not greatly disfigure the plants, much less kill them. The deciduous species, which are sometimes cut for their decorative fruit-covered branches, usually are pest free.

Pests that attack hollies vary with season and part of the country. In many areas, leaf miner and holly berry midge are two of the most severe problems. Holly leaf miner is an insect that tunnels through the leaves, resulting in individual leaves that resemble highway maps. The holly berry midge grows inside the berries and prevents them from ripening. Therefore the berries are green during the winter and not bright red or yellow. Both insects generally are most severe on American holly.

Other pests, such as spider mites, scale insects, leaf spots, canker and nematodes, can be local problems. If the problem is severe enough to warrant controls, the extension service and some nurseries and garden centers can help with the most up-to-date pesticide recommendations. Removal of infected leaves and fruits often reduces the level of infection.

Hollies react well (with increased and fuller growth) to fertilization. Almost any fertilizer will work; repeated appplications of a small amount are preferable to heavy annual applications. Mulching with an organic material, also will improve the health of most hollies.

Hollies are insect-pollinated, meaning that the plants only need to be within a bee's flight of each other. Supposedly males can pollinate females as far away as a mile. For best results, however, it is safest to plant both males and females in your garden. Generally one male is sufficient for a number of females (some experts recommend one male for every five females, but there is no definite rule).

Some of the finest plantings of holly are in public gardens. The Scott Arboretum in Swarthmore, Penn., has a large and well-labeled collection of hollies. In Washington, D.C., the U.S. National Arboretum is an excellent place to visit. Williamsburg, Va., uses hollies as specimens, hedges and clipped topiary.

It is a large, rich genus, well deserving use in our gardens. Its popularity in modern landscapes continues a long, venerable history in the garden.

CHOOSING AND CULTIVATING RHODODENDRONS

The large family of rhododendrons has a great deal to offer to the gardener. In sun or shade, few shrubs are showier than rhododendrons and azaleas. Flower color varies from white to pink to red to purple to orange, and some are nicely fragrant. The earliest begin to bloom in late winter and the last species may still be blooming on the first day of autumn. Evergreen species are valued for their winter effect and many of the deciduous forms have attractive autumn foliage. For complete descriptions of specific types, see Chapter 4.

Rhododendrons and azaleas are used in shrub plantings singly as specimens or, more frequently, in masses. Occasionally they are used for cut flowers. Small-leaved azaleas shear well and can be used as hedges. Sizes range from less than one foot tall to almost treelike.

The best growing conditions for the genus in the U.S. are found in the East and in the Pacific Northwest. The plants will tolerate sun and shade, but shade is advisable in warmer climates. Shelter from wind is usually beneficial. Soil is the major limiting factor in growing these plants. Hardiness, often considered a major problem, is actually much less limiting than soil. There are species that will grow in some of the coldest parts of the country and new hybrids greatly expand the range of available colors in the North. However, there are none that will tolerate highly alkaline soils.

Rhododendrons and azaleas grow best in acid, well-drained moist soil. In areas with unsuitable soils, there are alternate solutions. In all cases, ample moisture is essential and supplemental weekly irrigation may be necessary. One option is to grow the plants in containers. The container should have drainage holes and the potting soil should be acidic with a high percentage of organic matter. The "P.J.M." hybrids introduced by Western Nurseries are considered some of the best rhododendrons for containers.

Another alternative is to mound organic matter and acidic soil above your normal soil. This improves drainage and provides better soil for the roots. A third alternative is to amend the garden soil itself. Additions of organic matter, such as compost or peat moss as well as acidic soil amendments should help. The more organic matter there is in the soil, the less important is its relative alkalinity.

Rhododendrons and azaleas are usually transplanted balled-and-burlapped (with a ball of soil around the roots) or as containerized plants. Young deciduous plants may be moved bare root. Most members of the genus have brittle roots that are easily damaged. Try to disturb the roots as little as possible. Never carry the plant by its stem, but always support it from below. Do not let the root ball dry out and do not overwater, since flooding will suffocate the roots.

Do not dig the planting hole any deeper than the roots (it is better to plant them in a hole that is too shallow than too deep). Loosen the soil horizontally as much as you have the time and inclination for. This is because the roots do not go very deep, but instead usually stay within the top ten in. of soil. Loosening the soil will make the soil more conducive for root growth.

An addition of an organic mulch will help control weeds, keep the soil cool, and reduce moisture loss. Excellent mulches include composted oak leaves, pine needles and almost any compost that has not been supplemented with lime.

Transplant rhododendrons and azaleas any time of the year except when the plant is actively growing. During this time, the young leaves are very sensitive to wilting. Generally, one should not move the shrubs after they have started growth in late spring, until the new growth has hardened in late summer. This timing can be ignored if the plants are container-grown or were dug, balled-and-burlapped before growth started. Such plants can be planted anytime.

Young plants generally require no pruning. If a young or old shrub is leggy and you want to make it fuller, pruning back the main stems will help. Cut back to a bud, leaf or branch. New growth occurs just below where the cut was made.

Many gardeners deadhead (remove spent flower clusters) just after the blossoms fade. Deadhead by cutting or breaking off the old flower clusters. This action prevents the development of fruit capsules and seeds. It makes the plant look neater, wastes no energy making seeds and often improves the number and size of next year's flowers. It is dull work, however!

Pests are usually not very important on otherwise healthy plants. If insects or diseases are attacking a plant, check first to determine if the soil conditions are correct.

Often, correcting soil problems will improve the health of the plant so dramatically that pests may disappear.

There are public gardens throughout the country offering beautiful displays of rhododendrons and azaleas. They are often worth a visit when determining which type to grow at home. On the West Coast, there are the Strybing Arboretum in San Francisco, Ca., the Rhododendron Species Foundation outside of Seattle, Wash., and the University of Washington Arboretum in Seattle. The University of Minnesota Landscape Arboretum near Minneapolis and the Morton Arboretum, outside of Chicago, both have beautiful collections. The Chicago Botanic Garden is actively studying the plants and publishing cultivation recommendations. The Holdon Arboretum near Cleveland, Ohio, has hybridizer David Leach's collection. The Secret Arboretum in Wooster, Ohio, has been testing the genus for a number of years. Heritage Plantation in Sandwich, Mass., was the garden of hybridizer Charles Dexter. Winterthur Gardens, outside of Wilmington, De., and Callaway Gardens near Atlanta, Ga., have two of the most beautiful displays. The Scott, Morris and Tyler Arboretums, in and near Philadelphia, Penn., and the Birmingham Botanical Gardens in Ala. have fine collections.

Rhododendrons and azaleas are native throughout much of the Appalachian Mountain range, with the highest concentration in the Smoky Mountains. Few gardens can compare with the splendor of these wonderful natural stands. These settings are also excellent places to study the conditions under which rhododendrons and azaleas grow best.

FOUNDATION PLANTING

Foundation plantings usually consist of grouped evergreen shrubs and other permanent plants set around the base of a house. Visually these plants hide the foundation line and link the structure to the greens and browns of grass and soil. This sort of planting is used much more often than it should be: It is needed only if the house's foundation is ugly. Otherwise, lighter plantings, especially using fewer plants in general and specifically, fewer evergreens, will produce a much more attractive landscape and one that has a better chance of blending into the garden itself.

A common mistake made with small, young plants is to use more than are necessary and to plant them too close to the house. Within a few years, the plants grow out of proportion with nearby plantings or with the scale of the building. Use of acid-requiring plants, such as rhododendrons, in soil that is basically alkaline (due to leaching from the concrete foundation) is another common problem and results in the need for constant maintenance of soil acidity or eventual replacement of the plants.

The light requirements of the plants must be taken into account: on the north side, plant only specimens that flourish in shade; and for the south side, select those that grow best in full sun and can endure the high temperatures caused by the reflection of the sun from the building's wall. The warmth and protection offered by a south wall can be an advantage, since they allow the gardener to try specimens that cannot normally survive your zone's north winds and winter cold. Sometimes plants that are barely hardy within the general area will thrive in such a protected spot.

LOW HEDGE PLANTS

Buxus microphylla (Japanese box) cultivars are quite hardy and make good, fine-textured, evergreen hedges.

Buxus sempervirens var. *suffruticosa* (dwarf box) is the traditional edging box. It can have disease and hardiness problems, but remains the hedge by which all others are judged. Other cultivars of box, such as 'Vardar Valley', are tougher plants but have a different texture and color.

Euonymus alata 'Compacta' (dwarf winged euonymus) needs annual clipping to keep it low; it can be kept at heights from 1 ft. to 8 ft. Its foliage turns bright red in the fall.

Ilex crenata (Japanese holly) can be pruned as low as 1 ft. and is a good substitute for box as it has small boxlike, evergreen leaves.

Salix purpurea 'Nana' (dwarf blue-leaved arctic willow) has grayish blue-green foliage; these plants grow from 1 ft. to 6 ft. tall.

Taxus cuspidata 'Nana' (dwarf Japanese yew) makes good low, evergreen edging. Clip it as low as 1 ft.

chapter

3

PLANTING & CULTIVATION

The most important day in the life of a tree or shrub is the day it goes into the ground. If it is planted in the wrong climate, in the wrong kind of soil, or if is improperly planted, its future will be brief. But when the right specimen is set in the right place in the right way, it will flourish for years; trees planted in the 1700s still thrive in eastern U.S. gardens. One of the great joys of planting a tree is knowing that it is a legacy for future generations. Planting a young tree is a way of repaying previous generations for the trees they planted.

PLANTING BASICS

Begin with a nursery-grown plant from a reputable seller. To encourage the growth of fibrous roots, the tree—or shrub—will have been root pruned at least a year in advance of moving. This new root growth will reduce the shock it experiences when it is transplanted. The plant will be bare-root, in a container, or balled and burlapped. All three types are acceptible for planting but bare-root plants should only be planted during the dormant season. Container and balled-and-burlapped plants can be moved any time the soil can be dug. Fall planting is excellent wherever the winters are not too harsh. This includes zones 6 and warmer, although success is possible in even

colder areas. Consult with the professionals at a local nursery for suggestions.

A container-grown or balled-and-burlapped tree should be planted as soon as possible, although it should store well until planting if it is kept in the shade and watered regularly. Dig the hole no deeper than the root ball, but as wide as possible. (In arid areas, consult local nursery professionals for specific planting advice.)

Planting depth is controversial but important. Current research in gardens points to many problems with trees and shrubs planted too deeply, especially if the soil is heavy. Planting too deeply is less a problem in light, sandy soils. Often, trees come from nurseries where the soil was mounded up around the trunk and may already be several inches too deep in the ball of soil. If the tree is at its proper depth, the roots will start just below the top of the root ball. If it is too deep in the soil, they may be several inches below the top and the tree should be planted correspondingly higher.

The second reason not to dig the hole too deeply is that the loosened soil will settle in the year after planting. Thus, even if the tree is planted at the soil level, it will end up below grade if the hole was dug too deeply.

Loosening the soil and adding organic matter

around the hole is important. The young tree's roots rarely grow much deeper than the original root ball. Most of the roots grow out horizontally so that treatment of the soil level below the root ball is not of much help.

Remove sticks, stones and other debris from the hole. Put the topsoil in one pile, the clay and gravel in another, and any turf or other plant material in a third (this pile can be dumped directly on the compost heap). When ready to plant the tree, lay a length of 2-by-4 across the hole, to establish the ground level. Set the root ball so the juncture of trunk and soil is an inch or so above ground level.

If the plant is balled and burlapped, fill in about half of the hole first with topsoil and tap the soil to firm it. This amount of soil should hold the tree in place. Now loosen the burlap and unfold it from the top so that it will be completely covered by soil. However, if the burlap is synthetic or treated to resist rot, it should be removed from the hole. Untreated burlap, indentifiable by its tan color, will readily rot when buried, so it can be left in the planting hole. Fill in the rest of the hole with any of the remaining soil. Do not bury any lawn grass or leaves deeper than several inches because they will ferment and release toxic compounds into the soil.

Container-grown plants should be treated in a similar manner. Remove the plant from the container. If it is root-bound the container will be filled with roots growing in a circular direction. In such cases, cut or spread out the roots to keep them from continuing to grow in a circular direction. If allowed to continue growing around each other, the roots will not spread out and the plant may eventually die. Cut the roots with a knife on four sides of the root ball, remove the bottom half inch of the root ball, or slice one-third of the way up from the bottom (essentially butterflying the root ball).

Fertilizer (low nitrogen) can be added to the soil, but make sure it is well mixed in and does not come into contact directly with the roots. Finish the back fill of soil by forming a raised rim around the root ball just at the edge of the roots of the tree (rather than at the edge of the hole). This rim will hold water and allow for easier watering.

With bare root plants, the condition of the roots can be easily seen. Remember the roots are living and can dry out (and die) quickly. Never leave them sitting out, exposed to the sun and wind. Keep the roots covered with moist soil, sphagnum moss, or burlap until planting. Before planting, trim off broken roots. If there is time, soak the roots for four hours in a bucket of water. Avoid longer soaking, which can drown roots from lack of oxygen. Build a mound of soil in the center of the planting hole such that the roots can be set on it and the first roots will be about two inches above the hole's top rim. Fill in half of the hole with soil and pack the soil carefully around the roots. Avoid large air holes, but do not overly compact the soil. Then fill in the rest of the hole with soil, build a rim as with the other methods, and water.

CARE & MAINTENANCE

Water the tree immediately after planting and then, for the first year, whenever the top inch of soil is dry. Always water slowly so the moisture will seep in. Try to run the hose slowly enough that it can run for half an hour without flooding beyond the rim.

Avoid staking the young tree unless it seems to be in danger of tipping over. Staking inhibits the growth of strong roots and trunks and the guy wires and stakes can physically injure the tree.

In very windy locations, however, staking may be necessary. One method is to attach the tree firmly by guy wires to three solid stakes just beyond the area of the hole. Another is to use two or three wooden stakes spaced equally around the tree, several feet away from the hole, and attached with wires.

Use strips of tire or hose to keep the wires from chafing the tree. Leave the wires in place only as long as is necessary, usually not more than one year. A girdling wire or loop can kill the limb around which it draws tight. Wires that girdle at the base of the tree will kill the entire tree. The fact that a guy wire, for example, is enclosed in a piece of rubber hose is of little advantage if the whole thing becomes a strangling noose when trunk diameter increases.

Water and fertilizer are the best tools. Generally, frequent applications of low levels of fertilizer are better than infrequent heavy applications. Spring and fall are excellent times to apply fertilizers but in northern areas, avoid fertilizing between mid-summer and early fall. Organic fertilizers, such as composted manures, are perfect, but chemical fertilizers can be used. If using chemical fertilizers, apply ones that contain nitrogen, phosphorus, and potassium to promote root and top growth. The nitrogen level should be no higher than that of the other two elements.

Since most of the feeder roots of a tree are near the surface of the soil, it is not necessary to deep feed. Broadcast the fertilizer over the root zone, or use a crowbar to punch a ring of shallow holes and fill the holes with a mixture of fertilizer and organic matter. The roots of the tree often extend well beyond the edge of the branches, so be sure to fertilize at least to the edge of the branches.

A tree's worst pest is the human race. We remove all the leaves and natural mulch that fall to the ground. We cut the roots that are in the way of ditches and building foundations. We pave over the roots, change the grade, and compact the soil with heavy machinery so air and water can't penetrate the soil to the roots. We build fires under the branches and damage the leaves, or put a charcoal cooker so close to the bark that it damages the living cells. And, most frequently, we hit the base of the tree with a lawn mower and damage the bark. This weakens the tree, allows pests to attack healthy wood, and may kill the tree if the trunk is damaged all the way around.

The best control of tree problems is to avoid damaging the tree. Generally by the time trees show stress, it is too late to do anything other than mourn the eventual loss of the plant.

Pruning of young trees can prevent later structural problems. However, more harm is done by improper pruning than by not pruning. If you do not know how to prune, either hire someone to do it or skip it. Most trees will develop very well with no pruning at all.

Fertilizers and Mulches

A common misconception is that fertilizers are foods. Often, even well-educated professionals speak of "feeding plants." This is unfortunately misleading about a very basic fact. Whereas humans do not produce their own food within their bodies and must be fed, plants produce their own food through photosynthesis. What plants get from the soil is not food, but physical support (for the roots, which anchor the plant), water (a key ingredient used by the plant to make food), and nutrients. The nutrients are what some people call plant food. Nutrients are used by plants in the process of building their tissues and growing.

Three nutrients are used in larger amounts than the others. They are nitrogen (abbreviated by its chemical symbol N), phosphorus (P), and potassium (K). These are often called macronutrients, in contrast with micronutrients, which are needed by plants but in much smaller amounts. Some fertilizers also have micronutrients added, sometimes listed as minor elements.

Complete fertilizers have all three macro-nutrients. In general, nitrogen encourages the growth of the top of the plant. Excess nitrogen inhibits flowering and fruiting. Lawn fertilizer, for example, is high in nitrogen, to encourage top growth in lawn grasses. Phosphorus and potassium encourage root growth and flowering (which in turn encourages fruiting), respectively. Use high nitrogen fertilizers to encourage leafy growth on a plant. Use low nitrogen fertilizers when flowers and fruit are important.

The most commonly advertised fertilizers are chemical fertilizers, so called because they are produced in a factory. Unlike organic fertilizers, which are produced by plants or animals and vary in their chemical analysis, the only nutrients chemical fertilizers add to the soil are those listed on the bag. Organic fertilizers usually contain extras, such as micronutrients and organic matter, improve the quality of the soil by encouraging the growth of beneficial organisms. Overuse or misuse of chemical fertilizers, on the other hand, has a detrimental effect on beneficial soil microflora.

Most fertilizers use three numbers to indicate the relative composition of the three macro-nutrients. The first number lists the percentage of nitrogen; the second, of phosphorus; the third, potassium. Thus, 10-10-10 fertilizer, a typical complete fertilizer, is composed of 10% of each of the three basic nutrients. The remaining 70% is filler. An example of a low nitrogen, complete fertilizer is 5-10-5.

The pH of the soil refers to how acidic or alkaline the soil is. The term pH stands for potential of hydrogen, and is a measure of the hydrogen ions in the soil. The more hydrogen ions present, the more acid the soil. How the numbers are actually determined is more complicated than we can cover in this book, but it is helpful to know

that a pH of 7 is considered neutral. A pH of 6.5 is slightly acidic and is ideal for for most garden soils. A pH of 5 is considered very acidic; 8, very alkaline.

For every plant there is a pH range in which it grows best. Some plants are more exacting in the pH range they require than others. For instance, broadleaf evergreen trees and shrubs thrive in soil which is slightly more acidic than normal. Potentillas, on the other hand, will happily tolerate somewhat alkaline soil.

In the past, gardeners would measure the pH literally by tasting the soil! A sour tasting soil was acidic; a sweet tasting soil, alkaline. Some gardeners still discuss sweet and sour soils. Today, the pH is measured with a chemical test, which is much easier on the mouth. Home soil testing units can be used, or samples can be sent into the state for testing (contact the county Department of Agriculture extension service or the land grant university in your state). Soil tests can also determine the levels of nutrients in the soil but if everything is growing well and healthy, there probably is no need to have a soil test. If leaves that should be green are yellow, a soil test may help. But never try to change the soil pH without first having a test done.

A few last comments about fertilizers. Heavy applications of fertilizer can damage roots. It is much better to apply small amounts of fertilizer over a long period of time rather than applying a lot all at once. If a plant is over-fertilized (this is easily done with chemical fertilizers, especially high nitrogen ones), use extra water to help flush the burning, excess salts from the soil. Generally, it is wise to water more after fertilizing.

A mulch can also help the growth of plants. Mulch is, essentially, anything put on the top of the soil that reduces water loss and suppresses weed growth, while not damaging the plants. Organic mulches, such as compost, straw, hay, wood chips and bark, which slowly break down and become part of the soil are most preferable. They add to the content of the soil and act as very weak fertilizers.

Inorganic mulches include plastic and stones. These often work satisfactorily in the short run, but at some point they usually need to be removed (plastic, for instance, begins to get holes in it and lets weeds through). Removal is usually more work than the initial installation.

Pest Control

Entire books are written on pest control for trees and shrubs, identifying the pests (which are most often insects and fungi) and the various ways of controlling them. Often pests are a symptom of other problems, which, if solved, will also eliminate the pest. Several kinds of stress can increase a plant's susceptiblity to insects and diseases. Planting a tree or shrub outside of its hardiness zone, planting it where there is poor drainage or soil compaction, planting too deeply, giving it too much or too little water, or injuring its bark or branches are forms of stress that usually will be followed by an attack of pests. Instead of immediately spraying a pesticide to eliminate the pest, first study the situation to try to identify and eliminate one or more causes of the stress.

If control measures are necessary, either because the sources of stress cannot be eliminated or correction will take time, short term help may be necessary. Always try the least toxic method first. If an insect is causing the damage, find out whether there is a predator that can be released to attack the insect. If not, sprays of horticultural soaps and oils often can provide sufficient control. If more toxic sprays are called for, it is probably time to call in professional help. Many pesticides cannot be sold except to licensed professionals. Regardless of who does the application or which are used, the local extension agent can be a great help in recommending treatment. Reputable, full service garden centers and nurseries also can be of help.

THE ART OF PRUNING

The purpose of pruning ornamental trees and shrubs is to correct present and avoid future problems. If a plant is in poor health it may be cut back to remove diseased or dead portions and to encourage fresh, healthy, new growth. With orchard trees and shrubs, where fruit production is the goal, pruning is done to increase the yield crop.

Generally, selective cutting of individual branches is meant by "pruning," but shearing a hedge is also a form of pruning. So are disbudding, pinching, and cutting flowers for the house.

In order to prune properly, it is essential to understand how plants grow. New growth comes from buds. Buds on most plants are at the tips of stems, or along the sides of stems and at the base of the plant. Wherever there is a leaf, a bud will form in the leaf axil. To encourage a bud to grow make a pruning cut just above it or at the base of a branch. The bud will usually start to grow in the direction it is pointing. If the plant has opposite buds, that is two buds across from each other, both buds will usually grow.

Make clean, diagonal cuts with a pair of sharp pruning shears or knife. The face of the cut should slope away from the bud; the stub above the bud should be as short as possible without injuring the bud itself.

Larger pruning cuts usually involve the entire removal of a branch. In this case, make the cut with a pruning saw or with long handled lopping shears. Cut just above the branch collar, which is the swelling at the base of the branch. Pruning just beyond the branch collar actually leaves a small stump, but the wound will heal more satisfactorily and quickly.

When pruning a shrub or a tree, first remove any dead or diseased limbs. Next remove any crossing branches, choosing to remove the ones that interfere the most with the tree or the ones with the narrowest (and therefore, weakest) crotch angles. If a number of branches are clustered together, remove one or several of them to help strengthen the overall structure of the plant. Finally, look the plant over and remove any other limbs that detract from the form of the tree or shrub. When you are through, the plant ought to have a natural shape and preferably will look as if it had not been pruned at all.

Never top a tree. When a tree needs pruning that you cannot do from ground level, call in a professional arborist. He or she will selectively remove branches back to the trunk or to another branch. The limbs will be carefully dropped to avoid injury to the tree, people, vehicles and buildings. When finished, the overall shape of the tree should be as natural as it was in the beginning.

Keep several points in mind as you prune; they should guide your thinking, and, accordingly, your pruning tool.

1. Pruning during the dormant season results in a vigorous burst of growth the following spring. Pruning during early summer tends to inhibit much replacement growth. Thus, if your goal is to reduce the size of the plant, you will be most successful pruning during the summer.

2. Use the proper tool for the job. If you are using a pruning or lopping shear and have difficulty making the cut, the branch is too big for the tool.

3. Make all cuts clean and just above a bud or just beyond the branch collar when removing an entire branch. This may actually leave a small stub.

4. Do not use tree-wound dressing. Research has shown that wound dressing does not promote

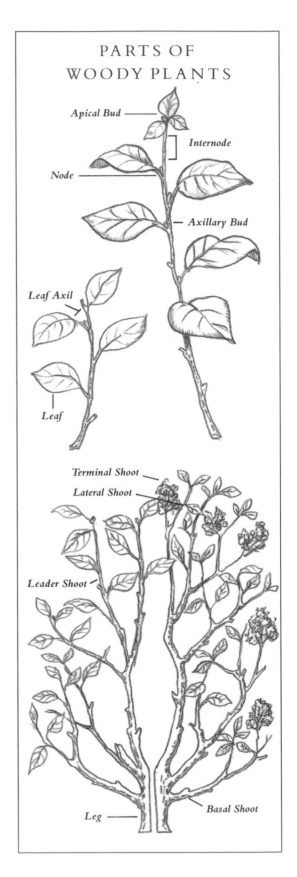

PARTS OF
WOODY PLANTS

Apical Bud

Internode

Node

Axillary Bud

Leaf Axil

Leaf

Terminal Shoot

Lateral Shoot

Leader Shoot

Basal Shoot

Leg

healing and can actually inhibit the healing of wounds.

5. When removing a tree limbs of any size, do it in steps. Attempting to cut off the entire branch at once will often damage the bark of the trunk. Make at least three cuts in a heavy branch to remove it. The first cut should be a fourth or a third of the way into the underside of the branch, about 8 in. from the branch collar (saw from the bottom upward). Start the second cut on the upperside of the limb, an inch out from the undercut. Once it is cut slightly more than halfway through, the branch should break off leaving a long stub. Now remove the stub just beyond the branch collar.

6. For aesthetic rather than tree-health reasons, you may wish to prune so bleeding is kept to a minimum. Several genera of trees, notably maples, birches, beeches and walnuts, will lose sap from the wound if pruned in winter or early spring. To avoid this bleeding, which does not harm the tree but is a bit unsightly, prune in the summer when growth has almost stopped.

7. If the plant that you are pruning is diseased, dip the pruning tool in denatured alcohol or in a weak solution of bleach after every cut you make.

ARBORICULTURE

Arboriculture is a general term to describe any work that is done on large trees. A good rule to follow is that if pruning cannot be done from the ground, a professional should be called in to do the work. The arborist should be certified and insured. Pruning, whether necessary to remove a live branch, a dead branch or a storm-damaged branch, requires great care to avoid further damage to the tree itself, to people under the tree, as well as to buildings and vehicles in the vicinity.

Reinforcing or cabling is sometimes necessary when a heavy branch or trunk threatens to split off from the rest of the tree. This is particularly likely to happen when a large branch forks into a Y. Narrow crotch angles are structurally weak and likely to split eventually. If the branch is too important to remove, even too important to thin to reduce its weight, cabling may be necessary to help hold the tree together.

Cavities in trees are among the most difficult wounds to cope with. Standard practice used to be to clean out the cavity and fill it with concrete. Recent research has proved that such "cleaning out" can actually cause a great deal of damage. Trees compartmentalize wounds and in doing so, prevent rot from attacking living wood. The wood in the center of the tree is dead, surrounded essentially by a shell of living tissue. The main concern is to keep the living tissue healthy. The old standard cleaning of wounds has been found to cut through the shield the tree makes around a wound, which allows fungi to attack living wood. Therefore, making any cuts through rotting wood into living, healthy wood is definitely not recommended. Concrete replaces the strength that would have been supplied by the heartwood, but when the tree dies, you have a pillar of concrete in its center, which may make removal very difficult. You will have to rely on the advice of your professional arborist in such matters.

Evergreen Trees and Shrubs

Evergreen plants do not lose all their foliage in the fall but retain their leaves the year round. However, all evergreens, like all deciduous plants, do lose their leaves periodically. Some species of the pine genus, for example, lose their needles after two growing seasons. Other evergreens retain their leaves for periods ranging up to five years.

You can prune evergreens during any season, as long as you cut back to a branch or bud. Heavy pruning is best done in late winter or early spring, before new growth starts, because the new growth will fill in holes that you may have made. This timing is recommended more for aesthetic reasons than for the health of the tree. Fairly heavy trimming is safe in winter for the holidays.

Specimen hemlocks, firs, spruces and Douglas firs should be left untouched if possible. Otherwise prune with hand shears, cutting back to a branch or bud. Or shear immediately after the new growth has been produced. Hedge shears can be used, but do not go deeper than the new growth and complete the pruning before the new growth has hardened.

Pines are the most tricky of the evergreens to prune. All of their buds are produced at the end of the branch so that when it is cut all the buds are removed. New buds will not be produced elsewhere on the branch and the branch will die, although the death of the branch will not take place until the needles naturally drop off, which may take several years. Therefore, all pruning of pines must be back to a branch or to the trunk.

The only exception to this pine pruning rule is just after the new growth has started in spring. Buds expand into new shoots, which are called "candles." Generally there is a central candle surrounded by a whorl of several slightly smaller ones. These candles can be cut or broken (they are very brittle and break easily) at any point and new buds will form at the tip of the broken candle.

Yews are probably the easiest conifer to prune. New growth will start wherever cuts are made and the plants can take heavy pruning at almost any time of year. Junipers can be cut back severely, but it is best to always leave some foliage on a branch because they do not always grow new foliage from old wood.

Deciduous Flowering Shrubs

Some pruning of deciduous flowering shrubs every other year will help avoid a massive overhaul job in the future. The basic philosophy is to keep the plant young; regular pruning can seem to give shrubs eternal youth.

First remove any dead wood that is present and one or two of the thickest, oldest shoots. If this is done every couple of years, there probably will not be any dead shoots to remove. Cut the shoot as close to ground level as possible so that new growth will come from the base of the plant. Removing the oldest shoots allows light into the center of the shrub, giving these new shoots better growing conditions.

With an overgrown shrub, remove about one fourth of the shoots, cutting at ground level. Remove the oldest and unhealthiest shoots first, and then any that are crossing with others.

Prune shrubs at any time of the year. If flowers are important, prune immediately after the flowers fade. This way, next year's flower buds will not be lost. If the fruit display is as important as the flowers, there may not be any time possible to prune without removing flower buds or fruits. In that case, prune at any time. Most pruning can be done any time of the year and in today's busy world, it is best just to go ahead and prune whenever it is convenient.

Removing spent flowers from a plant (known as deadheading) can be useful on shrubs like lilac and rhododendron, where the fruits are rather unattractive and their removal can shift the plant's energies to the production of next year's flowers. Deadhead by cutting or breaking off the spent flower heads as they go out of bloom. This is usually only done with rhododendrons and lilacs, since most gardeners consider it to be too time consuming and not worth the effort. Do not deadhead plants that have showy fruit displays, however, because the fruits are produced from the flowers.

Broadleaf Evergreen Shrubs

Hollies, euonymus, mahonias, aucubas and cherry laurels are some of the vigorous broadleaf evergreens that may be trimmed freely. These can be pruned much as one would prune the deciduous flowering shrubs mentioned above. Many people wait to prune these until late November or early December with an eye toward handsome sprays for holiday decorating.

Less vigorous broadleaf evergreens do not need much pruning except to remove unhealthy or crossing branches, only occasionally pruning if the form needs some help. Many rhododendrons need little pruning, but some of the large species and cultivars can become leggy and overgrown. These, too, can be cut back fairly hard, if necessary, to encourage fuller branching. They will start new growth even from old wood which has no leaves. Some broadleaf evergreens, such as the magnolias, are best pruned when young, because their wood does not heal well when cut.

Hedges

To keep sheared hedges in perfect condition, they need to be clipped with a sharp electric or manual hedge shear every time the new growth reaches 2 or 3 inches; otherwise, the hedge soon looks ragged. Many people compromise, however, and only shear their hedges once or twice a summer.

To make a perfectly straight hedge, stretch a guiding cord along both upper edges of the hedge so the surface is absolutely level and the edges square and then shear to the cords. Next, move one cord to the bottom of one side and again shear between the guides. Next, do the same on the back side of the hedge.

The bottom of a hedge should always be wider than the top. This allows light to reach to the base of the hedge on both sides, enabling the leaves to grow all the way down.

Hedges that have become overgrown, exhibit weak growth or have become too tall or bare at the base only have foliage on the surface and no leaves inside. Rejuvenative pruning can bring some of these problem hedges back to health. Cut a deciduous hedge to the ground in early spring before new growth starts. As new growth develops, let the shoots reach 1 ft. or so, then cut them back to half their height. Continue this sequence of growth and pruning throughout the summer, gradually building the hedge back to a dense barrier. It may take a few years to return it to the desired height.

Evergreen hedges do not rejuvenate as easily. In fact, such pruning cannot be done at all on any of the conifers except for yew (*Taxus*) and arborvitae (*Thuja*). With yew, arborvitae, and most of the broadleaved evergreens, it is generally best to cut no more than 1 ft. of growth off the plant.

Milder rejuvenation is possible with any hedge. This is done by opening holes in the foliage to allow light into the center of the plant. Use pruning shears and make the cuts at least every 10 in. to just above a point where a shoot branches. Following this procedure once a year for about three seasons will successfully bring the plant back to health. Continue shearing each year. Opening holes in the hedge is good for any hedge and can be done throughout its life.

R O O T   P R U N I N G

The roots of trees and shrubs, if left undisturbed, grow a substantial distance from the upper portion of the plant. These roots should be protected from any damage, such as being cut, being damaged by compaction of the soil in which they grow, or changes in the grade or level of the soil. When planning to transplant a tree or shrub, however, it is usually helpful to prune the roots one or two years (or more, if the plants are large) in advance of the move, to encourage the growth of fibrous roots nearer to the base of the plant.

There are several factors to keep in mind when root pruning. First, the roots must be cut in closer to the plant than the eventual root ball will be. New roots will grow where the cuts are made and it is important that they are not damaged in transplanting. Second, a trench is dug around a tree or shrub to prune the roots, back fill the trench with an excellent soil mix, to encourage root growth. Third, if the plant is large, only dig the trench on one side of the plant the first year, then on the other side the second year, and postpone transplanting until the third year.

Keep in mind that any time roots are cut, stress is placed on the plant. It is less able to draw water and nutrients from the soil. Therefore, water the plant during dry periods, mulch the trenched area to reduce water loss, and apply a dilute mixture of low-nitrogen fertilizer. Some horticulturists recommend pruning the top of the plant also, to counter the root loss. Other experts (it is never a good idea to ask more than one expert the same question, since any two experts are bound to disagree) feel that the plant needs all its leaves to produce the food that will fuel the growth of roots. Top-pruning, however, can reduce water loss. But if you are able to water the root-pruned plants, do not prune the top.

All good nursery stock is root-pruned several times before it is sold. Such stock is much more likely to survive transplanting than wild plants or those whose roots have not been pruned prior to digging.

Finally a broken, split or torn root is an invitation to trouble on any plant; cut it off cleanly. Use pruning shears, lopping shears or a saw to cut it cleanly.

chapter

4

ENCYCLOPEDIA OF TREES & SHRUBS

The following encyclopedia lists the trees and shrubs most suited for home landscape and garden use, including the most commonly available species and cultivars. It encapsulates most of the information necessary to make informed choices when selecting plants for the garden and identifies their essential characteristics and best qualities.

It includes many fruit trees and shrubs, such as highbush blueberry (*Vaccinium corymbosum*) and apricot (*Prunus armeniaca*), that can be enjoyed as much for their ornamental qualities as for their fruit. It does not, however, include roses, although they are generally considered to be shrubs, or woody ground covers, which can attain the heights of small shrubs; these two subjects will each be a volume unto themselves.

In this chapter plants are listed by genus under their botanical names (with a pronunciation key). Species of each genus appear in every entry, together with the varieties and cultivars. For instance, the various kinds of spruce trees are all listed under their genus, *Picea*. Conversely, if only the common name of a plant is known, the

Common Name Index will be helpful in finding its correct botanical name. Look up "Spruce" and it will lead to the genus entry for *Picea*, look up Norway spruce and it will lead to *Picea abies*, its botanical name.

The binomial system of nomenclature enables facts about related species to be readily available. Under this classification, for instance, you can see that the American cranberry bush, arrowwood and black haw are all species that belong to the same genus as viburnum. As noted in the Viburnum genus entry, members of the genus are among the most popular ornamental plants for their showy clusters of small flowers, attractive fruit and good fall color.

Plant Ratings

The encyclopedia has singled out the most outstanding landscape plants for the garden. Virtually indispensable genera, such as *Acer* (maples) and *Magnolia*, are noted with two asterisks (✳✳). Unusually outstanding species, such as *Cornus kousa* (Japanese dogwood), are indicated by a single asterisk (✳).

The Encyclopedia Entries

General horticultural information, such as the type of soil and amount of light plants require, their susceptibility to disease, overall hardiness, planting times and depths and appropriate methods of propagation appears with each genus. General gardening information, such as the valued ornamental aspects of the plants—flowers, fruit, form, foliage and branch structure, to name a few—that makes the plants worthy of a place in the garden are outlined to present an overview of the genus.

Each species entry contains a detailed description of the plant, which includes: average mature plant heights and widths; flower shape, size, color, and blooming period; leaf structure, color, size, and texture; fruit size, color, structure and season; and branch structure, form and color where pertinent.

Geographical information, such as the plant's place of origin (which is a key to the conditions under which it naturally thrives) and hardiness zones alert gardeners to the ability of each species to grow well in their region. Wherever possible, a complete zone range, which features the southern boundaries (beyond which the summers and winters are too warm for the plant to be healthy in the garden without protection) as well as the more commonly known northern limits, has been supplied for the most complete hardiness information available.

In addition, more detailed cultural and propagation information appears in features on such important plants as *Ilex* (holly), *Malus* (crabapple) and *Rhododendron* in Chapter 2. Where there has been a great deal of work done to create new hybrids, detailed sections and even a chart (for *Malus* species) offer quick reference for making informed selections of the new varieties.

UNDERSTANDING
THE ENCYCLOPEDIA ENTRIES

Genus, a plant group including many similar species.

Two stars indicate a genus indispensable to the home garden.

Common name for the genus *Ilex*.

Single star indicates species of outstanding landscape merit.

Stands for Ilex opaca, a species belonging to the Ilex (holly) genus.

Detailed plant description, including average mature plant heights and widths; flower shape, size, color and blooming period; leaf structure, color, size and texture; fruit size, color, structure and season; and branch structure, form and color where pertinent. In-depth cultivation information, including zone ranges, light and soil requirements and propagation techniques are covered. Design suggestions and reliable varieties, forms, cultivars, and hybrids complete the information.

Entry listed alphabetically under the plant's common name in the Index. All entries are listed under both the common and the correct botanical name so they can be located under either.

Pronunciation key. Accent on italicized syllable.

Common name of family to which this genus belongs.

Botanical name of the plant family.

Common name for *Ilex opaca*. Cross-reference entry appears listed in the Index of Common Names for American Holly, giving the correct botanical name, *Ilex opaca*.

Indicates this plant will survive cold weather generally prevailing in Zones 6 to 9. The U.S.D.A. Plant Hardiness Zone Map showing which areas of the continent these zones cover is reprinted on pages 194–195.

★★Ilex (*eye*-lex).

HOLLY.

Holly Family (*Aquifoliaceae*). Native primarily to temperate and tropical regions of N. and S. Amer. and Asia. Range from shrubs less than 1 ft. to trees over 80 ft. tall. Grown for their foliage and/or fruit effect. Many hollies are evergreen, and some are considered by gardeners the most valuable of our broad-leaved specimens. Some of the deciduous species are extremely showy for their fruit display.

★I. opaca (oh-*pay*-kuh).

AMERICAN HOLLY.

One of the important native broadleaf evergreens. Native to eastern U.S., it grows to 50 ft. tall by 30 ft. wide. If pruned will be an elegant pyramidal specimen. Leaves medium green and lustrous to dull above, greenish yellow beneath. Leaves are to 3 in. long, elliptical, with spined margins. Fruits are mostly bright red, though some varieties show orange or yellow fruits. There are hundreds of cultivars. 'Bountiful' bears an abundant supply of fruits every year and has dark green leaves. 'Croonenberg' bears dark red fruits heavily and is self-fruitful. Form *xanthocarpa* includes all the yellow-fruited cultivars. Zones 6 to 9.

BRIDAL WREATH.

See *Spiraea prunifolia*.

Abelia (ay-*bee*-lee-uh).

Honeysuckle Family (*Caprifoliaceae*).

Graceful, bushy shrubs from Asia and Mex.; small to medium in size, and widely useful in landscaping where winter temperatures are not too severe. Opposite, simple, pointed, small leaves. Tubular flowers are small but profuse and pretty, produced in leafy terminal clusters over a long period in summer and early fall. Sun encourages flowering, but abelias tolerate considerable shade. Plant in a well-drained sandy loam, rich in humus. Propagate by cuttings or seeds.

Abelia × *grandiflora*
GLOSSY ABELIA

A. × grandiflora (gran-di-*floh*-ruh).

GLOSSY ABELIA.

Hybrid of *A. chinensis* and *A. uniflora*. Grows to 6 ft. high and about 5 ft. wide. The lustrous, semi-evergreen leaves, on arching stems, assume a lovely bronze color in the fall. The bell-shaped, pinkish-white flowers bloom continuously from early summer through mid-autumn. The top

may be killed back in severe winters, but new growth from the base is vigorous and produces flowers the same summer. Especially useful as a border accent for landscape and unusual hedge plantings; even for single specimen display. 'Edward Goucher' is a desirable semi-evergreen hybrid of *A.* × *grandiflora* and *A. schumannii*. It grows to 5 ft., bears lilac-pink flowers all summer, and is slightly less hardy. Zones 6 to 9.

Abeliophyllum (a-bee-lee-oh-*fill*-um).

Olive Family (*Oleaceae*).

There is only one species, a deciduous shrub from Korea. Best in full sun but tolerant of shade. Propagate in spring from softwood cuttings, in midsummer using cuttings of half-ripened shoots or from seeds sown in autumn. New plants can be produced from self-layered/rooted shoots.

Abeliophyllum distichum
KOREAN ABELIA-LEAF

A. distichum (*diss*-ti-kum).
KOREAN ABELIA-LEAF.
WHITE FORSYTHIA.
Grows 3 to 4 ft. high, with an equal spread. Oval, opposite leaves to 2 in. long, on slender, arching stems. When young, it is an awkward shrub but becomes bushy with maturity. Dense clusters of small, white, fragrant flowers in early spring before the leaves appear—making it well worth planting in the shrub border and an excellent companion for the spring-flowering bulbs. An evergreen ground cover helps to show off the flowers. Zones 5 to 8.

Abies (*ay*-beez).
FIR.
Pine Family (*Pinaceae*).
Evergreen trees of pyramidal form, most growing to 50 ft. or more. They bear their cones, which shatter soon after maturity, erect, usually high on the trees, distinguishing them from spruces, which have cones that hang down. The leaves (needles) of both trees are attached directly to the twigs, but those of the fir leave a distinctive, round, depressed scar that resembles two white bands on the twig when they fall off. The needles of firs are flatter and their twigs smoother than those of the spruces. Firs grow best in full sun in moist, acid soil, becoming sparse under hot, dry conditions. Most do not tolerate summer heat. Landscape use is similar to that of spruces, often as screening plants or specimens. Propagate by seeds or grafting.

A. balsamea (bal-*suh*-mee-uh).
BALSAM FIR.
Native to the mountains of northeastern Amer., this species may reach a height of 60 ft. and a spread of 20 ft. Rounded leaves to 1 in. long and violet-purple cones 2 to 3 in. long. Among the most popular Christmas trees, but does not grow well in areas with hot summers. 'Nana' is a slow-growing dwarf with a mounded form that is occasionally grown in the West. Zones 3 to 5.

A. cephalonica (sef-a-*lon*-i-kuh).
GREEK FIR.
Native to Greece. Grows up to 90 ft. high and 25 ft. wide, with grayish-brown bark and shiny green leaves about 1 in. long. Greenish-purple cones, 3 to 5 in. long. Tolerates hot summers. Zones 6 to 7.

✳**A. concolor** (*kon*-kuh-lor).
CONCOLOR FIR.
WHITE FIR.
Native to the mountainous regions of south-western U.S. and northern Mex., this handsome tree grows about 80 ft. by 25 ft. Gray bark, bluish-green leaves about 2 in. long, and greenish-purple cones, 3 to 5 in. long. Similar to Blue Colorado Spruce in effect but often healthier. Several "blue" cultivars available. Fairly tolerant of heat. The variety *lowiana* is similar to the species, with longer needles that are notched at the tip. 'Compacta' is a dwarf form of the species. Zones 3 to 6.

A. firma (*fur*-muh).
MOMI FIR.
Native to Japan. Grows to 70 ft. with a spread of 30 ft. Dark green needles 1½ in. long. Attractive horizontal branches. Cones 3 to 5 in. long. One of the most heat-tolerant firs. Zones 6 to 9.

A. fraseri (*fray*-zer-ee).
FRASER FIR.
SOUTHERN BALSAM FIR.
Native to the mountains of W. Va., N. Car. and Tenn., it resembles the balsam fir that grows in the North, but has fuller branches and cones with prominent bracts. Excellent in cool, moist moun-

Abies concolor
CONCOLOR FIR

Abies grandis
GIANT FIR

tain areas, but unhealthy where summers are hot and dry. Zones 4 to 6.

A. grandis (*gran*–diss).
GIANT FIR.
Native from Vancouver Island as far south as Calif. and as far east as Mont. Leaves are up to 2¼ in. long, rounded and notched at the apex. Cones of the giant fir are cylindrical, bright green and about 4 in. long. Zones 5 to 6.

A. homolepis (ho-mo-*lep*-iss).
NIKKO FIR.
A valuable Japanese tree, growing to about 80 ft. by 40 ft. wide, with lustrous, dark green leaves about 1 in. long. Purplish to brown cones about 4 in. long. Beautiful, wide-spreading, heat-tolerant tree. Zones 4 to 7.

A. koreana (koh-ree-*ay*-nuh).
KOREAN FIR.
Native to Korea. Grows to about 30 ft. by 15 ft., with lustrous green leaves less than 1 in. long. The violet-purple cones are up to 3 in. long and may be produced on young trees. Tolerant of heat. There are several attractive dwarf forms. Zones 5 to 7.

A. lasiocarpa (lay-see-oh-*kar*-puh).
ROCKY MOUNTAIN FIR.
A mountain fir that is native from Alaska to northern Calif. The cones are purple, about 3 in. long, and the leaves are to 1 ½ in. long. Bark of the variety *arizonica* (ar-iz-*zon*-ik-uh) is a light grey and has a corky texture. This variety tolerates heat and does better in the East than the species. 'Compacta' is dwarf, with a conical form and bluish needles. 'Argentea' grows more slowly than the species and has brighter blue needles. Zones 5 to 7.

Abies koreana
KOREAN FIR

A. nordmanniana (nor-man-nee-*ay*-nuh).
NORDMANN FIR.
Native to the Caucasus, Asia Minor and Greece. One of the most attractive firs, with dark green, shiny foliage that appears as though it had been brushed forward. Needles an inch long or longer. Tree 60 ft. tall, 25 ft. wide, tolerant of heat. Zones 4 to 6.

Abies procera 'Glauca'
NOBLE FIR

A. pinsapo (pin-*say*-poh).
SPANISH FIR.
This beautiful, narrow, Spanish native grows to 60 ft. tall and 15 to 20 ft. wide, with rigid, dark green leaves to ¾ in. long. A tree of great distinction when adequately displayed. Tolerates heat. The purplish-brown cones are 4 to 5 in. long. Zones 6 to 7 (can be grown in Calif.).

A. procera (proh-*sair*-uh).
NOBLE FIR.
Although native to the mountains of Wash., Ore. and Calif., this fir tolerates some heat. It grows to about 75 ft. in cultivation, with a spread of about 20 ft. Cones start out green and turn brown when mature. They can be from 6 to 10 in. long. The cultivar 'Glauca' is a silvery-blue conifer and may tolerate heat and drought better than the species. Zones 5 to 6.

A. veitchii (*veetch*-ee-eye).
VEITCH FIR.
A handsome and hardy fir from Japan, it grows to 60 ft. high by 30 ft. wide. The leaves are crowded in a forward direction. They are up to 1 in. long. A lustrous dark green, they have two conspicuous silvery bands underneath. Bluish-purple cones are each about 2½ in. long. Zones 3 to 6.

Acacia (ak-*kay*-see-uh).
Pea Family (*Leguminosae*).
A large group of fast-growing evergreen trees and shrubs, native to many tropical and subtropical regions, including southwestern Amer., Mex. and Australia. The leaves are usually bipinnate with numerous small leaflets, but in some cases are reduced to flattened, leaflike stems called phyllodes. Showy yellow flowers in attractive clusters or spikes bloom in warm winters or spring. In northern areas, they can be grown in cool greenhouses. A number are handsome and

popular plants to grow outdoors in the Southwest and Fla., where they are free-flowering and reach considerable size. The fruits are typical legume pods. Grow in full sun. Propagate by seeds or cuttings.

A. dealbata (deal-*bah*-tuh).
SILVER WATTLE.

Native to Tasmania and southeastern Australia. This is the "mimosa" of florist shops. Grows to 60 ft., with silvery-gray foliage and heads of soft yellow flowers. Widely grown in Calif. as a florist's flower. Zones 8 to 10.

A. farnesiana (far-neez-ee-*ay*-nuh).
POPINAC.

SWEET ACACIA.

Native to subtrop. and trop. Amer. An attractive, thorny, much-branched shrub growing to 10 ft., with leaflets that are ⅛ in. long. Produces heads of yellow, very fragrant flowers that can bloom much of the year. Zones 8 to 10.

Acanthopanax (ah-kan-thoh-*pah*-naks).
Aralia family (*Araliaceae*).

Tough, thorny shrubs native from Asia to the Philippines. Flowers small, in globe-shaped umbels. Dark purple fruits. Leaves alternate and palmately compound. Propagate by seed or cuttings.

A. sieboldianus (see-bol-dee-*ay*-nus).
FIVELEAF ARALIA.

Useful in tough locations as a barrier or screening shrub. Fast growing and tolerant of sun or shade, shrubs reach 8 to 10 ft. in height with a similar spread. The cultivar 'Variegatus' has white-margined leaves. Zones 4 to 8.

✶✶Acer (*ay*-ser).
MAPLE.

BOX ELDER.

Maple Family (*Aceraceae*).

Deciduous trees ranging in height from 20 to 120 ft. and native to North Temperate Zones. They make good shade trees, although many have highly competitive surface roots. As a group they are among the most valuable landscape trees. The lobed or compound, opposite leaves turn a brilliant color in the fall on most species. They produce clusters of small flowers in spring and, in some species, colorful, long-winged fruits (samaras). Easily grown, maples thrive in ordinary soil, are mostly very hardy and tolerant of either full sun or fairly heavy shade. Established specimens grow better if fertilized from time to time and are often improved by removing weak or crossing branches. Propagate by seed, grafting, or rooted cuttings.

A. buergeranum (burr-jar-*ay*-num).
TRIDENT MAPLE.

A low, globe-shaped tree from China and Japan. To 20 ft. tall by 20 ft. wide. Small, three-lobed leaves usually produce good, red-orange fall color. Bark exfoliates with age. Zones 5 to 8.

A. campestre (kam-*pes*-tree).
HEDGE MAPLE.

Native to Eur., northern Turkey, Caucasus and northern Iran. Slow-growing shrub or round-headed tree to 40 ft. with an equal spread. Corky branchlets. The leaves, to 4 in. across, have three to five lobes and almost no autumn color. Greenish flowers in loose, erect corymbs (clusters). Makes an excellent bold screen or clipped hedge because of its dense growth. Frequently used as a roadside hedge in Great Britain. 'Compactum' (kom-*pak*-tum) is lower growing, exceptionally dense, reaching 6 ft. in height. Zones 5 to 8.

A. ginnala (gin-*nah*-la).
AMUR MAPLE.
Native to Asia. A picturesque small tree to 20 ft. tall by 20 ft. wide; craggy, with silver bark and a spreading, open crown. Often multiple-trunked or low-branched. Leaves small, toothed, shiny, with three lobes; they produce brilliant colors in autumn. Samaras showy red in early summer. Tolerant of adverse conditions. 'Compactum' and 'Durand Dwarf' are bushlike and dense. Zones 3 to 6.

A. griseum (*gris*-ee-um).
PAPERBARK MAPLE.
Native to China. A tree to 25 ft. tall with a 15 to 20 ft. spread. Valuable for its papery, cinnamon-colored bark, which peels freely. The three-leaflet leaves are small and glossy green. Attractive orange fall color. Zones 5 to 7.

Acer japonicum 'Aureum'
GOLDEN FULLMOON MAPLE

A. japonicum (ja-*pon*-i-kum).
FULLMOON MAPLE.
Native to Japan. Similar in most ways to Japanese maple, *A. palmatum*. Leaves generally wider, with more lobes. Excellent fall color. The cultivar 'Aconitifolium' has deeply lobed leaves; 'Aureum' has yellow leaves throughout the growing season. Zones 5 to 8.

A. negundo (nee-*goon*-doh).
BOX ELDER.
Very tough, often weedy tree, native throughout most of Amer. and southern Can. Grows 50 ft. tall by 40 to 50 ft. wide. Leaves compound with 3 or 5 leaflets. No fall color. Useful where other trees will not grow, such as urban landscapes and very cold areas. Plant male trees to avoid weedy seedlings. Zones 2 to 8.

Acer griseum
PAPERBARK MAPLE

✱**A. palmatum** (pal-*may*-tum).

JAPANESE MAPLE.

These are small, to 20 ft. by 20 ft., maples. In cultivation in Japan for centuries, hundreds of named cultivars are in the Japanese literature and many of these are grown in the U.S. The trees are usually round-headed, with gray, smooth, mature bark. The palmate leaves have five to nineteen lobes. The leaves of the variety *atropurpureum* (at-roh-per-*puh*-ree-um) are purple early in the season, fading slowly to deep green. Leaves similar to the species, and generally with good fall color. 'Bloodgood' is one of the best cultivars for holding its purple leaf color throughout the summer. 'Burgundy Lace' is a cutleaf, lacy small tree with reddish foliage. The green leaves of 'Scolopendrifolium' (sko-low-pen-*dree*-fohl-ee-um) are cut to center, with narrow divisions. 'Osakazuki' has large, yellow-green leaves that turn flame-red in fall. The variety *dissectum* (dis-*sek*-tum), the threadleaf Japanese maples, includes all Japanese maples with dissected leaves. Usually fairly slow growing, they reach only 8 to 10 ft. in height with a similar or greater spread and produce orange fall color. 'Waterfall' is an excellent green dissected form, with gold to orange fall color. The cultivars 'Red Filigree Lace' and 'Tamukeyama' of the variety *dissectum atropurpureum* (ah-troh-pur-*puh*-ree-um) have purple, dissected leaves. 'Sangokaku' (syn. 'Senkaki') has light green leaves and stems that are showy red in the winter. Zones 6 to 8.

A. platanoides (plat-an-*noy*-deez).

NORWAY MAPLE.

Native to Eur., Caucasus, northern Turkey and northern Iran. A wide tree of formal aspect. Densely branched, it forms a round head with age, up to about 50 ft. tall with a spread almost as wide. Withstands city conditions. Identified by the milky sap that exudes from the broken petiole

Acer palmatum var. *dissectum atropurpureum*
THREADLEAF JAPANESE MAPLE

Acer palmatum 'Sangokaku'
JAPANESE MAPLE

and bright yellow fall color, which occurs latest of the maples. Tends to be surface-rooted, making it very difficult to grow grass or other plants beneath it. Has a tendency to have many weed seedlings and often escapes to natural areas. There are many cultivars. 'Crimson King' has dark red leaves throughout summer; 'Erectum' (ee-*rek*-tum) and 'Columnare' (ko-*lum*-nare) are upright, narrow trees. 'Globosum' (gloh-*boh*-sum), round-headed and dense, is usually grafted onto a 6- to 7-foot tree. 'Schwedleri' (shwed-*ler*-eye) is red-leaved in spring, but bronze-green throughout summer and fall. 'Summer Shade' is upright-growing with a single trunk and may be resistant to leaf-scorch. 'Drummondii' (dra-mon-*dee*-eye) has green leaves edged in white, but it often reverts to green. Zones 3 to 7.

Acer platanoides 'Drummondii'
Norway Maple

A. rubrum (*roo*-brum).
Red Maple.
Swamp Maple.
Native to east and central U.S. A fast-growing, silver-barked tree to 80 ft. with a 40 to 60 ft. spread. Its three-lobed leaves are 2½ to 4 in. wide. Showy clusters of red flowers and fruits in spring and flame-red fall coloration make this an ornamental shade tree. Tolerates poor drainage. Because it is native over a wide north-south range, hardiness varies among the cultivars and seedlings. 'Armstrong' and 'Columnare' (ko-*lum*-nare) are narrow, columnar trees ('Armstrong' is usually considered a hybrid, *Acer* × *freemanii* 'Armstrong', with silver maple as its other parent). A number have been selected for excellent autumn color. Generally the ones that color early are better adapted to colder climates. Zones 3 to 9.

A. saccharinum (sak-ar-*rye*-num).
Silver Maple.
Native to most of eastern N. Amer., this tree grows rapidly to as much as 120 ft. high and 80 ft. wide. The leaves are handsome, deeply five-lobed, 5 in. broad (or more) and silver-green below; they have a tannish-yellow fall color. Silver maple has surface roots that invade beds, borders and lawns. The wood is weak and crotches tend to be narrow, a combination that leads to trees self-destructing with age. Zones 3 to 8.

✴**A. saccharum** (sak-*kar*-um).
Sugar Maple.
Hard Maple.
Native from Quebec to Fla., and as far west as Minn. and Okla. A formal-appearing, stately tree with a massive trunk (to 75 ft. tall, with a spread of about 50 ft.) and glossy, dark green leaves to 6 in. across, which are usually five-lobed. Turns a wonderful orange in autumn. Al-

Acer rubrum
RED MAPLE

Acer saccharum
SUGAR MAPLE

though beautiful, these can be difficult in the garden as the surface roots allow little to grow under the tree. Trees are easily injured by ice-melting salt and some herbicides. Most sugar maples color beautifully in the fall. 'Green Mountain' tolerates dry conditions better than the species and in colder areas has excellent orange fall color. 'Temple's Upright' and 'Newton Sentry' are both narrow, columnar plants. Zones 3 to 7.

Aesculus (*ess*-kew-lus).

HORSE CHESTNUT.

BUCKEYE.

Horse chestnut Family (*Hippocastanaceae*).

Native to N. Amer., southeastern Eur. and eastern Asia. Large, deciduous, compound leaves with three to nine leaflets arranged in fingerlike fashion. Showy flowers are borne in large, many-flowered panicles (clusters) in spring. The fruit consists of large, smooth or spiny capsules, usually containing one big inedible seed. They thrive in ordinary, well-drained soil. All horse chestnut trees are messy, shedding twigs, leaves, bark, fruit hulls or fruit. Many lose their leaves before coloring in the fall. Propagate by seeds sown immediately upon ripening, or by grafting.

A. × carnea (*karr*-nee-uh).

RED HORSE CHESTNUT.

Hybrid of *A. hippocastanum* and *A. pavia*. It grows to 50 ft. with a similar spread. Produces leathery leaflets to 6 in. long and slightly prickly fruit. The winter buds are sticky and resinous. Red flowers appear in panicles to 8 in. long. 'Briotii' (bry-*ott*-ee-eye), ruby horse chestnut, has larger panicles and deeper red flowers. Zones 5 to 8.

A. glabra (*gla*-bra).

OHIO BUCKEYE.

Tree to 40 ft. high with 40 ft. spread. Yellowish-green flowers not as showy as other species. Leaf blotch often causes early defoliation. Buds not sticky; fruits slightly prickly. Zones 3 to 7.

A. hippocastanum (hip-poh-kas-*ta*-num).
COMMON HORSE CHESTNUT.
A large and handsome tree to 75 ft. with a 60 ft. spread and very sticky buds. Leaflets to 10 in. long; white flowers with a reddish tinge bloom in clusters to 12 in. long. Prickly fruit. One of the showiest of all flowering trees, but many people find the dropping of fruit and early leaf drop to be strong drawbacks. The cultivar 'Baumannii' (bow-*man*-ee-eye), Baumann's horse chestnut, has double-white, sterile flowers with red streaks in tight clusters on 9-in. spikes. No fruit litter. Zones 4 to 8.

A. parviflora (par-vi-*floh*-ruh).
BOTTLEBRUSH BUCKEYE.
A wide-spreading shrub that may grow to 12 ft. tall and 12 ft. wide. Easily kept smaller by pruning immediately after bloom. Produces leaflets 8 in. long, white flowers. in narrow clusters, and smooth fruit. Zones 5 to 8.

A. pavia (pay-*vee*-uh).
RED BUCKEYE.
Small tree to 20 ft. high and 20 ft. wide. Native to southeastern U.S. In mid- to late spring bears widely spaced tubular scarlet flowers on 4- to 8-in. panicles. Zones 5 to 8.

Albizia (al-*biz*-ee-uh).
Pea Family (*Leguminosae*).
Deciduous trees and shrubs, usually of tropical and subtropical regions. The trees are spreading, umbrellalike; the wood is very weak. Propagate by seeds, budding or grafting.

Aesculus hippocastanum
COMMON HORSE CHESTNUT

Aesculus parviflora
BOTTLEBRUSH BUCKEYE

A. julibrissin (ju-li-*bri*-sin).

SILK-TREE.

MIMOSA.

Much planted in the South, mimosa grows to 40 ft. tall with a similar spread. Farther north it is likely to be lower, very wide-spreading, and often has much dead wood. The alternate leaves are pinnately compound (feathery) with 40 to 60 leaflets. Feathery, fragrant flower heads bloom in late spring and intermittently afterwards. Flowers range from whitish to dark rose-pink. Flat brown seeds are produced in 6-in.-long flat pods. Generally short-lived and frequently subject to insect and disease problems. Cultivars 'Charlotte' and 'Tryon' are said to be disease resistant. 'E. H. Wilson' originated in Korea, is hardier, and has deeper pink flowers. Zones 6 to 9.

Albizia julibrissin
SILK-TREE

Alnus (*al*-nus).

ALDER.

Birch Family (*Betulaceae*).

A large group of deciduous trees and shrubs native to the Northern Hemisphere and the Andes. Alternate, generally coarse-toothed leaves that drop in autumn, usually while still green. Buds are on short stalks, making the tree easy to identify. Most species fix nitrogen in their roots, allowing them to grow in infertile soil. The flowers are in the form of catkins, which appear in early spring before the leaves. Female catkins are short and become small woody cones. Tolerant of urban conditions and wet areas. Propagate by grafts, cuttings, or seeds.

A. glutinosa (glew-tee-*noh*-suh).

COMMON ALDER.

Tree to 50 ft. high with horizontal branches spreading to 30 ft. Tolerates a wide range of soil types. Zones 4 to 7.

A. incana (in-*kay*-nuh).

SPECKLED ALDER.

Shrub or tree to 50 ft. Yellow catkins in March, followed by round leaves, which are bluish-gray beneath. 'Aurea' (*aw*-ree-uh) has young shoots yellow-green; 'Pendula' (pen-*dew*-luh) has drooping branches. Zones 3 to 6.

Alnus incana
SPECKLED ALDER

Amelanchier (am-el-lang-*kee*-uhr).
SHADBUSH.
SARVICEBERRY.
SERVICEBERRY.
Rose Family (*Rosaceae*).
Deciduous shrubs or small trees, found chiefly in the Temperate Zone. Alternate, toothed leaves and profuse, airy clusters of white flowers appear briefly in early spring before the foliage. Effective at the edge of woodlands or the back of large-scale shrub plantings during spring bloom and when the foliage colors in autumn. Will grow in almost any soil. Propagate by seeds, grafts or softwood cuttings.

A. arborea (ar-*boor*-ee-uh).
DOWNY SERVICEBERRY.
Native to N. Amer. One of the most decorative small, shrublike trees of early spring, this species grows to 30 ft. and spreads to 20 ft. This plant is

Amelanchier arborea
DOWNY SERVICEBERRY

often listed as *A. canadensis*. The oblong leaves, 2 in. long, are silvery when young. Fall color is yellow to orange. The nodding clusters of flowers, to 4 in. long, appear before the leaves, filling the early woodlands with airy drifts of white. The small, sweet, dark purple fruits look and taste like very seedy blueberries and are loved by birds. Zones 3 to 8.

A. canadensis. See *A. arborea*.

A. × grandiflora (gran-dee-*floh*-ruh).
APPLE SERVICEBERRY.
A hybrid between *A. laevis* and *A. arborea*. Flowers tend to be larger. Zones 3 to 8.

A. laevis (*lee*-vis).
Native to eastern and midwestern N. Amer. Very similar to *A. arborea*, but the new leaves have a purplish tinge in the spring. Zones 5 to 7.

Aralia (ar-*ray*-lee-uh).
Aralia Family (*Araliaceae*).
A genus of ornamental herbs, shrubs and trees of N. Amer., Asia and Australia. The woody species make imposing, coarse-textured plants for the large shrub border or for use as bold lawn specimens. The two species listed have spiny stems and sucker profusely. Propagate by seeds, root cuttings or division.

A. elata (ee-*lay*-tuh).
JAPANESE ANGELICA.
Native to northeast Asia. A handsome, exotic-looking tree with striking foliage, growing to 40 ft. high and 20 ft. wide. Entire plant is less spiny than *A. spinosa*. Showy, alternate and bipinnately compound leaves to 3 ft. long, with small leaflets. Large clusters of whitish flowers bloom above the foliage in late summer. Soft black fruit. 'Aureovariegata' (*or*-ree-oh var-ee-*ga*-ta) and 'Variegata' have mottled foliage. Zones 4 to 9.

Aralia elata 'Aureo-variegata'
JAPANESE ANGELICA

A. spinosa (spye-*noh*-suh).
DEVIL'S-WALKING STICK.
HERCULES'-CLUB.
Much like *A. elata* but has spiny leaves. It is native to N. Amer. and grows to 20 ft. high with a similar spread. It has large compound leaves and immense clusters of small white flowers in late summer, borne above the leaves. Zones 5 to 9.

Araucaria (or-roh-*cay*-ri-a).
Araucaria family (*Araucariaceae*).
A genus of large, evergreen conifers that are usually dioecious (male and female cones on separate plants). Native to S. Amer. and some Pacific Islands.

A. araucana (are-*roh*-cay-nuh).
MONKEY-PUZZLE TREE.
Leaves spirally arranged, very stiff and spiny, to 2 in. long. Trees grow to 80 ft. with a spread of 30 to 40 ft. Branches whorled with distinct spaces between whorls. Propagate by seed. Zones 7 to 10.

Araucaria araucana
MONKEY-PUZZLE TREE

Aronia (ar-*roh*-nee-uh).
CHOKEBERRY.
Rose Family (*Rosaceae*).
Decorative, deciduous shrubs, native to N. Amer. Leaves are alternate in arrangement and turn red in the fall. Clusters of showy white flowers, blooming in spring, are followed by brightly colored but bitter-tasting red, purplish or black fruit. Readily adaptable to informal plantings, these shrubs are good in woods, in the wild garden and in shrub borders, in full sun or shade. Grow well in almost any soil but do best in a moist situation. Propagate by seeds, cuttings, layers or simply by division or sucker growth.

✱**A. arbutifolia** (ar-bew-ti-*foh*-lee-uh).
RED CHOKEBERRY.
A dependable and attractive shrub about 6 ft. high and 5 ft. wide. The oblongish leaves, 3 in. long, turn a brilliant red in the fall. Dense clusters of white or pink-tinged florets bloom in mid-spring. Bright red fruits appear in late autumn and remain colorful well into winter. Zones 4 to 8.

Aucuba (aw-*kew*-buh).
Dogwood Family (*Cornaceae*).
Evergreen shrubs with handsome foliage on stout branches. Leaves are opposite, deep green or variegated. Small, purplish, dioecious flowers (male and female on separate plants). Attractive, bright scarlet berries on females. They need a partially shaded position in moist, well-drained soil. Propagate by seeds or cuttings.

A. japonica (ja-*pon*-ik-uh).
JAPANESE AUCUBA.
JAPANESE LAUREL.
Vigorous, spreading shrub that grows to 8 ft. tall by 6 ft. wide. Grown by florists as a decorative

Aronia arbutifolia
RED CHOKEBERRY

Aucuba japonica var. *variegata*
GOLD-DUST PLANT

pot plant. Glossy, dark green leaves, to 7 in. long, coarsely toothed in the upper half. Conspicuous, scarlet fruit in dense clusters to 3 in. long.

The variety *variegata* (var-ee-uh-*gay*-tuh), with yellow-spotted leaves, is known as the gold-dust plant. At least six other variegated forms are described, but they are seldom available in the U.S. nursery trade. Zones 6 to 8.

Berberis (*ber*-ber-iss).
BARBERRY.
Barberry Family (*Berberidaceae*).

Widely varied deciduous or evergreen spiny shrubs that are native to N. Amer., Eur. and Asia. Simple leaves (alternate) turn a colorful scarlet, orange or yellow in fall. The small but attractive yellow flowers bloom in the spring. Valuable for specimen and hedge plantings.

The barberries, whether deciduous species or those with evergreen foliage, are moderate-sized, slow-growing and adaptable ornamental shrubs. Their flowers and fruits, usually red or frosty blue, are neither very large nor generally remarkable. But the busy exuberance of the stems and branches and the precise gloss of the leaves combine to give us plants of substance and quality. Not the least of their virtues (one native species excepted) is their relative freedom from insect attack and disease. Perhaps their greatest service is to remain handsome throughout the garden year. Deciduous species are generally hardier than the evergreens. Not particular as to soil, they grow best in full sun, although all will tolerate considerable shade. Some species (notably *B. vulgaris*) are hosts of wheat rust and are not suitable for general planting. Propagate by seeds or cuttings of young growth.

The species listed below (there are many more) are among the most valuable—and most available—barberries for ornamental use.

B. julianae (jew-lee-*ann*-ee).
WINTERGREEN BARBERRY.

From China, this is one of the best evergreen species, growing to 8 ft. tall and 6 ft. wide, with yellowish stems and upright growth habit. Its dense, dark, spiny leaves, to 3 in. long, make it a useful background shrub. Conspicuous, decorative yellow flowers, up to 15 in a cluster. Blue-black berries have a silvery bloom. Winter foliage turns purplish bronze in the sun but remains dark green in partial shade. Zones 6 to 8.

B. koreana (koh-ree-*ay*-nuh).
KOREAN BARBERRY.

Erect, deciduous shrub from Korea growing to 6 ft. high and wide, with leaves to 3 in. long, that take on brilliant fall coloration. Yellow flowers in dense clusters are followed by long-lasting, bright red fruits. Zones 3 to 7.

B. × mentorensis (men-tor-*ren*-sis).
MENTOR BARBERRY.

Partly evergreen hybrid of *B. darwinii* and *B. empetrifolia*. Will grow to 7 ft., with slender, arching branches, giving a graceful effect. Good hedge plant. Yellow flowers, up to six in a nodding cluster. It tolerates both low and high temperatures better than most evergreen or near-evergreen species. Zones 5 to 8.

B. thunbergii (thun-*ber*-jee-eye).
JAPANESE BARBERRY.

Deciduous shrub to 6 ft. tall and wide, of dense habit, with leaves to 1½ in. long that turn a brilliant scarlet in autumn. Persistent red berries remain until spring. Seedlings can become weeds in natural areas. The cultivar 'Atropurpurea' (at-row-pur-*puh*-ree-ah) has purple leaves when grown in the sun. One of the most popular hedge plants. Zones 4 to 8.

Berberis

Berberis thunbergii 'Atropurpurea'
JAPANESE BARBERRY

B. verruculosa (vehr-rook-yew-*loh*-suh).
WARTY BARBERRY.
Delicate and choice Chinese evergreen to 3 ft. Of
compact form, it has glossy green leaves, to 1 in.
long, whitish beneath, that turn a handsome
bronze shade in autumn. Golden-yellow flowers,
larger than in most barberries, occur one or two
in a cluster. Blue-black fruit with bloom. Zones
5 to 8.

Betula (*bet*-yew-la).
BIRCH.
Birch Family (*Betulaceae*).
Trees and shrubs of the Northern Hemisphere,
usually boreal or northern, are deciduous and
produce catkins. Toothed leaves are alternate,
simple, usually broadly lance-shaped. Many are
grown for their graceful form or handsome bark.
While most grow naturally in moist, high-
humus soil, they will do almost as well under
average garden conditions so long as the soil is not

a heavy, tight clay. Should be transplanted with a
ball in the spring. Plant in the open to take advantage of their form and showy bark. Most turn
yellow in fall. Propagate by seed, or graft selected
cultivars onto seedling stock. Birch leaf miner
produces blotched and falling leaves and threatens
birches in the Northeast. Some authorities report
that watering during drought and substantial
feeding in early spring can do as much to offset
birch leaf miner attack as spraying programs.

B. nigra (*ni*-grah).
RIVER BIRCH.
RED BIRCH.
In nature, this tree thrives in areas where there is
excess moisture. It occurs along stream or river
banks from Mass. to Fla. and out to the Midwest.
The tree will tolerate dry soils, however. Mature
height can reach 60 to 80 ft. tall and even taller. It
typically breaks into two to three main stems low
on the trunk and its growth habit is rounded to
oval. The bark is reddish on the young twigs and
peels freely. The older bark is gray-brown to
cinnamon-brown and flakes, but bark colors vary
considerably because of the inherent diversity of
seedling-raised populations. The leaves are 1 to 3
in. long, pointed at the tip, broad at the base, and
doubly serrate with the veins impressed into the
surface. The male catkins, 2 to 3 in. long, appear
in the spring. Plant in deep, rich, acid soils in full
sun. 'Heritage' is a vigorous cultivar, with whiter
bark than the species. Zones 5 to 8.

B. papyrifera (pap-eh-*rif*-er-uh).
PAPER BIRCH.
CANOE BIRCH.
WHITE BIRCH.
This very hardy birch is native to northern N.
Amer. Its distinctive, shiny white bark makes this
species one of the best known of the birches. The
bark was used by Indians to build canoes. When

the thin, papery layers of peeling bark are pulled back, they reveal an orange under bark. With maturity, the bark starts to turn black. The leaf is 2 to 4 in. long, pointed at the tip, broad at the base and doubly serrate. It has a good yellow fall color. In spring, its catkins are 2 to 4 in. long. This tree has an oval habit at maturity with a height of up to 90 ft. but normally only grows to 50 to 70 ft. This species is highly susceptible to bronze birch borer in regions where the summers are hot. Plant in sun in well-drained, moist, acid, sandy soil. Zones 2 to 6.

Betula pendula
EUROPEAN WHITE BIRCH

Betula papyrifera
PAPER BIRCH

B. pendula (*pen*-doo-lah).
EUROPEAN WHITE BIRCH.
SILVER BIRCH.
This European native has been widely planted in the U.S. It is very similar to *B. papyrifera* but it has a pendulous branching habit and usually does not grow as tall (40 to 50 ft.). The bark is white turning black with age and the leaves are pointed

at the tip and broad at the base. In the spring the catkins are 2 in. long with the nutlike fruit maturing in the fall. The growth habit is pyramidal when young and oval at maturity. Strikingly beautiful when ice storms hit, these trees arch to the ground and form tunnels for eager children to run through in the Winter Wonderland. Unfortunately, the ice often causes serious damage to these brittle trees. Plant in full sun in well-drained, moist, sandy soil. Zones 3 to 5.

Buddleia (*bud*-lee-uh).
BUTTERFLY BUSH.
Logania Family (*Loganiaceae*).
Attractive deciduous or semi-evergreen shrubs that do best in rich, well-drained soil and full sun. Propagate by cuttings taken in late summer or by seeds.

B. alternifolia (al-ter-ni-*foh*-lee-uh).
A beautiful shrub from China, growing 10 to 15

ft. tall and 15 ft. wide, with graceful, arching branches. Alternate, lance-shaped leaves to 4 in. long are held late in the fall. Decorative lavender-purple flowers—in dense clusters along stems grown the previous year—bloom in early summer. Although this species is less well-known and generally less winter-hardy than the following more publicized species, it has greater grace and refinement of form. The cultivar 'Argentea' (are-*gen*-tea-ah) has silver leaves. Zones 4 to 7.

Buddleia alternifolia 'Argentea'

B. davidii (day-*vid*-ee-eye).
SUMMER-LILAC.
An upright shrub that grows to 10 ft., less where stems are winter-killed. Soft gray-green leaves are whitish beneath, grow to 8 in. long, are toothed and occur on tall, slender branches. Beautiful fragrant lilac flowers with orange eyes bloom in dense spikes to 10 in. long. Popular for its midsummer bloom even where it is not reliably top-hardy; however, new growth starts

quickly from the base if the stems are cut low in the spring. This species is a favorite of butterflies. Several varieties with different colorings are available. The cultivar 'Black Knight' has dark purplish flowers. The variety *nanhoensis* only grows to about 5 ft. in height. Zones 5 to 7.

Buddleia davidii
BUTTERFLY BUSH

Buxus (*buck*-sus).
BOX.
BOXWOOD.
Box Family (*Buxaceae*).
Traditionally popular, boxwoods are densely-branched evergreen shrubs. Native to Eur. and Asia, they have small opposite leaves and clusters of tiny flowers without petals that bloom in the spring. Slow-growing plants, they grow best in well-drained soil and can tolerate both sun and shade. One of the most valuable plants for hedges and edgings, box tolerates shearing and shaping very well. Prune in late spring after new growth has formed. When established, the plants thrive

for years. Clean out dead leaves and twigs from the inside every spring. Eating even small quantities of leaves has caused the death of animals. Propagate by cuttings in late summer; the dwarf form is popular for edgings and is propagated by division in the spring.

B. microphylla (my-kroh-*fill*-uh).
JAPANESE BOX.

An attractive, compact shrub that grows to 5 ft. and tolerates both sun and considerable shade. Angled, winged stems: leaves, to 1 in. long, are broadest above the middle. Zones 5 to 8.

The variety *japonica* (juh-*pon*-ik-uh), grows to be a 6-ft. shrub. (Zones 6 to 8). The hardiest variety is the lower-growing variety *koreana* (koh-ree-*ay*-nuh), which spreads to 4 or 5 ft. but reaches only 3 ft. in height. Korean box foliage turns brownish in winter, but the plant is a good substitute in regions where other species suffer excessive winter damage. 'Wintergreen' tends to stay green all winter. Zones 4 to 8.

Buxus microphylla
JAPANESE BOX

B. sempervirens (sem-per-*vye*-rens).
COMMON BOX.

A broad, dense shrub or small tree, common box grows to 25 ft. in a mild climate. Larger growing than *B. microphylla* (my-crow-*fil*-uh), this is the species that includes the traditional English and American box of historic veneration. Many

plants from Colonial days are still flourishing in Va. Its dark green, glossy foliage is pale on the underside. Each leaf is about 1½ in. long, and stems are slightly winged. There are many forms in cultivation, notably the dwarf variety *suffruticosa* (suf-frew-ti-*koh*-suh), long prized for garden edgings. A few forms have gold- and silver-variegated foliage. Zones 6 to 8 with considerable winter protection. 'Vardar Valley' is one of the hardier, low-growing forms. Some forms are hardy to Zone 5.

Buxus sempervirens
COMMON BOX

Callicarpa (kal-i-*kar*-puh).
BEAUTYBERRY.

Verbena Family (*Verbenaceae*).

Deciduous shrubs or small trees of tropical and temperate regions of N. and S. Amer., Asia and Australia. Opposite leaves and small pink, blue or white flowers in clusters. These plants are grown chiefly for the uniquely colorful berries that appear in the fall and last until after the leaves have fallen. Stems may sometimes be winter-killed in the North, but new growth from the base will flower and fruit the same year. Sun and rich soil are needed for best fruiting, but plants will tolerate shade. Propagate by seeds, layers or cuttings.

C. americana (am-eh-rik-*kay*-nuh).
To about 6 ft. tall, with leaves 4 to 6 in. long. It has small bluish flowers and a profusion of bright purple berries in the fall. There is also a white variety, *lactea* (lak-*tee*-uh), which is especially effective when planted with the purple. Zones 6 to 8.

C. bodinieri (boh-dee-nee-*ay*-ree).
Reaching 8 ft. tall, with erect branches. This species is more showy and a bit coarser than the others. The variety *giraldii* is very similar to the species.

Callicarpa dichotoma

C. dichotoma (dye-*kot*-oh-muh).
This is the most attractive and the hardiest species, growing to 4 ft. tall. Leaves, to 3 in. long, are toothed in the upper half. Pink flowers are followed by clusters of lilac-violet fruits, for which the species has considerable garden merit in late summer. Zones 5 to 8.

C. japonica (ja-*pon*-ik-uh).
Grows to 4 ft. Leaves to 5 in. long and finely toothed. Pink flowers are followed by violet berries. Zones 5 to 8.

Callistemon (kal-*liss*-tuh-mun).
BOTTLE BRUSH.
Myrtle Family (*Myrtaceae*).
Showy, fast-growing evergreen shrubs or small trees of Australia with narrow, alternate leaves and handsome flowers. Grown indoors and in cool greenhouses in the Northeast, and outdoors in Fla., southern Calif. and southern Ariz. where they bloom in spring and summer. They are not particular as to soil and are tolerant of dry conditions. Propagate by seeds or cuttings.

C. citrinus: See C. lanceolatus.

Callistemon citrinus 'Splendens'
LEMON BOTTLEBUSH

C. lanceolatus (lan-see-oh-*lay*-tus).
LEMON BOTTLEBRUSH.
Often listed in catalogs as *C. citrinus* (sit-*trin*-ous). Grows to 30 ft. high, with lance-shaped leaves 3 in. long. The flowers have tufted, bright red stamens in rather loose clusters to 4 in. long. *C. citrinus* 'Splendens' (*splen*-denz) has dense, showy flowers. Zones 9 to 10.

Calycanthus (kal-ee-*kanth*-us).
SWEETSHRUB.
Calycanthus Family (*Calycanthaceae*).
Fragrant, deciduous shrubs of N. Amer. with opposite, glossy but rather coarse leaves. These plants will grow in ordinary garden soil in sun or

shade, but do best in rich, well-drained soil. Of chief interest for their aromatic leaves and spicy flowers in spring. The fruits are brown capsules 2 in. or more long. Propagate by seeds, layers or division.

Calycanthus floridus
CAROLINA ALLSPICE

C. floridus (*flo*-ree-dus).
CAROLINA ALLSPICE.
A densely hairy shrub, 4 to 8 ft. high, with dark green elliptical leaves to 5 in. long that are pale beneath. Reddish-brown flowers to 2 in. across. This is the most fragrant and therefore the most commonly grown species—and also the hardiest. Some individual plants have flowers that are very fragrant, whereas other plants may lack fragrance. Zone 4.

Camellia (kuh-*meal*-ee-uh).
Tea Family (*Theaceae*).
Spectacularly handsome evergreen shrubs and trees from Asia that are grown in warm-temperate Amer. for their glossy foliage and showy, waxlike flowers. Alternate leaves. Shallow-rooted, they thrive in cool, moist, humus-rich acidic soil and partial shade. They can stand variable amounts of frost without harm, depending on species and variety. They tolerate shade well. There are scores of excellent hybrids and cultivars. Grown also in cool greenhouses for winter and spring bloom, and, increasingly with new varieties, in sheltered locations outdoors in regions thought to be unfavorable to them. Propagate by seeds, cuttings or grafting.

Camellia japonica 'Arajishi'
CAMELLIA

C. japonica (ja-*pon*-ik-uh).
COMMON CAMELLIA.
This, together with its hybrids, is the most widely grown species. Shrub or tree, it grows to 30 ft. or more. Its oval leaves, dark green and glossy foliage grow to 4 in. long. Its decorative flowers are up to 5 in. across, blooming in late

Camellia

winter and early spring. The many named varieties are selected for their white, pink or red flowers. With winter protection, some have survived outdoors as far north as Westchester County, N.Y. Otherwise a sure thing only in a cool, well-ventilated greenhouse, in pots, tubs or ground beds. Some attractive cultivars are: 'Amabilis', white, single; 'Imura', white, semidouble; 'Purity', white, double; 'Debutante', an older pink double, but very popular; 'Sweetii Vera', a large pink double; 'Arajishi', red, double; 'Lady Vansittart', red, semidouble; 'Herme', variegated double, scented; 'Sara-Sa', semidouble and variegated. Zones 7 to 9.

Camellia sasanqua

C. sasanqua (suh-*san*-quah).

Grows to only about 12 ft. high. Except for certain hybrids, generally blooms earlier and is hardier than *C. japonica*. Loose in habit, with lustrous green leaves to 2 in. long. The white flowers are smaller (to 2 in. across) and more fragile-looking than those of other species, but

the profusion of bloom is a delightful addition to the shrub border or hedge. Numerous semidouble and double flower forms of varying habit and color are known, some hardier than others. For bloom from Sept. to Dec., here are some cultivars of C. sasanqua: 'Blanchette', single, white; 'Hebe', single, pink; 'Mini-no-yuki', double, white, with a faint scent; 'Tanya', single, a dark rose color. Zones 7 to 9.

Caragana (kar-uh-*gay*-nuh).

PEA TREE.
PEA SHRUB.
Pea Family (*Leguminosae*).

Decorative deciduous shrubs or small trees, mostly from Asia. Alternate pinnately compound leaves with small leaflets. Attractive, mostly yellow flowers growing singly or in clusters. Very hardy, growing well in sandy soil and full sun. Propagate by seeds, layers or grafting.

Carpinus betulus
EUROPEAN HORNBEAM

C. arborescens (ar-boh-*ress*-enz).

SIBERIAN PEA TREE.

Erect shrub or shrubby tree to 20 ft. Leaves to 3 in. long, with four to six pairs of leaflets. Yellow flowers, one to four in a cluster, bloom in late spring. A good accent shrub, but of greatest value for cold climate hedges in poor dry soils, or in windbreak in prairie regions of the U.S. Dwarf forms are available. The variety *pendula* (pen-*dew*-luh) has drooping branches and is used in northern landscapes. The cultivar 'Lorbergii' (lor-*bur*-gee-eye) has graceful, almost grassy leaves and smaller flowers than those of some varieties. Best grafted to tall stems of *C. arborescens*. Without grafting, this caragana is a superb soil binder and ground cover for steep, dry banks. Zones 2 to 4.

Carpinus (kar-*pye*-nus).

HORNBEAM.

Birch Family (*Betulaceae*).

Useful and ornamental deciduous trees of the Northern Hemisphere. Their attractive, compact growth habit and interesting fruit recommend these small trees for the home landscape, although (sometimes perhaps because) they are slow growers in poor soil. They may be used for hedges or as specimen plants, and will give good shade when mature. Smooth gray-brown bark, alternate toothed leaves, catkins for flowers and small nutlets enclosed in leaflike bracts. They will grow in any soil. Propagate by seeds, which must be stratified, or, in special varieties, by grafting.

C. americana: See *C. caroliniana*.

C. betulus (bet-*yew*-lus).

EUROPEAN HORNBEAM.

A fine foliage tree up to 50 ft. in its native habitat, but usually shorter and more compact in cultivation. Oval leaves to 4 in. long turn yellow-green in the fall. The massed foliage effect of the mature tree is handsome. Catkins to 4 in. long. Drooping clusters of fruit are decorative in summer and fall. It is widely used for hedges and allees in Europe, as it withstands shearing well. There are many varieties, one with a pyramidal habit, one with drooping branches and an especially handsome form with a densely rounded outline. Zones 5 to 7.

C. caroliniana (ka-roh-lin-ee-*ay*-nuh).

AMERICAN HORNBEAM.

IRONWOOD.

BLUE BEECH.

Often listed in catalogs as *C. americana*. Native to the woods of eastern N. Amer., this species rarely grows over 20 ft. high. It has less compact massing of foliage than the European species. Of a rounded and bushy habit, it often has several trunks. Tolerates wet soil and shade, and has good yellow-to-orange fall coloring. Not easy to transplant, but a fine small, shrublike tree for landscape use. Zones 3 to 8.

Caryopteris (kar-ee-*op*-ter-iss).

Verbena Family (*Verbenaceae*).

Attractive Asiatic shrubs grown for their handsome bloom. Small and deciduous, they are characterized by toothed, opposite leaves. A profusion of showy clusters of blue flowers appears in the fall. Wood is winter-injured where temperatures fall below 20°F.; cut back to stubs in the spring as basal shoots appear. Blooms on new wood in late summer. Easy and popular pot plants for the cool greenhouse, they are useful in the border as well. Should have well-drained light soil and a sunny position. Propagate by seeds or cuttings.

Caryopteris × clandonensis
BLUEBEARD

C. × clandonensis (klan-doh-*nen*-sis).
BLUEBEARD.
A hybrid of *C. incana* and *C. mongholica*. A rounded shrub to about 3 ft., with many clusters of powder blue flowers in late summer. Somewhat hardier than *C. incana*. 'Blue Mist' and 'Heavenly Blue' are excellent clones. Zones 4 to 9.

C. incana (in-*kay*-nuh).
A pleasing plant that occasionally grows to 5 ft., but is generally less than 2 ft. In colder areas it must be cut back to the ground each spring. Grayish leaves to 3 in. long. It makes a useful ground cover or massed effect in a large border. Dense clusters of lavender-blue flowers in the fall. 'Candida' is a white-flowered form. Zones 5 to 9.

Catalpa (kuh-*tal*-puh).
Bignonia Family (*Bignoniaceae*).
Flowering, deciduous trees of N. Amer. and Asia with large, opposite leaves and showy clusters of flowers blooming in early summer, when few other trees are in flower. Long, slender pods follow the blossoms. Although they are short-lived, they make imposing street and specimen trees, and grow well in extreme conditions from deep, moist, fertile soil to wet, dry and alkaline conditions, in sun or partial shade, even desert environments. Tend to be messy trees. Propagate by seeds or root cuttings.

C. bignonioides (big-noh-nee-*oy*-deez).
INDIAN BEAN TREE.
Grows to 40 ft. by 40 ft., with a broad head. Oval leaves to 8 in. long, whorled or opposite in arrangement, emitting an unpleasant odor when bruised. Attractive flowers, 2 in. across and in

Catalpa speciosa
WESTERN CATALPA

broad panicles to 8 in. long, are white with yellow stripes and purple spots. Pods to 15 in. long. The cultivar 'Nana' (*nay*-nuh) is a dwarf, globe-shaped form that rarely blooms but is used for occasional accent in formal plantings. Zones 5 to 8.

C. speciosa (spee-see-*oh*-suh).
WESTERN CATALPA.
Tall, bold tree to 60 ft. tall by 40 ft. wide. Oval leaves to 1 ft. long, downy underneath, are without odor. The white flowers, 2 ½ in. across, with brown spots, bloom in early summer in clusters about 8 in. long. Zones 4 to 8.

Ceanothus 'Puget Blue'

Ceanothus (see–uh–*noth*–us).
Buckthorn Family (*Rhamnaceae*).
A large genus of very handsome deciduous and evergreen shrubs and small trees of N. Amer. Alternate or opposite leaves. The majority of species are hardy only in mild climates. Some are grown for their strongly blue flowers although species' flower colors range from blue to purple, pink and white. Few ceanothuses are cultivated away from the West Coast states. Many may be grown as wall shrubs or as espaliers, but most are warm-climate plants and react badly to winter frosts and root rot from water mold organisms. Grow best in light, well-drained sandy soil in a sunny position. Propagate by seeds or by cuttings.

C. arboreus (ar-*boh*-ree-us).
CATALINA CEANOTHUS.
Evergreen shrub or tree to 20 ft., with oval leaves, white beneath. Fragrant, pale to dark blue flowers. It is native to the islands off the coast of Calif. Zones 8 to 9.

Ceanothus thyrsiflorus
BLUE-BLOSSOM

C. cyaneus (sye-*ay*-nee-us).
San Diego Ceanothus.
Evergreen shrub, growing to 8 ft., with shiny, alternate leaves 2 in. long and rich dark blue flowers in panicles to 10 in. long. Popular for the deep blue color and large and showy flower clusters. Drought resistant. Zones 8 to 9.

C. thyrsiflorus (thir-sif-*floh*-rus).
Blue-blossom.
Evergreen shrub or tree to 20 ft. tall, wider than it is tall, with angled branchlets and glossy green, alternate leaves to 2 in. long. Pale blue flowers. Zones 8 to 9.

Cedrus (*seed*-rus).
Cedar.
Pine Family (*Pinaceae*).
True cedars are large, handsome, evergreen trees of N. Africa and Asia. Magnificent in maturity, they are among the most impressive of all the trees that may be grown in a landscape setting of large scale. The species resemble one another closely in general appearance and in their esthetic merit. They are long-lived and relatively slow-growing. These trees have dark gray bark, smooth at first, later furrowed and scaly. Alternate, single leaves occur on young shoots, but become densely clustered in spurs on older branches. Leaves are stiff and needlelike. Cones are erect. Cedars need full sun and rich moist soil. Propagate by seeds, cuttings or grafts.

C. atlantica (at-*lan*-ti-kuh).
Atlas Cedar.
Upright tree to 75 ft. by 50 ft. wide. Awkward pyramid when young, becoming loose and wide-spreading with age. Green to bluish green leaves, less than 1 in. long. Light brown cones, to 4 in. long. The cultivar 'Glauca' (*glaw*-kuh), the blue atlas cedar, is an especially striking form with

Cedrus deodora
Deodar Cedar

Cedrus libani
Cedar of Lebanon

steel-blue needles. 'Glauca Pendula' (pen-*dew*-luh) has weeping branches; 'Fastigiata' (fas-tig-ee-*eye*-tuh) is an upright, narrow form. Zones 6 to 8.

C. deodara (dee-oh-*dar*-uh).
DEODAR CEDAR.
A tall tree, to 75 ft. by 50 ft. wide, with gracefully pendulous branches (only slightly pendulous in the north). Bluish-green leaves to 2 in. long. Cones to 5 in. long. The cultivars 'Kashmir', 'Kingsville' and 'Shalimar' are all somewhat hardier than the species. Interesting variations are available on the West Coast for yellow foliage and dwarf and prostrate forms. Zones 7 to 9.

C. libani (*lib*-an-eye).
CEDAR OF LEBANON.
Perhaps the hardiest species, it grows to 75 ft. tall, with wide-spreading, horizontal branches to 50 ft. in length. Dark green leaves to 1¼ in. long and brown cones to 4 in. long. Zones 6 to 8.

Celtis (*sell*-tiss).
HACKBERRY.
Elm Family (*Ulmaceae*).
Mostly deciduous trees of the Northern Hemisphere, grown in northern, north-central and southern states as shade and street trees. Alternate, elmlike leaves. The fruit is oval, with scanty pulp. Tolerant of various soils, sun or shade, and city conditions. Propagate by seeds or cuttings.

C. laevigata (lee-vig-*gay*-tuh).
SUGARBERRY.
SUGAR HACKBERRY.
This species is generally resistant to a witches'-broom disease that attacks other species, especially *C. occidentalis*. Tree to 70 ft. tall and 60 ft. wide. Thin leaves to 4 in. long. Very small orange-red to bluish-purple fruits. Zones 6 to 9.

Cercidiphyllum japonicum
KATSURA TREE

C. occidentalis (ox-si-den-*tay*-lis).
COMMON HACKBERRY.
Grows to 60 ft. tall and 50 ft. wide. It has a rounded head, bright green leaves 5 in. long that turn light yellow in the fall, and small, orange-red to purple fruit. Susceptible to leaf galls and witches'-broom disease, which is mainly an esthetic problem in that it disfigures the trees, not one that physically threatens them. Zones 3 to 8.

Cercidiphyllum (ser-si-di-*fill*-um).
KATSURA TREE.
Cercidiphyllum Family (*Cercidiphyllaceae*).
Native to Japan. Ornamental, deciduous trees of dense habit, usually with several trunks. Grow best in rich, moist soil. Propagate by seeds or grafts.

C. japonicum (ja-*pon*-ik-um).
Grows 60 ft. tall and up to 50 ft. wide (some trees

Cercidiphyllum

Cercis canadensis 'Forest Pansy'
EASTERN REDBUD

are much narrower). Handsome blue-green foliage. The leaves, opposite and bluntly toothed, turn a colorful yellow to scarlet in the fall. Flowers are inconspicuous, with male and female occurring on separate trees. Fruits are inconspicuous, small dry capsules. Intolerant of drought. Zones 5 to 8.

Cercis (*ser*-sis).
REDBUD.
Pea Family (*Leguminosae*).
Attractive deciduous shrubs or small trees of N. Amer., Eur. and Asia. Simple, alternate leaves turn yellow in autumn. The showy clusters bloom in early spring on both old and young wood. Trees thrive in well-drained, moist soils and tolerate sun and shade. Propagate by seeds and grafts.

C. canadensis (kan-uh-*den*-sis).
EASTERN REDBUD.
Hardy shrub or tree, native to eastern N. Amer. Grows to 40 ft. high by 30 ft. wide. Spreading branches and light green, heart-shaped leaves to 6 in. long. Slender, pealike, magenta-pink flowers in small clusters, before the leaves appear. Seedlings vary in hardiness. For northern areas, be sure the seed source was also northern. The cultivar 'Alba' (*al*-buh) has distinctive white flowers. 'Wither's Pink Charm' has pale pink flowers. 'Forest Pansy' has leaves that are purplish when grown in the sun but green in the shade. Zones 5 to 9.

C. chinensis (chi-*nen*-sis).
CHINESE REDBUD.
Generally a large, multi-stemmed shrub. 10 ft. tall by 6 ft. wide. Flowers are rosy purple and bloom at about the same time as Eastern Redbud. Leaves are smaller and more leathery. Zones 6 to 9.

C. reniformis (ren-i-*for*-mus).
TEXAS REDBUD.
A small tree, similar to Eastern Redbud, that shows great promise to be healthier and more attractive in warmer regions. Foliage is leathery, slightly smaller, and more rounded in shape. Zones 7 to 9.

Chaenomeles (kee-*nom*-eh-lez).
FLOWERING QUINCE.
Rose Family (*Rosaceae*).
The genus is sometimes included with *Cydonia* (cy-*don*-ee-uh), the true quinces. Ornamental, deciduous, mostly spiny shrubs of Asia. Popular especially for their dense habit and showy, bright-colored (red, pink, or white; single or double) mid-spring flowers, which usually appear in advance of the leaves. Leaves are alternate

in arrangement. The fruit is a hard, yellowish, quincelike pome. They are edible and sometimes used in making preserves. These plants thrive in good garden soil and sun. Propagate by seeds or cuttings.

C. japonica (ja-*pon*-ik-uh).
JAPANESE QUINCE.

Low, much-branched, spreading shrub to 3 ft. tall by 4 ft. wide, with spiny branches and lustrous green leaves. A wide variety of flower colors are available. Zones 5 to 8.

Chaenomeles speciosa
FLOWERING QUINCE

C. speciosa (spee-see-*oh*-suh).
FLOWERING QUINCE.

Spreading shrub to 6 ft. tall and 6 ft. wide. Shiny, oval leaves to 3 in. long remain green until well into the fall. 'Apple Blossom' has pale pink flowers; 'Nivalis' is white. Zones 5 to 8.

✶✶Chamaecyparis (kam-ee-*sip*-a-ris).
FALSE CYPRESS.

Cypress Family (*Cupressaceae*).

Attractive, large, evergreen trees of N. Amer. and Asia, growing up to 80 ft. tall yet rarely spreading beyond 20 ft. There are many dwarf forms. These trees are valuable because of their narrow width, tolerance of sun and shade, and large number of cultivars. Scaly or fissured bark and frondlike branchlets characterize the genus. Leaves are scalelike on mature growth but are needle-like on seedlings, in heavy shade, and on certain cultivars. Cones are small, erect, and globose. They grow best where humidity is high. Propagate by seeds, cuttings or grafting.

Chamaecyparis lawsoniana 'Aurea'
GOLDEN LAWSON FALSE CYPRESS

C. lawsoniana (law-soh-nee-*ay*-nuh).
LAWSON FALSE CYPRESS.
PORT ORFORD CEDAR.

Reddish-brown bark and spreading branches, horizontal or sometimes drooping. Bright green

Chamaecyparis

leaves, with slight whitish markings underneath. Cones to ⅓ in. wide, with small points on each scale; purplish brown when ripe. There are several hundred cultivars of this species, varying in form from dwarf and nearly as broad as tall to tall and narrow. Colors vary from green to blue to yellow. This species grows very well on the west coast but is quite variable in its success in the East. 'Allumii', blue foliage, narrowly pyramidal; 'Aurea': yellowed leaves and grows as tall as the species; 'Ellwoodii': slow-growing shrub with glaucous-blue foliage; 'Fletcheri': feathery blue foliage, dwarf, 'Howarth's Gold': yellow foliage and a dense conical form. Zones 6 to 8.

C. nootkatensis (noot-ka-*ten*-sis).
NOOTKA FALSE CYPRESS.
ALASKA CEDAR.
Brownish-gray bark and erect branches with pendulous branchlets and bluish-green, dense, evergreen foliage. 'Pendula' has horizontal branches with drooping branchlets. Zones 5 to 7.

✴**C. obtusa** (ob-*tew*-suh).
HINOKI CYPRESS.
Has reddish-brown bark, horizontal branches, frondlike pendulous branchlets and dark green leaves with white lines beneath. Numerous named cultivars that vary in color and habit; most are slower growing than the species. A useful substitute for Canada hemlock in regions of hot, dry summers. 'Gracilis' (gra-*sil*-iss) has dark green foliage and forms a compact pyramid. 'Nana' (*nay*-nuh), a very dwarf form growing not much more than 1 in. per year, rarely reaches 2 ft. in height. 'Nana Lutea' (loo-*tee*-uh) is a dwarf yellow plant slightly larger than 'Nana'; 'Coralliformis' (cor-al-i-*for*-mis) a slow growing shrub with twisted branches; 'Crippsii' (*crip*-see-eye) golden yellow leaves and a slightly slower growth rate than the species; 'Magnifica'

Chamaecyparis nootkatensis 'Pendula'
WEEPING NOOTKA FALSE CYPRESS

Chamaecyparis obtusa 'Nana Gracilis'
HINOKI CYPRESS

Chamaecyparis pisifera 'Boulevard'
SAWARA FALSE CYPRESS

(mag-*nif*-ah-cuh) grows vigorously, with slightly denser foliage than the species; 'Nana Gracilis' (gra-*sil*-is) is a beautiful dense dark green form growing about 3 to 4 in. per year. Zones 5 to 8.

C. pisifera (pye-*siff*-er-uh).

SAWARA FALSE CYPRESS.

Pyramidal tree with reddish-brown bark and flattened, somewhat drooping branchlets. Dark green, lustrous scale-like leaves have white lines beneath. Leaves more pointed than Hinoki false cypress. 'Boulevard' has light blue, soft, needle-like foliage that tends to open up with age; 'Filifera' (fil-*if*-er-uh) features long, threadlike, drooping branches; 'Filifera Aurea' (*aw*-ree-uh) has yellow, threadlike, drooping branches; 'Golden Mop' is similar to 'Filifera Aurea' but is a bit slower in growth and presents a better yellow in winter; 'Plumosa Feathery' (ploo-*moh*-suh) has light green branches. Zones 5 to 8.

C. thyoides (thye-*oy*-deez).

ATLANTIC WHITE CEDAR.

Native to areas along the eastern coast of the U.S. Very similar in appearance to eastern red cedar, *Juniperus virginiana* (joo-*nip*-er-us vir-gin-ee-*ay*-nuh) but has small, pointy round cones that turn purplish brown when ripe. Tolerates almost any acid soil, sun and shade. Often brownish in full sun in the winter. Zones 5 to 9.

Chimonanthus (kye-moh-*nan*-thus).

Calycanthus Family (*Calycanthaceae*).

A genus of shrubs from Asia. Grown for very early spring flowers that are golden yellow and very fragrant. Full sun or light shade. Well-drained soil. Propagate by seeds or cuttings.

Chimonanthus praecox
WINTERSWEET

C. praecox (*pree*-cox).

WINTERSWEET.

Deciduous Chinese shrub to 10 ft. tall and 6 ft. wide. Has coarse opposite, lustrous green, de-

Chimonanthus

Chionanthus virginicus
FRINGETREE

ciduous leaves to 6 in. long. The very fragrant yellow flowers bloom in late winter, well before the leaves appear. It can be effectively trained on walls. Zones 6 to 9.

Chionanthus (kye-oh-*nan*-thus).
FRINGETREE.
Olive Family (*Oleaceae*).
A group of small, hardy, deciduous trees or large shrubs. In spring they bear large panicles of small white flowers. Male and female flowers on separate plants. Dark blue fruit is produced on female plants and is fairly showy. Tolerate sun or shade, but bloom best in bright light conditions. Propagate by cuttings or seed.

C. retusus (reh-*tew*-sus).
CHINESE FRINGETREE.
Native to China. Leaves more leathery and smaller than *C. virginicus*. The flowers are more showy and appear later. Grows to 20 ft. high with a similar spread. Zones 6 to 8. The variety *ser-*

rulatus has very attractive, rugged brown bark, but may be less hardy.

✳C. virginicus (vir-*jin*-i-cus).
FRINGETREE.
This native of the southeastern U.S. grows about 20 ft. tall and 20 ft. wide. It bears lacy white flowers on panicles 6 in. long in late spring as the leaves are emerging. Yellow fall color. Zones 5 to 8.

Choisya (*koy*-see-uh).
Rue Family (*Rutaceae*).
The primary species in cultivation is a handsome evergreen shrub from Mexico with opposite, trifoliate leaves and fragrant white flowers. Propagate by seeds and cuttings.

C. ternata (ter-*nay*-tuh).
MEXICAN ORANGE.
Grows to 8 ft. high and wide with attractive, bright green foliage and showy clusters of fra-

Choisya ternata
MEXICAN ORANGE

Cistus ladanifer
LAUDANUM

grant white flowers, each to 1 in. across. Blooms in spring, sometimes continuing throughout the summer. Does best in full sun. Zones 8 to 10.

Cistus (*sis*-tus).
ROCK ROSE.
Rock rose Family (*Cistaceae*).
Handsome shrubs of the Mediterranean region, mostly evergreen. They have simple, opposite leaves and showy delicate flowers that usually last only a day but are produced for several weeks in succession. Rock roses thrive in well-drained limestone soil in a sunny location. They tolerate salt spray and strong winds. They look very much like roses at first glance. Propagate by seeds and cuttings.

C. ladanifer (la-*dan*-if-er).
LAUDANUM.
Erect, branched shrub to 5 ft. tall, with dark green, sticky leaves, white beneath. Flowers to 3½ in. across, white with yellow center. Zones 9 to 10.

Cladrastis (kla-*dras*-tiss).
YELLOWWOOD.
Pea Family (*Leguminosae*).
Vigorous and handsome deciduous trees of N. Amer. and Asia. Alternate, pinnate leaves and attractive white flowers in long clusters. Propagate by seed.

C. lutea (lew-*tee*-uh).
AMERICAN YELLOWWOOD.
Also known as *C. kentukea*. A beautiful flowering tree growing 30 to 50 ft. high and spreading about 40 ft. Worth growing in landscapes for its modest size at maturity, its very decorative foliage effect through the season and its showy flowers. Flowers have a tendency to be borne in alternate years. Smooth gray bark and bright green leaves, with seven to nine leaflets, which turn bright yellow in the fall. Fragrant, white flowers in loose, drooping clusters, 1 ft. long, bloom in late spring. Zones 5 to 8.

Clerodendrum (kleer-oh-*den*-drum).
GLORY-BOWER.
Verbena Family (*Verbenaceae*).
Rapid-growing, deciduous and evergreen

shrubs, vines and trees of tropical regions (mostly Asia). Leaves simple, opposite or in whorls. Flowers showy and in terminal clusters. Propagate by seeds or cuttings.

C. trichotomum. (tri-koh-*toh*-mum)
HARLEQUIN GLORY-BOWER.
Native to China and Japan. A showy shrub growing to 10 ft. tall and 8 ft. wide. Has oval leaves to 8 in. long, with a strong medicinal odor. Fragrant, white flowers with red bases (calyces), followed by showy blue berries in round clusters. May freeze to the ground in Zones 5 and 6 but will regrow from the roots. Zones 6 to 8.

Clethra (*kleth*-ruh).
WHITE ALDER.
White-alder Family (*Clethraceae*).
Ornamental shrubs or small trees of tropical and temperate regions of the world. They have white flowers in spirelike clusters. Some species are especially fragrant and all are valued for their abundant late-summer bloom. Simple, toothed, alternate leaves. They thrive in moist soils, in sun or shade. Propagate by seeds or cuttings.

C. alnifolia (al-ni-*foh*-lee-uh).
SWEET PEPPERBUSH.
SUMMER-SWEET.
A suckering, deciduous shrub to 8 ft. tall and about 5 ft. wide. Native to the Atlantic Coast. Fall color yellow. Very fragrant white flowers in erect clusters to 6 in. long. Tolerates wet and dry soils. Propagate by seeds, division, or cuttings. 'Rosea' (roh-*zee*-uh) has pink flowers. Zones 5 to 9.

C. barbinervis (bar-bin-*er*-vis).
JAPANESE CLETHRA.
Large shrub or small tree to 15 ft. tall and 6 ft. wide. Non-suckering, with attractive exfoliating bark on old shoots. Flowers white, held horizon-

tally on the plant. Leaves larger and darker green than the preceding species. Fall color orange. Zones 6 to 8.

Comptonia (komp-*toh*-nee-uh).
SWEET FERN.
Sweet-gale Family (*Myricaceae*).
There is only one species—an aromatic, deciduous shrub of eastern N. Amer. Tolerates infertile soils, since it is able to fix its own nitrogen, but does best in acid soils. Tolerates drought, sun and shade. Does not transplant well. Propagate by seeds or division of clumps.

C. peregrina (per-i-*grye*-nuh).
Sometimes mistakenly listed as *Myrica asplenifolia* (*meer*-uh-cuh ass-*plen*-uh-fohl-ee-uh). Grows to 4 ft. tall by 4 ft. wide, with deeply cut, alternate leaves that resemble ferns. Insignificant green flowers in catkins. Zones 4 to 7.

Clethra alnifolia
SWEET PEPPERBUSH

✳✳Cornus (*kor*-nus).

DOGWOOD.

Dogwood Family (*Cornaceae*).

A large genus of shrubs and trees containing some of the choicest and most ornamental woody plants. Mostly deciduous, with simple, usually opposite leaves. Valued for their generally attractive appearance, showy floral effect in spring or early summer, colorful fruit displays, and colorful autumn foliage. Some also display strongly colored stems in winter. The latter provide better color in the stems when cut to the ground in late winter to ensure growth of colorful new shoots. They grow in sun or shade, but will be most colorful in full sun. Propagate by seeds, cuttings, layers or grafting.

C. alba (*al*-buh).

TATARIAN DOGWOOD.

Deciduous shrub from eastern Asia. Grows to 8 ft. tall by 8 ft. wide with stems that are bright red in winter but turn green during the growing season. Leaves to 4 in. long, whitish beneath. Fall color yellow to red. White spring flowers in clusters, about 2 in. across, but only moderately showy. White to bluish fruits. 'Argenteomarginata' (ar-jen-*tee*-oh mar-ji-*nay*-tuh) has leaves edged with white, but it tends to be less vigorous than the species; 'Spaethii' (*spayth*-ee-eye) has yellow-edged leaves; 'Sibirica' (sye-*bear*-i-kuh) was selected for its outstanding winter coral-red bark. Zones 3 to 7.

C. alternifolia (al-ter-ni-*foh*-lee-uh).

PAGODA DOGWOOD.

Hardy, deciduous shrub or tree to 20 ft. tall by 20 ft. wide, is a native of eastern N. America. Grows best in cool shade. The branches are whorled in horizontal tiers, resulting in a somewhat oriental effect. Alternate leaves, to 4 in. long, turn orange to purple in autumn. Small,

creamy-white spring flowers borne in showy, flattened clusters. Dark blue fruit, which is showy but quickly eaten by birds. The cultivar 'Argentea' (ar-gen-*tee*-uh) has white variegated leaves. Zones 4 to 7.

Cornus alternifolia
PAGODA DOGWOOD

✳C. florida (*flor*-i-duh).

FLOWERING DOGWOOD.

The most ornamental and famous dogwood, attractive in every season of the year. Grows to 20 ft. tall and wide, with leaves to 6 in. long. Autumn foliage color is an attractive deep red. Greenish-yellow flowers in mid-spring above four large, white bracts, producing a very showy effect. Scarlet fruit adds to the autumnal and early winter display (until eaten by birds). The cultivar 'Rubra' (*roo*-bruh) has pink bracts. 'Welchii' (*welch*-ee-eye) and 'Rainbow' have leaves with both pink and creamy-white variegation. 'Eddie's White Wonder', which has 5½-in. bracts and a longer bloom period, is a cross between *C. florida* and *C. nuttallii*. 'Welch's Junior Miss' has large attractive pink and white bracts and is especially useful in warm areas. It is probably less cold hardy than other cultivars. 'Cherokee Chief' has flower bracts of a rich ruby-red. 'Cherokee Princess', 'Springtime' and 'Cloud 9' were selected for very attractive blooms, which begin when the plant is very young; 'Alba Plena' ('Plu-

Cornus florida 'Rubra'
PINK FLOWERING DOGWOOD

ribracteata') is double-flowering, blooms for a longer period of time and is usually fruitless. Zones 5 to 8.

✱ **C. kousa** (*koo*-suh).
JAPANESE DOGWOOD.
KOREAN DOGWOOD.
Asian shrub or tree to 25 ft. tall with a 20 ft. spread. Leaves, to 4 in. long, turn orange in autumn. Greenish-yellow flowers bloom above extremely showy, creamy-white, pointed bracts in June and remain for at least four weeks. Bracts may remain showy even longer, turning pink with age. Rounded, pinkish-orange fruit hangs below branches in late summer. 'Milky Way' was selected for heavier flowering and 'Summer Stars' retains its floral bracts until late summer. Zones 5 to 7.

C. mas (*mass*).
CORNELIAN CHERRY.
Vigorous spreading tree to 20 ft. tall by 20 ft.

wide. Oval leaves of lustrous green grow to 4 in. long, coloring late in autumn to a reddish-orange. Tolerates shade, but blooms and colors best in full sun. Small, showy clusters of yellow flowers bloom in early spring. Scarlet, edible fruits ripen in late summer. 'Golden Glory' bears deeper yellow flowers and is more showy in bloom than the species. 'Flava' has yellow fruit. Zones 5 to 7.

C. nuttallii (nuh-*tall*-ee-eye).
PACIFIC DOGWOOD.
The Pacific Northwest counterpart to *C. florida*, but growing taller and usually bearing 6 floral bracts. May bloom twice, spectacularly in spring. Generally unsuccessful in the East. Zones 6 to 8.

C. officinalis (oh-fis-i-*na*-lis).
JAPANESE CORNEL.
Similar in most aspects to *C. mas*. Bark exfoliates, and thus is more attractive. Usually blooms a week earlier and ripens its fruits later. Zones 5 to 7.

Cornus kousa
JAPANESE DOGWOOD

Cornus mas
CORNELIAN CHERRY

C. sericea (ser-*eh*-see-uh).
REDOSIER DOGWOOD.
Also known as *C. stolonifera* (stoh-lon-*if*-er-uh). Valued for its brilliant red winter twigs, this eastern U.S. native grows to 12 ft. and self-layers, making large clumps that may spread to 15 ft. Grows naturally in wet areas, but tolerates drought. Leaves to 4 in. long. Small, white flowers in flat clusters about 2 in. across in late spring are not very showy. White fruit. This species is at its best massed or in naturalistic shrub plantings that are readily visible in winter. 'Flaviramea' (flay-vir-ray-*mee*-uh) is conspicuous in winter with its yellow stems. 'Kelseyi' (*kel*-see-eye) is a dwarf form, but is often disappointing due to health problems and lack of winter stem color. Zones 3 to 7.

Corylopsis (kor-i-*lop*-sis).
WINTER HAZEL.
Witch-hazel Family (*Hamamelidaceae*).

Cornus nuttallii
PACIFIC DOGWOOD

Corylopsis

Deciduous shrubs from Asia, with alternate leaves and charming yellow flowers in nodding clusters that bloom in early spring before the leaves appear. They thrive in light, peaty soil. Generally best in light shade, but will tolerate heavy shade or full sun, if the soil is sufficiently moist. Propagate by seeds or cuttings.

Corylopsis glabrescens
FRAGRANT WINTER HAZEL

C. glabrescens (gla-*bres*-enz).
FRAGRANT WINTER HAZEL.
A neat, dense shrub, growing to 12 ft. by 12 ft., with leaves to 3 in. long. Delicate, fragrant, pale yellow flowers in ample clusters, 1 in. or more long. Zones 5 to 8.

C. pauciflora (paw-si-*floh*-ruh).
BUTTERCUP WINTER HAZEL.
Charming, low shrub, from 4 to 6 ft. high, spreading horizontally to about 6 ft. Ovate leaves to 3 in. long, pale beneath, with attractive veination. Young leaves have a touch of red on the margins. Pale yellow flowers, two or three in a cluster. Zones 6 to 8.

Corylus (*kor*-i-lus).
HAZEL.
HAZELNUT.
FILBERT.
Birch Family (*Betulaceae*).
Deciduous bushy shrubs or small trees from northern temperate regions. Valued for their ornamental catkins, which appear in early spring, as well as for their nuts. The rather large, broad, ovate leaves are toothed and often hairy. Male and female flowers borne separately on the same plant, males in drooping catkins, females inconspicuously in clusters from a small bud, with only red styles showing. Propagate by seeds, cuttings, suckers or budding.

C. americana (uh-mer-i-*kay*-nuh).
AMERICAN FILBERT.
A bold shrub 5 to 10 ft. tall with a similar spread. Native to N. Amer. Leaves grow to 5 in. long and turn yellow in the fall. Produce two to four small roundish nuts in a cluster in a lobed, leafy enclosure twice as long as the nuts. The flavor is excellent. Zones 3 to 8.

C. avellana (av-el-*lay*-nuh).
EUROPEAN HAZEL.
Grows 15 ft. to 25 ft. high and about 10 ft. wide. Leaves to 4 in. long. Clusters of one to four nuts in a leafy covering. Native to Eur. The cultivar 'Aurea' (*aw*-ree-uh) has yellow leaves. 'Contorta' (kon-*tor*-tuh) has oddly twisted and somewhat pendulous branches and is often called "Harry Lauder's Walking Stick." Zones 3 to 9.

C. colurna (coh-*lur*-nuh).
TURKISH FILBERT.
Usually a small tree to 40 ft. tall and about 20 ft.

wide but can grow to 80 ft. Native to southeastern Eur. and W. Asia. Attractive, slightly exfoliating bark. Coarse leaves turn yellow in autumn. Zones 5 to 8.

C. maxima 'Purpurea' (*max*-uh-muh per-*puh*-ree-uh)
GIANT FILBERT

Native to southeastern Eur. Grows to 30 ft. Produces large nuts and has purplish-red foliage. Zones 4 to 8.

Cotinus (ko-*ti*-nus).
Cashew Family (*Anacardiaceae*).

Deciduous shrubs or small trees with alternate leaves. Desirable for landscapes for the handsome foliage and large, loose clusters of flowers. Grow in sun or light shade. Propagate by seeds, layers or cuttings.

C. coggygria (coh-*gig*-ree-uh).
SMOKE TREE.
SMOKEBUSH.

Eurasian shrub or small tree to 15 ft. high and 12 ft. wide. Has roundish leaves to 3 in. long, turning yellow to orange to purple in the fall. Profuse, feathery, pinkish flowering and fruiting clusters, to 10 in. long, are much branched and give a "smoky" appearance in summer. 'Royal Purple' and 'Velvet Cloak' have dark purplish leaves and fruiting panicles. Plants can be cut back hard in the spring to promote colorful new foliage and to prevent bloom. Zones 5 to 8.

C. obovatus (ab-oh-*vay*-tus).
AMERICAN SMOKETREE.

Small tree to 35 ft. tall and 20 ft. wide. Flowers and fruits less showy and leaves a bit larger than the preceding species. Fall color an excellent red-orange. Zones 4 to 8.

Corylus avellana 'Contorta'
HARRY LAUDER'S WALKING STICK

Cotinus coggygria
SMOKE TREE

Cotoneaster (koh-toh-nee-*ass*-ter).

Rose Family (*Rosaceae*).

Handsome and varied deciduous or evergreen shrubs and ground covers, mostly from temperate regions of northern Asia. Valued for graceful branch structure, fine foliage and ornamental berries, which usually appear in the fall. Small, alternate leaves; the small white or pinkish flowers are borne singly or in clusters in the spring and some are rather showy. The fruit is generally bright red, looking like tiny apples. The form varies from very low to 15 ft. Only the taller, shrubby species are covered in this book. All species grow best in well-drained soil and full sun or slight shade. Since they do not transplant well with bare roots, use pots or ball and burlap. They may be attacked by fire blight. Propagate by seeds, layers or cuttings.

C. divaricatus (di-var-i-*kay*-tus).

SPREADING COTONEASTER.

Native to China. Grows to 6 ft. high by 6 ft. wide, with dense, spreading branches. Small, shiny, deciduous leaves turn red before falling in mid-autumn. Pinkish flowers and deep red fruit. Zones 5 to 8.

C. lacteus (lak-*tay*-us).

MILKY COTONEASTER.

Semi-evergreen shrub, native to China. It produces very hairy leaves and extremely showy, persistent, red fruit. Zones 7 to 9.

C. multiflorus (mull-ti-*floh*-rus).

This deciduous shrub grows to 10 ft. by 10 ft., with handsome, arching branches. Native to western China. Leaves grow to 2 in. long, dull above and whitish beneath, and turn a pale yellow before dropping. White flowers in loose, showy clusters. This is one of the showiest Cotoneasters in bloom. Large, red, conspicuous fruit. Zones 5 to 7.

Cotoneaster lacteus
MILKY COTONEASTER

Crataegus crus-galli
COCKSPUR HAWTHORN

C. salicifolius (sal-is-i-*foh*-lee-us).
Native to western China. Semi-evergreen, gracefully arching, upright shrub to 12 ft. high and 8 ft. wide. Leaves, to 3 in. long, are fairly narrow. White flowers are fairly inconspicuous. Red fruit. Zones 6 to 8.

C. × watereri (wat-er-*er*-eye).
WATERER COTONEASTER.
A hybrid of *C. frigidus × C. henryanus*. A large shrub to 15 ft. in height. Large dark red fruit in clusters with dark green, evergreen leaves 4 to 5 in. long. Zones 7 to 9.

Crataegus (kruh-*tee*-gus).
HAWTHORN.
THORN APPLE.
Rose Family (*Rosaceae*).
A large group of spiny, deciduous small trees, native in the North Temperate Zone, a great many in N. Amer. Alternate, toothed or lobed leaves, some with good fall color. Clusters of white flowers (pink or red in a few) appear in late spring or early summer, followed by colorful fruit that resembles miniature apples. Tolerate sun or light shade. Propagate by seeds or grafting. All tolerate shearing well.

C. crus-galli (crus-*gal*-ee).
COCKSPUR HAWTHORN.
Native to eastern North Amer. A horizontally branching hawthorn, which grows to 25 ft. high by 25 or 30 ft. wide. Quantities of slender but strong spines to 4 in. long. Excellent wine-red fall color. Flowers are ½ in. wide, showy, occurring after the leaves. Fruit dull red. Zones 4 to 6.

C. laevigata (lee-vi-*ga*-tuh).
ENGLISH HAWTHORN.
Small tree, to 20 ft. by 20 ft., is native to Eur. Leaves have three to five lobes with little fall color. The flowers   pink, white or dark red—

appear in mid-spring with the leaves. Fruit is scarlet, small and not very showy. Prone to attack by insects and diseases. 'Paul's Scarlet' has showy red double flowers. Zones 5 to 7.

C. × lavallei (lav-*val*-ee-eye).
LAVALLE HAWTHORN.
Hybrid between *C. crus-galli* and *C. pubescens*. A rounded tree to 20 ft. tall by 15 ft. wide. Thornless or with a few stout spines. Leaves to 4 in. long, turning bronzy-red in fall. Late spring white flowers are ¾ in. across, occurring in clusters. Showy, orange-red fruit remains into winter. Zones 4 to 7.

C. phaenopyrum (fee-no-*pye*-rum).
WASHINGTON HAWTHORN.
Pyramidal tree from eastern and midwestern U.S., to 30 ft. tall and 25 ft. wide. Leaves, to 2½ in. long, look a bit like miniature maple leaves, and turn scarlet to orange in autumn. Small, bright orange fruit in large clusters that are colorful throughout the winter. Zones 4 to 7.

✳**C. viridis** (vir-*ree*-dees).
GREEN HAWTHORN.
Small, wide-spreading tree; 25 ft. to 40 ft. tall and as wide. Lustrous green leaves and orange fall color. White flowers in late spring show nicely in contrast with the new foliage. Orange-red fruits last into late winter. Bark exfoliates attractively. 'Winter King' has slightly larger fruits that are often showy until spring. Zones 5 to 8.

Cryptomeria (krip-toh-*meh*-ree-uh).
Bald-cypress family (*Taxodiaceae*).
A one-species genus, native to Japan. This evergreen tree of pyramidal form produces densely whorled, curved, bluish-green needles, ¾ in. long. It grows best in moist soil, protected from the wind. Extremely important timber tree in

Cryptomeria

Asia. Propagate by seeds, grafts, or cuttings. Zones 6 to 9.

Cryptomeria japonica
JAPANESE CEDAR

C. japonica (ja-*pon*-ik-uh).

JAPANESE CEDAR.

A majestic tree, the tallest in Japan, becomes about 60 ft. tall and 25 ft. wide in the U.S. Foliage has a tendency to brown. Its reddish-brown shredding bark is very attractive. Cones are round, to 1 in. across, with unique pointed projections. 'Lobbii' (*lob*-ee-eye) has branches clustered ball-like, almost like pom-poms; it grows 40 to 60 ft. tall. 'Bandai-sugi' (ban-*day*-eye *soo*-gee) is a round, dwarf plant to about 6 ft. tall; 'Elegans' (*ell*-uh-ganz) is rounded in form, has longer needles than the species, and turns purplish in winter. 'Yoshino' (yo-*shee*-no) is a narrow, pyramidal form that becomes as tall as the species but stays a better green during the winter; it is perhaps hardier.

Cunninghamia (kun-ing-*ham*-ee-uh).
Bald-cypress Family (*Taxodiaceae*).
Evergreen, coniferous trees. Native to eastern Asia. Flat leaves spreading in two ranks. Propagate by seed or cuttings.

C. lanceolata (lan-see-oh-*lay*-tuh).
CHINA-FIR.
A somewhat rare evergreen coniferous tree native to China. It grows about 60 ft. tall and about 30 ft. wide. Bluish-green, sharp-pointed, flat needles, with two white lines on the underside. Tends to hold old brown foliage. Bark attractive, reddish brown. Has the unique ability to sprout new branches on old wood and even from stumps. Tolerates full sun or shade. Wind protection advisable in northern regions. 'Glauca' (*glau*-ka) is a very attractive blue form, somewhat hardier than the species. Zones 6 to 9.

× *Cupressocyparis leylandii* 'Castellwellan Gold'
LEYLAND CYPRESS CULTIVAR

× **Cupressocyparis** (kew-press-oh-*si*-pa-ris).

Cypress Family (*Cupressaceae*).

A hybrid genus resulting from the cross between *Cupressus* and *Chamaecyparis*. Evergreen, scale-like foliage. Round cones intermediate in size between the two genera. Propagate from cuttings. Grow in full sun or shade.

× **C. leylandii** (lay-*lan*-dee-eye).

LEYLAND CYPRESS.

A hybrid between *Cupressus macrocarpa* and *Chamaecyparis nootkatensis*. An extremely fast-growing narrow, columnar tree, 70 ft. tall by 10 ft. wide. Green, flat foliage on upright branches. 'Naylor's Blue' has bluish foliage; 'Leighton Green' is deep green in color; 'Silver Dust' is white variegated, 'Castlewellan Gold' has yellow foliage. Zones 6 to 9.

Cupressus (kew-*press*-us).

CYPRESS.

Cypress Family (*Cupressaceae*).

This is the genus of true cypress. Magnificent evergreen trees, native in N. Amer., southern Eur. and Asia. Small, aromatic, opposite leaves are needle- or scalelike. Require well drained soil and do best in full sun. Propagate by sowing seeds or by cuttings.

C. arizonica (ah-ree-*zohn*-ih-kuh).

ARIZONA CYPRESS.

Native to the Southwest, from Ariz. to Tex. and Mexico, it is one of the hardiest cypresses. Grows to 40 ft. high and 15 ft. wide, with a narrow form. Attractive, exfoliating bark. Fine-textured, bluish-green leaves are sharp and resinous. Cones to 1 in. long. Zones 7 to 9.

C. macrocarpa (mak-roh-*kar*-puh).

MONTEREY CYPRESS.

Grows to 40 ft. high and 30 ft. wide. Although it is pyramidal when young, it becomes broad and spreading later. Dark green leaves and cones to 1½ in. across. Fast growing, this cypress withstands shearing well. It is the best cypress for the seashore, especially in S. Calif. where it is a native. Does not grow well in the East. 'Aurea' and 'Goldcrest' have golden foliage. Zones 8 to 9.

Cupressus macrocarpa 'Goldcrest'
MONTEREY CYPRESS CULTIVAR

C. sempervirens (sem-per-*vye*-rens).

ITALIAN CYPRESS.

Tall, naturally narrow tree with dark green foliage. The typical cypress of Italy, it is native to southern Eur. and western Asia. Does not grow well in areas of high humidity but is drought tolerant in Calif. and S. Ariz. Zones 9 to 10.

Cytisus (*si*-ti-sus).

BROOM.

Pea Family (*Leguminosae*).

Attractive, deciduous or evergreen shrubs from

Cytisus

Eur. and Asia, with simple or trifoliate leaves; some are almost leafless. Valued especially for their profuse bright-colored blossoms and for providing green stems and/or leaves in winter. Most species grow best in a sunny location where they have excellent drainage. They are free-flowering in yellow, white, or pink. Propagate by seeds or cuttings.

Cytisus × praecox
WARMINSTER BROOM

C. × praecox (*pree*-cox).
WARMINSTER BROOM.
A handsome hybrid between *C. multiflorus* (multi-*flo*-rus)—white—and *C. purgans* (*pur*-gans)—yellow. A vigorous, deciduous shrub, growing to 6 ft. tall and wide. Branches are green (effective in a winter garden), slender, erect or spreading. Leaves are small. Pale yellow flowers are produced in abundance in the spring. Zones 6 to 9.

C. scoparius (sko-*pay*-ree-us).
SCOTCH BROOM.
Naturalized in N. Amer. Deciduous, green-stemmed shrub to 8 ft. with an equal spread. Yellow flowers in spring. Zones 6 to 8.

Daphne (*daff*-nee).
Mezereum Family (*Thymelaeaceae*).
Small evergreen and deciduous shrubs from Eur. and Asia. They are characterized by graceful form, flowers that are often highly fragrant, and fine-textured foliage. Fruits are rarely produced; many are poisonous. They grow best in a well-drained soil and in full sun. Propagate by seeds, cuttings, or layers.

Daphne × burkwoodii 'Somerset'
BURKWOOD DAPHNE

D. × burkwoodii (burk-*wood*-ee-eye).
BURKWOOD DAPHNE.
Hybrid of *D. caucasica* and *D. cneorum*. A compact bush to about 4 ft., with narrow leaves that are evergreen or nearly so. Profuse, fragrant, white

to pink flowers in spring. The clone 'Somerset' bears more flowers and is more compact than the species; 'Carol Mackie' has creamy-white edges to its leaves and produces light pink flowers. Zones 5 to 7.

D. cneorum (nee-*oh*-rum).
GARLAND FLOWER.
ROSE DAPHNE.

Native to mountains in Eur. A dense, evergreen shrub to about 1 ft. high and about 2 ft. wide. Alternate, dark green leaves. Short clusters of bright, fragrant, rose-pink flowers in spring. Zones 4 to 7.

D. mezereum (mee-*zeer*-ee-um).
FEBRUARY DAPHNE.

Deciduous, upright shrub to 3 ft. with an equal spread. Leaves to 3 in. long and alternate in arrangement. Flowers very fragrant, rosy-purple, in early spring before the leaves appear. Bright red berries in the summer. Zones 3 to 7.

D. odora (oh-*doh*-ruh).
WINTER DAPHNE.

Evergreen shrub to 4 ft. by 4 ft. Extremely fragrant flowers in late winter, rosy white in color. 'Alba' has white flowers; 'Aureomarginata' (or-ree-oh-mar-gin-*ah*-tuh) has leaves edged in yellow and may be slightly hardier. Zones 7 to 8.

Davidia involucrata var. *vilmoriniana*
DOVE TREE

Davidia (da-*vid*-ee-uh).
DOVE TREE.
Tupelo Family (*Nyssaceae*).

The only species is an ornamental, deciduous tree from China. The common name derives from the striking effect of the two showy, creamy-white bracts of unequal length that appear beneath each flower, giving the fanciful impression that doves have settled all over the tree. Propagate by seeds or by cuttings.

D. involucrata var. vilmoriniana (in-voh-loo-*kray*-tah vil-more-in-ee-*ay*-nah).
DOVE TREE.
HANDKERCHIEF TREE.

Blooms in mid-spring. Actually the flowers are inconspicuous but the two creamy white bracts that appear around the little ball of flowers are the real show. The leaves are alternate, heart shaped, 3 to 6 in. long, and coarsely toothed. Yellow fall color. This variety is hardier than the species. The tree is broadly pyramidal and will grow to from 20 to 40 ft. tall and will spread up to 40 ft. The fruit is small, green, nutlike and not showy. Plant in full sun to partial shade in deep, moist, rich, well-drained soil. Zones 6 to 8.

Deutzia (*dewt*-see-uh).
Saxifrage Family (*Saxifragaceae*).

Attractive, deciduous shrubs, mostly from eastern Asia and the mountains of Cent. Amer. Grown chiefly for the wealth of clustered flowers (mostly white) in spring and early summer. Opposite, toothed leaves. Grow in full sun and a well-drained soil for best flowering. Propagate by seeds, cuttings or layers.

D. gracilis (*grass*-il-iss).
SLENDER DEUTZIA.

A compact shrub growing about 4 ft. high and wide. Slender stems in spreading clumps. Narrow, pale green leaves to 2½ in. long, with a slight yellow coloration in the fall. Profuse clusters of pure white flowers in mid-spring, just before the leaves emerge. Zones 5 to 8.

D. × lemoinei (lee-*moy*-nee-eye).
LEMOINE DEUTZIA.
Hybrid between *D. parviflora* and *D. gracilis*. Shrub to 7 ft., spreading to 5 ft. Leaves to 4 in. long. Broad clusters of white flowers about ¾ in. long, freely produced. Zones 5 to 8.

Deutzia scabra 'Plena'
FUZZY DEUTZIA

D. scabra (*skay*-bruh).
FUZZY DEUTZIA.
Grows to 8 ft. in height and spreads 6 ft. Bark eventually exfoliates on old wood. Leaves to 3 in. long, rough and hairy on both sides. White flowers in narrow, loose, erect clusters to 5 in. long appear in late spring and early summer. 'Pride of Rochester' and 'Plena' have double white flowers. Zones 6 to 8.

Diospyros (dye-*oss*-pihr-os).
PERSIMMON.
Ebony Family (*Ebenaceae*).
Trees of N. Amer. and Asia with deciduous leaves. Bold foliage and decorative, edible fruit. Flowers are not very showy. More than one tree is needed for best fruit set. The fruit is a juicy, tasty, edible berry with large seeds. Persimmons will

grow in almost any well-drained soil. They tolerate sun or shade, but fruit best in the sun. A number of cultivars have been selected. Some ripen fruit early; others only after frost. Propagate by grafting or seeds.

D. kaki (*kay*-kye).
KAKI.
Sometimes referred to as oriental persimmon. Grows 40 ft. high and spreads about 20 ft. Leaves, 4 to 6 in. long, turn yellow in the fall. The orange to reddish fruit, about 3 in. long, ripens in late fall and has a delicious taste when fully ripe. It is much larger than the American species. It is said that Japan has as many cultivars of Kaki as the U.S. has of the apple. Zones 7 to 9, although some cultivars are hardier.

D. virginiana (vir-jin-ee-*ay*-nuh).
COMMON PERSIMMON.
This is a native American tree found wild in southeastern and southcentral states. Considerably hardier than the above and taller (to 60 ft. with a 35-ft. spread). Yellow or orange fruit to 1½ in. across; generally with a much stronger flavor than the oriental species. Zones 5 to 9.

Dirca (*dir*-cuh).
LEATHERWOOD.
Mezereum Family (*Thymelaeceae*).
Erect, deciduous shrubs with very flexible branches, native to the U.S.

D. palustris (pa-*lus*-tris).
Eastern N. Amer. Deciduous shrub to 6 ft. tall by 6 ft. wide. Small yellow flowers in early spring. Foliage of medium texture; green during the summer, turning yellow in autumn. Twigs so flexible they can be tied together. Propagate by seed or layers. Zones 3 to 8.

Disanthus (diz-*an*-thus)

Witch hazel family (*Hamamelidaceae*).
A genus of only one species, a deciduous shrub from Japan.

D. cercidifolius (sir-sid-i-*foh*-lee-us).

Alternate, deciduous leaves, dull green during the summer, turning a rich purple in autumn. Tolerates sun or shade; best with ample moisture but needs good drainage. Flowers, small and red, appear in autumn as the leaves are coloring and remain in bloom for about a week after leaf drop. Propagate by seed or cuttings. Zones 5 to 8.

Edgeworthia (edge-*worth*-ee-uh).

PAPERBUSH.
EDGEWORTHIA.
Mezereum family (*Thymelaeaceae*).
Deciduous shrubs from China and the Himalayas, with very flexible branches.

Elaeagnus angustifolia 'Caspica'
RUSSIAN-OLIVE

E. papyrifera (pa-pye-ri-*fur*-uh).

PAPERBUSH
Grows to about 6 ft. by 6 ft., with an open, loose habit. Flower buds, showy much of the winter, are covered with bright white hairs. These open in early spring to display showy yellow or rarely orange flowers. Propagate by seed or cuttings. Zones 8 to 9.

Elaeagnus (eh-lee-*ag*-nus).

Oleaster Family (*Elaeagnaceae*).
Ornamental shrubs or trees, evergreen or deciduous. Native to Eur., Asia and N. Amer. Alternate silvery leaves, covered with scales. Fragrant, small tubular flowers. Berrylike fruit, which may or may not be showy. Grow in any well-drained soil. Propagate by seeds or by cuttings.

E. angustifolia (an-gus-ti-*foh*-lee-uh).

RUSSIAN-OLIVE.
A small, silvery tree, growing to 20 ft. tall with a similar spread. Twigs are often spiny. Deciduous leaves, about 2 in. long, are gray-green and silvery beneath. Its yellow flowers are insignificant ornamentally. Fruit is about ½ in. long and yellow with silvery scales; it is mealy, but edible. Tends to be short-lived in most gardens. Zones 3 to 6.

E. pungens (*pun*-jenz).

THORNY ELAEAGNUS.
Evergreen, Japanese shrub to 12 ft. high and 12 ft. wide. Extremely fragrant, creamy-white flowers appear in autumn. Tolerates sun or shade, although in the northern part of its range it should be sheltered from the wind. 'Fruitlandii' is an attractive clone with very dark green leaves. 'Maculata' has a yellow spot in the center of each leaf. Zones 6 to 9.

Elaeagnus

E. umbellata (uhm-bel-*lay*-tuh).
Autumn-olive.
Autumn Elaeagnus.
Native to China, Japan and the Himalayas, but has escaped and is weedy in much of the eastern U.S. This spreading shrub is attractive over several seasons, yielding silvery leaves in the spring, creamy-yellow flowers in late spring and early summer, and silvery berries that turn red in the fall. Each plant can grow to 15 ft. tall and 15 to 20 ft. wide. The deciduous leaves are 1 to 3 in. long, alternate and elliptical, and are bright green above and silvery-green below. The flowers appear in leaf axils. Many thorns can be found on the branches. Plant in full sun. Zones 5 to 8.

Enkianthus (en-kee-*an*-thus).
Heath Family (*Ericaceae*).
Deciduous upright shrubs from Asia, with whorled branches and alternate leaves. Lovely fall color, usually red to orange. Attractive flowers in drooping clusters bloom in late spring, soon after the leaves expand. Thrive in moist, well-drained, slightly acid soil. Propagate by seeds, cuttings or layers.

Enkianthus campanulatus
Redvein Enkianthus

E. campanulatus (kam-pan-yew-*lay*-tus).
Redvein Enkianthus.
Distinctive shrub from Japan. Grows 10 to 15 ft. high and about 8 ft. wide. Its leaves, to 3 in. long, turn a brilliant scarlet in autumn. Produces dainty, bell-shaped flowers, yellowish with red veins, to ½ in. long in mid-spring. 'Albiflorus' has flowers that are nearly white. Zones 5 to 8.

E. perulatus (per-yoo-*lay*-tus).
White Enkianthus.
Small shrub to 6 ft. with a similar spread. Leaves about 2 in. long. The foliage turns a striking yellow, orange or scarlet in fall. White, bell-shaped flowers in mid-spring. Zones 6 to 8.

Erica (*ehr*-i-kuh).
Heath.
Heath Family (*Ericaceae*).
A large group of evergreen shrubs from Eur. and Africa, popular for their attractive, compact growth and profuse bloom. Small, narrow, needle-like leaves in whorls. Clusters of tiny, bright-colored, tubular flowers. Grow best in acid soil. Propagate by seeds or cuttings.

E. arborea (ar-*boh*-ree-uh).
Tree Heath.
Large shrub or tree to 15 ft. tall and about 12 ft. wide. Large clusters of fragrant white flowers bloom in winter and spring. Zones 8 to 9.

Escallonia × *langleyensis*
Langley Escallonia

Escallonia (ess-kal-*loh*-nee-uh).
Saxifrage Family (*Saxifragaceae*).
Generally evergreen trees and shrubs native to S.

Amer. Late fall flowers are valued in gardens. Propagate by cuttings.

E. × langleyensis (lang-*lee*-en-sis).
LANGLEY ESCALLONIA.
A hybrid of *E. rubra* and *E. virgata*. Flowers pink to rose-red on shrubs that are usually smaller than *E. rubra*. Zones 8 to 10.

E. rubra (*roo*-bruh).
RED ESCALLONIA.
Large shrub, to 12 ft., with sticky leaves on reddish twigs. Red flowers in open clusters. Zones 8 to 10.

Eucommia (yew-*kom*-ee-uh).
Eucommia family (*Eucommiaceae*).
Native to China. Elm-like deciduous trees. Green leaves, barely turning pale yellow before dropping in autumn. Grow to 60 ft. tall and about 50 ft. wide.

E. ulmoides (ul-*moy*-dez).
HARDY RUBBER TREE.
Tolerates hot, dry conditions well. Leaves contain latex, which can be seen in long strands when a leaf is pulled apart. Fast growing. Zones 6 to 8.

Euonymus (yew-*on*-i-mus and rarely *ee*-von-uh-mus).
SPINDLE-TREE.
Staff-tree Family (*Celastraceae*).
A large group of woody, small trees, shrubs and vines, some deciduous, some evergreen. Attractive fall color and fruits. Flowers are small, occur after the leaves appear, and are generally insignificant in effect. A characteristic of the spindle-tree berry is that it splits open in fall to reveal brilliantly colored seeds. Grow in full sun or shade; require good drainage. Propagate by seed or cuttings.

Euonymus alata
CORKBUSH

E. alata (al-*lay*-tuh).
CORKBUSH.
WINGED EUONYMUS.
A deciduous, large shrub or small tree to 15 ft. tall and 15 ft. wide. Native to northeastern Asia, in the U.S. it can escape to natural areas and become a weed. Leaves turn brilliant rosy red in fall. Tolerates heavy shade, but fall color is not as showy as in full sun. Twigs are characterized by big corky ridges. Flowers are yellow; fruits red. Both are insignificant ornamentally. 'Compacta' only grows to about 10 ft., has less corky twigs, and red fall color. Both this cultivar and the species shear well and are excellent for use in hedges. Zones 4 to 8.

E. europaea (yew-roh-*pee*-uh).
EUROPEAN SPINDLE-TREE.
Native to Europe. Deciduous with yellow to pinkish-orange fall color. Tall, growing to 20 ft., with a spread of 15 ft. Very showy fruits in au-

tumn; red with orange berries. 'Alba' (*al*-buh) has whitish fruit; 'Atrorubens' (at-roh-*roo*-benz) has red fruit. 'Red Cascade' has large, bright red fruits. Zones 4 to 7.

E. japonica (ja-*pon*-ik-uh).
EVERGREEN EUONYMUS.
Useful as a hedge or tall shrub, growing 12 ft. tall by 6 ft. wide. It has decorative glossy leaves reminiscent of box. Native to Japan. 'Albo-marginata' (*al*-boh mar-jin-*nay*-ta) and 'Silver King' have leaves rimmed with white. 'Aureo-variegata' (*aw*-ree-oh var-ee-uh-*gay*-ta) is blotched with yellow. Zones 7 to 9.

E. kiautschovica (kee-atch-*oh*-ee-kah).
SPREADING EUONYMUS.
This evergreen shrub will grow to 10 ft. in height, with a similar spread. In the south it is fully evergreen, but in the north the winters can be hard on the foliage, making it look ragged and sparse by spring. The opposite leaves are 2 to 3 in. long, elliptic to oblong and a dark green. Often used as a formal or informal hedge. Plant in full to partial sun in any soil. Zones 6 to 9.

Evodia (eh-*voh*-dee-uh).
Rue family (*Rutaceae*).
Tall, summer-blooming trees. Propagate by seeds, cuttings or root cuttings.

E. danielii (dan-*yell*-ee-eye).
KOREAN EVODIA.
This small flowering tree is one of the few in bloom in mid-to-late summer. This tree is native to Korea and China; it can escape to the wild in the U.S. The large, showy, 4- to 6-in. flat clusters of tiny whitish flowers are borne abundantly. When in bloom, this tree is very attractive to bees. Usually grows to be 25 to 30 ft. tall and as wide. Its pinnately compound leaves are a rich,

dark green. The bark is a smooth gray. The fruit starts to mature immediately after the flowers fade and becomes quite ornamental. The capsules are red and when they split open they reveal a black seed. Plant in full sun for best color. Zones 5 to 8.

Exochorda (ex-oh-*kor*-duh).
PEARLBUSH.
Rose Family (*Rosaceae*).
Deciduous shrubs from Asia, with slender branching habit and alternate leaves. Showy clusters of white flowers in spring, just before the leaves appear. Pearl-like buds. Bark becomes exfoliating and very attractive with age.

E. macrantha (ma-*kran*-thuh).
Similar to *E. racemosa*, but flowers are 2 in. wide. Plant is slightly less cold hardy. The cultivar 'The Bride' is a compact plant, reaching about 5 ft. in height. Zones 5 to 8.

E. racemosa (ra-see-*moh*-suh).
Shrub to 12 ft. tall and 12 ft. wide. Has elliptic leaves to 3 in. long. Flowers about 1½ in. across. Zones 5 to 9.

Fagus (*fay*-gus).
BEECH.
Beech Family (*Fagaceae*).
Ornamental deciduous trees of stately height, the beeches are 80 to 100 ft. tall at maturity with an almost equal spread. They show to wonderful advantage when their branches are allowed to sweep to the ground on all sides. Foliage is handsome and lustrous and the bark is a showy light gray, a bit like an elephant's hide. Can be sheared for use as hedges. Tend to hold some of their leaves into the winter, when they become a bleached tan. Flowers are insignificant and the fruits (nuts) are triangular and enclosed in a bris-

tly husk. Beeches prefer a well-drained soil and will grow in full sun or heavy shade. Propagate by seed or grafts.

F. grandifolia (gran-di-*foh*-lee-uh).
AMERICAN BEECH.

This species has coarsely toothed green leaves that turn a yellowish bronze in autumn. Native to eastern N. America. Zones 4 to 8.

Exochorda macrantha 'The Bride'
DWARF PEARLBUSH

Fagus sylvatica 'Purpurea'
EUROPEAN BEECH

✱ F. sylvatica (sil-*vat*-ik-uh).
EUROPEAN BEECH.

A European native that is usually grown for its cultivars. Very similar to the above species, but has leaves with smooth edges, slightly darker bark, and is slightly more drought tolerant. 'Asplenifolia' (ass-plen-eh-*foh*-lee-uh) and 'Laciniata' (las-in-ee-*ay*-tuh) have finely divided leaves. 'Atropunicea' (at-roh-pew-*niss*-ee-uh), 'Cuprea' (kew-*pree*-uh), 'Purpurea' (per-*puh*-ree-uh), and 'Riversii' (riv-vehr-*see*-eye) have dark purple leaves. 'Spaethiana' (spa-uh-thee-*ay*-nuh) is similar but is the best for remaining purple all summer. 'Pendula' (pen-*dew*-luh), the weeping beech, has drooping branches. Very awkward as a young specimen, it becomes stunningly handsome with age. 'Fastigiata' (fas-tij-ee-*ay*-tuh), the Dawyck beech, is a narrow column. Zones 5 to 9.

Ficus (*fye*-kus).
FIG.

Mulberry Family (*Moraceae*).

A large group of trees, shrubs and vines of tropical and warm-temperate regions. Mostly evergreen, with large alternate leaves and milky juice. They have no floral value and only one species is important for its fruits. Propagate by air layering, seeds, or cuttings. All grow best in full sun, but tolerate shade.

F. carica (*kar*-ee-kuh).
COMMON FIG.

Native to western Asia and eastern Mediterranean. Small tree or shrub, deciduous, to 15 ft. high and 15 ft. wide. Large leaves to 8 in. long, hairy beneath, usually with three to five lobes. Pear-shaped, green, yellow or purplish edible fruit. In northern areas, plants will often die to the ground in winter. Some, but not all, cultivars will ripen fruit the following summer. Require full sun for fruit production. Many cultivars are available, varying in fruit color, flavor, and hardiness. Zones 7 to 9.

Ficus carica
COMMON FIG

Firmiana (fir-mee-*ay*-nuh).
Sterculia family (*Sterculiaceae*).
Trees primarily of warm regions. Propagate by seeds.

F. simplex (*sim*-plex).
CHINESE PARASOL TREE.
Relatively rare tree grown for its midsummer flowers, large green, deciduous leaves, and green stems and trunk. Native to China and Japan. Flowers are small and whitish in large showy clusters. Fruits are somewhat showy, lasting through the winter. The fruits are long green capsules that open up, exposing the seeds. Fall color is gold. Branches are generally whorled. Tree may reach 45 ft. in height. Zones 7 to 9.

Forsythia (for-*sith*-ee-uh).
GOLDEN BELLS.
Olive Family (*Oleaceae*).
Handsome deciduous shrubs of Asia and southern Europe, popular for their dramatic spring blossoms. Simple or three-parted, opposite leaves. The bright yellow flowers open along the stems before the leaves appear in the spring. Occasionally there may be a scattering of bloom in late fall and sometimes bloom may be scanty after a hard winter with late frosts. Flowers best in sun, but will tolerate shade. Propagate by cuttings, seeds, or layers. Cut branches in late winter to force into bloom indoors. Zones 5 to 8.

Forsythia × *intermedia*
BORDER FORSYTHIA

F. × intermedia (in-ter-*mee*-dee-uh).
BORDER FORSYTHIA.
Hybrid between *F. suspensa* and *F. viridissima*. An upright shrub to 10 ft. high and 10 ft. wide, with arching or spreading branches. The leaves are up

to 5 in. long and may turn slightly purple in autumn. Golden-yellow flowers in numerous small clusters along the stems. Cultivars have been selected for larger and more golden flowers.

F. ovata (oh-*vay*-tuh).
EARLY FORSYTHIA.
Shrub to 6 ft. tall and 5 ft. wide. Flowers are pale yellow. Plants and flower buds are somewhat more hardy than the above species.

Fothergilla (foth-er-*gill*-uh).
Witch hazel Family (*Hamamelidaceae*).
Spring-blooming, deciduous shrubs of N. Amer. Alternate, coarsely toothed leaves that take on yellow to orange-red fall color. Fragrant white flowers in dense heads or spikes, minus petals but with a mass of showy stamens. Fruits are clustered, non-showy capsules that turn tan when ripe. These ornamental shrubs thrive in light shade and rich, moist soil. Propagate by seeds or cuttings.

Fothergilla gardenii
DWARF FOTHERGILLA

✶**F. gardenii** (gar-*deen*-ee-eye).
DWARF FOTHERGILLA.
Low, bushy shrub to 2 or 3 ft. tall and equally wide, with leaves to 2 in. long, pale beneath. Flowers in oblong clusters, about 1 in. long, either before the leaves come out or appearing just as the leaves are emerging. Zones 6 to 9.

F. major (*may*-jor).
LARGE FOTHERGILLA.
Upright shrub to 10 ft. tall and about 7 ft. wide. Leaves to 4 in. long, slightly whitish beneath. Flower clusters are to 2 in. long, the flowers opening with the leaves. Zones 5 to 9.

Franklinia (frank-*lin*-ee-uh).
Tea Family (*Theaceae*).
A single beautiful species becoming a tall, oval, large shrub or small tree. The tree was named for Benjamin Franklin. The long, alternate leaves open late in spring on erect, smooth gray branches. In autumn, foliage is wine red in color, often while gold-centered white flowers are present. Seeds, hard and nutlike when open and dry, last all winter. Needs moist soil. Withstands light shade as well as full sun. Propagate by seeds or by cuttings.

Franklinia alatamaha
FRANKLIN TREE

✶**F. alatamaha** (uh-lay-tuh-*may*-huh).
FRANKLIN TREE.
May attain 30 ft. in height and a spread of 15 ft. Leaves are bright green and shiny. Its lovely white, cup-shaped flowers to 3 in. across, are very short stemmed. Bloom starts in mid-summer and continues into fall. Zones 6 to 7.

Fraxinus (*frax*-in-us).

ASH.

Olive Family (*Oleaceae*).

Handsome, rapid-growing, often brittle-wooded deciduous trees, mostly of the North Temperate Zone. Opposite, pinnate leaves. Its small flowers are generally not showy. Winged fruit occurs on female plants. Seedlings can become weedy. Not particular as to soil, but grows best in full sun. Propagate by seeds or by grafting.

F. americana (uh-mer-ee-*kay*-nuh).

WHITE ASH.

Vigorous tree, to 80 ft. wide, 60 to 80 ft. high and taller. Leaves are bluish-green during the summer, with whitish undersides, and turn an attractive yellow, orange, or purple in autumn. Several cultivars have been selected for excellent fall color and seedlessness, including 'Autumn Purple.' Zones 4 to 8.

F. excelsior (ex-*sel*-see-or).

EUROPEAN ASH.

A roundheaded tree, to 70 ft. tall and 80 ft. wide, with conspicuous black winter buds. Leaves remain green late and often have poor fall color. 'Pendula' (pen-*dew*-luh) has a weeping habit. 'Aurea' (*aw*-ree-uh) has golden twigs and wonderful golden fall color. 'Hessei' (hess-ee-eye) has simple (rather than compound), dark green leaves. Zones 5 to 7.

F. ornus (*or*-nus).

FLOWERING ASH.

The showiest ash for flowers. Native to S. Eur. and southwestern Asia. Tree to 40 ft. tall and 40 ft. wide. Leaves green during the summer, sometimes turning yellow before dropping. Large winter buds. Fragrant white flowers in dense clusters to 5 in. long, appearing in late spring with the leaves. Zones 6 to 8.

Fraxinus ornus
FLOWERING ASH

Gardenia jasminoides
CAPE JASMINE

F. pennsylvanica (pen-sil-*van*-ik-uh).

GREEN ASH.

RED ASH.

A somewhat narrow tree to 60 ft. tall and 30 ft. wide. Similar in effect to white ash, but leaves are green to yellowish-green, yellow in autumn, with narrower leaflets. A number of male, non-seeding cultivars have been selected. Zones 2 to 8.

Gardenia (gar-*dee*-nee-uh).

Madder Family (*Rubiaceae*).

Shrubs or small trees with opposite, mostly evergreen leaves and large, fragrant flowers. They require a moist soil and protection from winter winds. Propagate by cuttings or seeds. Zones 8 to 10.

G. jasminoides (jas-min-*noy*-deez).

Cape Jasmine.

Gardenia.

Evergreen shrub to 6 ft. tall and wide. Thick, glossy leaves and white waxy flowers to 3 in. across, often double, often fragrant.

Garrya elliptica
Silk-tassel Tree

Garrya (*gar*-ee-uh).

Silk-tassel Tree.

Garrya Family (*Garryaceae*).

Evergreen shrubs of the coastal range of western N. Amer., with opposite, thick leaves. Flowers in pendulous, catkin-like clusters. Male and female flowers on separate plants, both of which must be present to produce the attractive berrylike fruits. Propagate by cuttings, seeds, or by layers.

G. elliptica (eh-*lip*-ti-kuh).

Hairy-branched shrub or small tree to 20 ft. tall, with dark green, leathery leaves to 3 in. long, hairy beneath. Zones 8 to 9.

Genista (jen-*nis*-tuh).

Pea Family (*Leguminosae*).

Ornamental deciduous or semi-evergreen shrubs similar to Cytisus, from Europe, Africa and Asia. Sparse leaves, mostly alternate, simple or trifoliate. Showy, pealike, yellow flowers. They thrive in poor, dry, sandy soil and show to advantage on sunny slopes. Propagate by seeds or cuttings.

Genista tinctoria
Dyers' Greenweed

G. tinctoria (tink-*toh*-ree-uh).
DYERS' GREENWEED.
Low yet erect shrub to 3 ft. high and 3 ft. wide. Stems are green year round with deciduous, narrow green leaves to 1 in. long. Prominent yellow blooms in many-flowered clusters in early summer. Zones 3 to 8.

Gingko biloba
MAIDENHAIR TREE

Ginkgo (*gink*-go).
MAIDENHAIR TREE.
Ginkgo Family (*Ginkgoaceae*).
Deciduous tree of China. It is a tall, wide-spreading tree of distinctive appearance. Because the fleshy coating of the seed on the female tree has an unpleasant odor (although the nut inside is a popular food in the Orient), only male trees should be used. Propagate by seeds, grafting, or rooted cuttings. Fossils of ginkgo have been dated at over 100 million years old.

G. biloba (bye-*loh*-buh).
Thought to be extinct in the wild, ginkgo has been kept alive at Buddhist temples in China, Japan and Korea. Grows up to 80 ft. tall and 60 ft. wide. Fan-shaped leaves, alternate or clustered, are dull green in summer and turn a glorious yellow in the fall. Inconspicuous flowers. Male and female flowers on separate trees. 'Fastigiata' (fas-tidge-ee-*ay*-tuh) has a narrow, pyramidal top. Zones 5 to 8.

Gleditsia triacanthos 'Sunburst'
HONEY LOCUST

Gleditsia (gle-*dit*-see-uh).
HONEY LOCUST.
Pea Family (*Leguminosae*).
Large, broad-headed, deciduous trees, found chiefly in Amer. and Asia. Alternate, fine-textured, compound leaves. Its small, greenish flowers are not showy. Large pods occur on female (fruiting) trees. Cultivars selected for form, fruitlessness, and thornlessness. They thrive in open, sunny positions in well-drained soil.

G. triacanthos (try-uh-*kan*-thos).
COMMON HONEY LOCUST.
Handsome tree that withstands city conditions well. To 70 ft. tall and 50 ft. wide. The species (rarely grown) is armed with stout thorns to 4 in. long and female trees bear large, 12-in. long pods. Yellow autumn color. The variety *inermis* (in-*er*-mis) is thornless and is the variety from which most of the ornamental cultivars have been selected. The newly opened leaves of 'Sunburst,' are bright yellow, turning green during the summer. 'Imperial', 'Majestic', 'Shademaster' and 'Skyline' have green leaves and consistently upright growth habits. Zones 4 to 8.

Gymnocladus (jim-*nok*-la-dus).

Pea Family (*Leguminosae*).
Deciduous trees of China and N. Amer. Leaves are large, generally twice compound, with small leaflets. After the leaves drop in mid-autumn, the trees appear twigless. Propagate by root cuttings or seeds.

G. dioica (dye-oh-*i*-kuh).
KENTUCKY COFFEE TREE.
One of the most handsome and healthy shade trees, growing to 75 ft. tall by 60 ft. wide. An eastern N. Amer. native. Tolerant of sun and light shade. Twice-pinnate leaves grow to 18 in. or more long, with three to seven pairs of ovalish leaflets about 3 in. long. Autumn color a bright yellow. Greenish-white flowers are rarely noticed. Male and female flowers usually on separate plants. The brown fruit is a thick, flat, pulpy pod to 7 in. long. Zones 4 to 7.

Halesia (hay-*lee*-zee-uh).

SILVER-BELL.
Storax Family (*Styracaceae*).
Attractive deciduous trees of N. Amer., with alternate toothed leaves. Small, hanging clusters of white, bell-shaped flowers. Especially handsome when in bloom in spring. They grow best in rich, well-drained soil in full sun or shade. Propagate by seeds or cuttings.

H. carolina (ka-rol-*lye*-nuh).
CAROLINA SILVER-BELL.
Small tree growing to 40 ft. tall and spreading 30 ft. Leaves to 4 in. long, turning yellow in the fall.

Halesia carolina
CAROLINA SILVER-BELL

Hamamelis × *intermedia*
HYBRID WITCH HAZEL

Delicate, pendulous flowers about ¾ in. long in mid-May. Dry, four-winged fruits to 1½ in. long. Zones 5 to 9.

H. diptera (*dip*-tehr-uh).
TWO-WINGED SILVER-BELL.
Similar to the above species, but blooms after the leaves emerge. Flowers are more open and flat, and less bell-like. Fruits are two-winged. Variety magniflora has significantly larger flowers. Zones 6 to 9.

H. monticola (mon-*tee*-coh-luh).
While it grows taller, it is so similar to *H. carolina* that some botanists group these two species as *H. tetraptera*. Zones 5 to 9.

H. tetraptera: *H. carolina* or *H. monticola*.

✶✶Hamamelis (ham-uh-*mee*-lis).
WITCH HAZEL.
Witch hazel Family (*Hamamelidaceae*).
Large, deciduous shrubs of N. Amer. and Asia, growing to 20 ft. tall by 20 ft. wide. Have alternate leaves that turn yellow and orange in the fall. Fragrant flowers with ribbonlike petals are of special interest because of their time of bloom (late fall and winter). They tolerate full sun and shade. Are best if planted where one gets close to the flowers. Propagate by seeds, cuttings, or grafts. Grafted plant is often plagued by sprouting rootstock which can overpower the main plant.

✶H. × intermedia (in-tur-*mee*-dee-uh).
HYBRID WITCH HAZEL.
The result of a cross between *H. mollis* and *H. japonica*, it bears showy yellow or orange flowers in winter. 'Arnold Promise' has a vase-shaped form when young and bears bright yellow flowers. 'Jelena' has very showy orange flowers

and excellent orange fall color. 'Diane' has coppery red flowers. Zones 5 to 8.

H. mollis (*moll*-iss).
CHINESE WITCH HAZEL.
The leaves and twigs are covered with dense hairs. Very fragrant, golden-yellow flowers with a reddish base blooming in winter. 'Brevipetala' has yellow-orange flowers with short, strap-like petals. It often holds its brown leaves all winter, which can detract from the show of the flowers. 'Pallida' has pale yellow flowers and excellent yellow fall color. Is thought by many to be the finest witch hazel. Zones 5 to 8.

H. vernalis (ver-*nay*-liss).
VERNAL WITCH HAZEL.
This Ozark native is slightly smaller in size than the other species and is the least showy in bloom. Blooms about the same time in winter as the Asian species. Bears small, yellow to orange flowers. Primarily useful in areas where the Asian species are not hardy. Zones 5 to 8.

H. virginiana (vir-jin-ee-*ay*-nuh).
COMMON WITCH HAZEL.
A native spreading shrub with bright yellow flowers that is especially valued for its late fall bloom, which coincides with and follows excellent yellow autumn foliage color. Zones 4 to 8.

Hibiscus (hye-*bis*-kus).
ROSE-MALLOW.
Mallow Family (*Malvaceae*).
A large and horticulturally important genus of handsome, spreading annuals, perennials and shrubs that are native to temperate and tropical areas. Bloom on new wood, so they can be pruned hard without loss of bloom. Grow best in full sun or very light shade, with ample moisture. Propagate by seeds or cuttings.

Hibiscus syriacus 'Blue Bird'
ROSE-OF-SHARON CULTIVAR

Hippophae rhamnoides
SEA BUCKTHORN

H. rosa-sinensis (*roh*-zuh-sin-*nen*-sis).
CHINESE HIBISCUS.

A lush, evergreen shrub, growing to 15 ft. tall and about 12 ft. wide. Colors range from white through pinkish yellow and pink to darkest red. There are a number of hybrids, some with dramatically ruffled, fringed or doubled blossoms up to 8 in. across. These bloom quickly on new wood and flower throughout summer. Often grown in greenhouses in the North. Zones 9 to 10.

H. syriacus (sihr-rye-*a*-kus).
ROSE-OF-SHARON.

Hardy deciduous shrub, 10 to 12 ft. high, and to 10 ft. wide, from eastern Asia. Blooms abundantly in mid- to late summer. The flowers are 2 to 4 in. across, in shades of white, pink, blue or lavender. The individual blossoms are short-lived, but heavily produced. Leaves appear very late in the spring. Fruits are dry capsules that remain on the plant all winter. Weed seedlings can be a problem. Some of the newer cultivars are sterile. 'Diana' has large, pure white, sterile flowers. 'Helene' has white sterile flowers with a deep pink center. Zones 5 to 9.

Hippophae (hi-*poff*-uh-ee).
SEA BUCKTHORN.
Oleaster Family (*Elaeagnaceae*).

Deciduous shrubs or small trees of Europe and Asia, with spiny branches and alternate leaves. Inconspicuous flowers, male and female on separate plants. Not particular as to soil and thrives near the seacoast, where it is especially valued for the silvery leaves and showy fruits. Propagate by seeds and root cuttings. Zones 3 to 7.

H. rhamnoides (ram-*noy*-deez).
Slender, ornamental shrub, usually not growing over 12 ft. tall and 8 ft. wide. Narrow silvery-gray

Hydrangea arborescens 'Grandiflora'
HILLS-OF-SNOW CULTIVAR

Hydrangea macrophylla 'Souvenir du
President Doumer'
BIGLEAF HYDRANGEA

leaves to 3 in. long. Small, yellowish flowers and profuse, long-lasting, orange-yellow fruits.

Hydrangea (hye-*dran*-jee-uh).
Saxifrage Family (*Saxifragaceae*).

Ornamental and widely grown woody shrubs, most deciduous, and handsome climbing vines from Asia and N. and S. Amer. Opposite, toothed leaves and small flowers in dense clusters, with few or many showy, large, sterile flowers that are the chief attraction of the genus. All hydrangeas thrive in rich soil on the moist side, in full sun or partial shade, and all tolerate sea air. Propagate by cuttings and seeds.

H. arborescens (ar-boh-*ress*-enz).
HILLS-OF-SNOW.

Erect shrub to 5 ft. tall and 6 ft. wide. Roundish leaves to 6 in. long, and clusters of tiny, but fairly conspicuous, white flowers to 5 in. across, with a few sterile flowers in each cluster. Blooms on new wood in early to mid-summer. Can be pruned heavily in the winter. The cultivar 'Grandiflora' (gran-di-*floh*-ruh), is more often planted than the species. Large round heads of showy, white, sterile flowers appear in early summer and turn tannish later. Larger flower heads are obtained when all shoots are cut to the ground in spring. 'Annabelle' has even larger clusters of sterile flowers. Zones 4 to 8.

H. macrophylla (mak-roh-*fill*-uh).
BIGLEAF HYDRANGEA.
FLORIST'S HYDRANGEA.

A stout, roundish Asian shrub to 6 ft. tall and wide. Has bright green, somewhat glossy leaves to 6 in. long. Showy pink, blue or white flowers in large, flat or rounded clusters, to 8 in. across, occur in summer. Blooms are on old wood, meaning that plants should only be pruned immediately following flowering. Numerous varieties are grown by florists as pot plants for Easter flowering. Blue-flowering kinds turn pink unless the soil is quite acid. Many cultivars are available, varying in color and amount of sterile flowers. Plants bearing a mixture of sterile and fertile flowers are called lace-caps. Plants are hardy further north, but flower buds are usually killed. Hardiness of the cultivars varies greatly. Zones 6 to 9.

H. paniculata (pan-ik-yew-*lay*-tuh).
PANICLE HYDRANGEA.
A Japanese shrub, often treelike, to 20 ft. high and 15 ft. wide. Leaves to 5 in. long with almost no fall color (sometimes turning yellow). White flowers in conical clusters to 10 in. long, with some showy, sterile flowers that later turn pinkish. Flowers in late summer. 'Grandiflora' (grandi-*floh*-ruh), the "PeeGee" Hydrangea, has large clusters of nearly all-sterile flowers. 'Tardiva' bears a mixture of sterile and fertile flowers later than the species. 'Praecox' is similar, but bears flowers earlier than the species. Zones 4 to 8.

✳**H. quercifolia** (kwer-si-*foh*-lee-uh).
OAK-LEAF HYDRANGEA.
An eastern American shrub to 5 ft. high by 5 ft. wide. Coarse twigs become attractive with age, having reddish-brown exfoliating bark. Leaves to 8 in. long and wide, lobed like an oak leaf. The leaves are white-felty beneath and turn an attractive reddish-purple in the fall. Flowers occur in long, cone-shaped clusters to 12 in., with numerous white sterile flowers to 2 in. wide, and turn pink and then tan for the winter. 'Harmony' and 'Roanoke' have sterile flowers. 'Snowflake' has large double flowers. Zones 5 to 9, but may not bloom every year in Zone 5 due to winter injury.

Hydrangea quercifolia
OAK-LEAF HYDRANGEA

Hypericum (hye-*per*-i-kum).
ST. JOHN'S-WORT.
St. John's-wort Family (*Hypericaceae*).
Shrubby perennials with clusters of attractive golden-yellow flowers, in appearance somewhat like a single rose, with conspicuous gold or red stamens adding to the showiness of the blooms. Most grow best in full sun with good drainage. Many are ground covers. Propagate by seeds and cuttings.

H. prolificum (proh-lif-*ik*-um).
SHRUBBY ST. JOHN'S-WORT.
Small shrub to 4 ft. high and 3 ft. across that is native to eastern and midwestern N. Amer. Small, bright yellow blooms, ¾ in. across with prominent stamens, are produced in abundant clusters in mid-summer. Bark reddish-brown and exfoliating. Zones 4 to 8.

Idesia

Idesia (i-*deez*-ee-uh).

IDESIA.

IIGIRI TREE.

Flacourtia Family (*Flacourtiaceae*).

Deciduous tree to 60 ft. tall by 60 feet wide. Native to Japan and China. Most showy feature is its red-orange fruits, produced in drooping clusters that are showy from autumn through early winter.

I. polycarpa (poh-lee-*car*-puh).

Male and female flowers are usually borne on separate trees. Both sexes are needed, since the males pollinate the female trees, which produce red-orange fruit in the form of many-seeded berries. A grove of seedlings is usually needed for best effect. Leaves large, pink-orange petioles (leaf stalks). The flowers are green, not showy, but fragrant. Zones 7 to 9.

✶✶**Ilex** (*eye*-lex).

HOLLY.

Holly Family (*Aquifoliaceae*).

Native primarily to temperate and tropical regions of N. and S. Amer. and Asia. Range from shrubs less than 1 ft. to trees over 80 ft. tall. Grown for their foliage and/or fruit effect. Many hollies are evergreen, and some are considered by gardeners the most valuable of our broad-leaved specimens. Some of the deciduous species are extremely showy for their fruit display.

Leaves are alternate, often tipped with sharp spines. Shading ranges from a dark musty green to a bright glossy green. Flowers are inconspicuous, generally white, sometimes greenish white, with males and females on separate plants. Both sexes needed for fruiting. Red-fruited species are popular, but there are a number of forms with yellow fruit, which are equally showy. Black-fruited species are not grown for their fruit, which is only noticed upon close inspection. Ev-

ergreen species make handsome hedges and very effective screens. They grow well in sun or shade. In full sun, hollies tend to be more dense. In partial shade they tend to be more open, but will still fruit well. Propagate by seed or cuttings.

I. aquifolium (ak-wif-*foh*-lee-um).

ENGLISH HOLLY.

Extensively cultivated in the Pacific Northwest and marketed throughout the U.S. for Christmas decorations, this evergreen is considered by many to be the best of all hollies. The species and many cultivars grow 50 ft. tall and 25 ft. wide. Foliage is dense, glossy dark green, wavy, 1½ to 3 in. long with sharp spines along the margin. Fruits are bright red, thickly set, round, about ⅜ in. across and generally remain well into winter. Zones 7 to 9. There are many cultivars. 'Albomarginata' (al-boh-mar-jin-*nay*-tuh), 'Argenteo-marginata' (ar-gen-*tee*-oh mar-gin-*a*-tuh),

Ilex aquifolium
ENGLISH HOLLY

'Argentea Regina' and 'Silver Beauty' have leaves variegated with white or silver. 'Ferox' (*fer*-ox) is known as Hedgehog Holly because it has spines all over the leaf, not just on the margins. 'Angustifolia' (an-gus-ti-*foh*-lee-uh), the narrowleaf English holly, has narrower leaves than the species. 'Camelliifolia' (ka-*mell*-ee-uh-*foh*-lee-uh), a handsome specimen, is dense with dark green oblong leaves and often has no spines. Plant is pyramidal in growth. Fruits are large and dark red. This is probably a hybrid and could be included in the hybrid species, *I.* × *altaclarensis* (all-tuh-clay-*ren*-sis). Another possible hybrid cultivar is 'James G. Esson', which has very dark leaves and bright red fruits. Leaves are somewhat spiny. Probably hardy north to Zone 6.

I. cornuta (kor-*new*-tuh).
CHINESE HOLLY.

A native of China, this evergreen has been popular in the U.S. for many years. Grows to 12 ft. high and about 15 ft. wide. Dark, lustrous green leaves, somewhat rectangular in shape, generally with three down-turned spines at the tip. Fruits are red and generally last through the winter. Female plants can produce fruit without normal cross-pollination, therefore males are not required for fruit set. Zones 7 to 9. 'Burfordii' (bur-*ford*-ee-eye) has bright green, concave leaves that have only one spine, which is at the tip. Fruits are bright red and the plant bears abundantly. Very popular in the South. Zone 7.

I. crenata (kruh-*nay*-tuh).
JAPANESE HOLLY.
An evergreen shrub, often resembling *Buxus*. Easily distinguished from *Buxus* since all hollies have alternately arranged leaves, while boxwood has opposite leaves. Compact and dense, with smooth, dark green leaves to 1½ in. long that are finely toothed. The species can reach 15 ft. high

and wide, but most cultivars are smaller. 'Convexa' (kon-*vex*-uh) has dark green, glossy leaves that are noticeably convex. It usually stays under 5 ft. high and 8 ft. wide. 'Helleri' (hel-*air*-eye) is compact, rarely exceeding 4 ft. in height (about 5 ft. wide). Its leaves are flat. 'Latifolia' (lat-uh-*foh*-lee-uh), 'Rotundifolia' (roh-tun-di-*foh*-lee-uh) and 'Fortunei' (for-*tew*-nee-eye) are all very similar. They are rapid growing with relatively large leaves and will reach 15 ft. heights. 'Microphylla' (mye-kroh-*fill*-uh) has small leaves and an upright growth habit. Very adaptable as a sheared or informal hedge. Fruits are black, small and often hidden among foliage and branches. Zones 6 to 9.

I. decidua (des-*sid*-yew-uh).
POSSUM HAW.
A deciduous shrub or small tree, native to the southeastern U.S., averaging between 10 and 20 ft. tall and 12 ft. wide. Leaves dark lustrous green, 1 to 3 in. long. Fruits are a bright orange-red to scarlet, ripen in Sept. and are very showy well into winter. Male plants needed for pollination. Tolerates sun or shade (best fruiting in sun), wet or dry soil. Zones 5 to 9.

I. glabra (*glay*-bruh).
INKBERRY.
WINTERBERRY.
A hardy evergreen that grows to 8 ft. high by 10 ft. wide. Grows in dense clumps with upright branches. Leaves are flat, dark lustrous green, wide at the tip, from 1 to 2 in. long. Their margins are nearly entire (spineless) with only a few teeth at the tip. Fruits are black, appear in autumn and stay through the winter. Tolerates sun or shade, wet or dry soil. Zones 5 to 9.

Ilex

Ilex opaca
AMERICAN HOLLY

I. × meserveae (meh-zer-*vay*-ee).
BLUE HOLLY.
MESERVE HOLLY.

This cross between *I. rugosa* (rew-*go*-suh), a very hardy but not terribly attractive shrub, and *I. aquifolium* has provided us with hardy plants with attractive, shiny, evergreen, dark bluish-green leaves, on purplish stems. The leaves are edged with coarse teeth. The berries on female plants mature to a brilliant red. Plant in full sun or shade. 'Blue Boy' and 'Blue Girl' were the first cultivars to be marketed from this cross and have been replaced in the trade by newer cultivars. 'Blue Prince' is male, low and compact in growth and an excellent pollinator. 'Blue Angel' and 'Blue Princess' are females that have attractive fruit. 'China Boy' and 'China Girl' are hybrids that resulted from a cross between *I. rugosa* and *I. cornuta*. Both have bold, attractive foliage reminiscent of Chinese holly, but are significantly more hardy. Zones 5 to 8.

✶I. opaca (op-*pay*-kuh).
AMERICAN HOLLY.

One of the important native broadleaf evergreens. Native to eastern U.S., it grows to 50 ft. tall by 30 ft. wide. Tends to somewhat loose growth (especially in shade), but if pruned will be an elegant pyramidal specimen. Leaves medium green and lustrous to dull above, greenish yellow beneath, making the branches less in demand as Christmas ornaments than the glossy green sprays of English holly. Leaves are to 3 in. long, elliptical, with spined margins. Fruits are mostly bright red, though some varieties show orange or yellow fruits. Male trees are needed to ensure fruit-bearing female trees. There are hundreds of cultivars. 'Bountiful' bears an abundant supply of fruits every year and has dark green leaves. 'Croonenberg' bears dark red fruits heavily and is self-fruitful. 'Howard', a columnar plant, has leaves that are sparsely spined, if at all. 'Old Heavy Berry,' another good fruit-bearing tree, displays fruits that are a deep dark red. Its leaves are a dark glossy green. 'Taber #3', has a compact, conical growth form. Its fruits are red and abundant. Form *xanthocarpa* includes all the yellow-fruited cultivars. Zones 6 to 9.

I. pedunculosa (peh-dunk-yew-*loh*-suh).
LONG-STALK HOLLY.
An upright, Asian evergreen to 20 ft. tall and 12 ft. wide. Leaves green, elliptical, 1½ to 2¾ in.

Ilex verticillata 'Aurantiaca'
ORANGE WINTERBERRY

long, margins entire and spineless. Pea-size, bright red fruits (on female plants) are borne on long stalks. Zones 6 to 9.

I. verticillata (ver-tiss-sil-*lay*-tuh).
WINTERBERRY.
Sometimes called black-alder, this interesting native deciduous shrub is useful for its fantastic red-orange berries that last well into the winter and are sold in florist shops as cut branches. Grows to about 8 ft. tall and 6 ft. wide. Spineless leaves are oval, dull green with serrated margins, and they turn yellowish in the fall. Fruits are on female plants, and males are required for pollination.

I. vomitoria (vom-i-*toh*-ree-uh).
YAUPON.
Native to the southern U.S. Evergreen shrub to 18 ft. tall by 12 ft. wide. Its grayish green leaves contrast with its attractive light gray bark. Fruits

are small, red and showy. Tolerates sun and shade. Grows well in dry and wet soils. 'Nana' is a mounding cultivar, to about 5 ft. high. Zones 7 to 10.

Illicium (il-*iss*-ee-um).
ANISE TREE.
Illicium Family (*Illiciaceae*).
Evergreen small trees and shrubs that are native to Asia and Amer. Leaves are fragrant and glossy. Flowers—white, yellow or red—are partially hidden by the foliage. Propagate by seeds or cuttings.

I. floridanum (flor-i-*day*-num).
FLORIDA ANISE TREE.
Large shrub, native from Fla. to La., grows to 10 ft. high and 6 ft. wide. Flowers brick red, up to 2 in. across. Zones 7 to 9.

Itea ilicifolia
HOLLY LEAF SWEETSPICE

Itea (eye-*tee*-uh).

Saxifrage Family (*Saxifragaceae*).

Deciduous and evergreen shrubs of Asia and the U.S. Alternate leaves and clusters of white flowers occur in early summer. Tolerate dry and wet soils and grow in sun or shade. Propagate mostly by division, cuttings, and by seed.

I. ilicifolia (ill-is-see-*foh*-lee-uh).

HOLLY LEAF SWEETSPICE.

Native of China. An evergreen species with unique, long,. drooping flower clusters. Very handsome specimen. Zones 9 to 10.

I. virginica (vir-*jin*-ik-uh).

SWEETSPIRE.

Deciduous shrub to 6 ft. tall and 6 ft. wide (suckering may spread it much wider). Native to swamps in the eastern U.S. but grows well in any garden soil. Leaves to 3 in. long, turning yellow to red in the fall. Showy, white, fragrant flowers in horizontal clusters to 6 in. long. 'Henry's Garnet' has good green foliage during the summer. Leaves turn a deep red in mid- to late autumn, effective for several weeks. Stems attractively red in winter. Zones 6 to 9.

Juglans (joo-*glanz*).

WALNUT.

Walnut Family (*Juglandaceae*).

Large deciduous trees of N. and S. Amer., Eur. and Asia. Produces large, alternate, odd-pinnate leaves that drop early in autumn, often before turning bright yellow. Flowers of separate sexes occur on the same plant. Grown for ornament, edible nuts and valuable timber. Grows best in rich, moist soil. Propagate by seed or by grafting. Leaves and roots produce a toxin that inhibits the growth of some plants (although not lawn grass). This can make it difficult to use these trees in a landscape with other plants. Squirrels love the nuts and will bury (plant) them throughout the neighborhood, resulting in weed seedlings appearing unexpectedly.

J. cinerea (sin-*ur*-ee-uh).

BUTTERNUT.

Large, round-headed tree to 60 ft. tall and 50 ft. wide. Has gray, moderately smooth bark. Sticky, hairy leaflets, to 5 in. long, 11 to 19 per leaf. Fruit is oblong, 2½ in. long. Zones 4 to 7.

J. nigra (*nye*-gruh).

BLACK WALNUT.

Grows to 75 ft. tall and 60 ft. wide, with a spreading, round head and brown, furrowed bark. Leaflets, 15 to 23, each to 5 in. Round fruit to 2 in. across. Zones 4 to 9.

J. regia (reh-*jee*-uh).

ENGLISH WALNUT.

PERSIAN WALNUT.

Dense tree to 50 ft. tall and 50 ft. wide. Has smooth, silvery gray bark and five to nine leaflets to 5 in. long. Nearly round fruit to 2 in. across. This is the nut that is generally sold as walnut. Hardy in Zone 7, but Carpathian walnut, which comes from the coldest part of its native range in the Carpathian Mts., is hardy to Zone 5.

Juniperus (joo-*nip*-er-us).

JUNIPER.

Cypress Family (*Cupressaceae*).

Plants of the Northern Hemisphere. These evergreens vary in size from ground covers to shrubs to tall slender trees. The ground covers are not covered in this volume. Junipers are among the most drought-tolerant conifers. They require sunny growing conditions and are well suited to urban conditions. Junipers do well on most well-drained soils. Leaves may be of two types. Seedlings have leaves that are needle-shaped. These are

Juglans nigra
BLACK WALNUT

Juniperus communis 'Hibernica'
IRISH JUNIPER

Juniperus chinensis 'Kuriwad Gold'
CHINESE JUNIPER

Juniperus scopulorum 'Skyrocket'
WESTERN RED CEDAR

Juniperus

called juvenile leaves. Some species keep such foliage throughout life, while others only have these leaves if they are in shade. On adult plants, small scale-like leaves are more characteristic. Most junipers are dioecious, meaning that an individual plant is either male or female. The female cones are small, fleshy and have the effect of small bluish berries. These berrylike cones are edible and taste like gin. Propagated by seeds, cuttings, layers or, rarely, by grafting.

J. chinensis (chi-*nen*-sis).
CHINESE JUNIPER.
Ranges in size from ground cover to trees 60 ft. tall and 20 ft. wide. Berrylike cones to ⅜ in. diameter. Leaves vary from medium green to blue in color. The species itself is rarely grown in this country. Instead, a wide range of cultivars are available. They include: 'Ames', a pyramidal shrub with bluish, needlelike foliage. Its eventual height is over 6 ft. 'Armstrongii' (arm-*strong*-ee-eye) has green foliage and grows to 4 ft. by 4 ft. A male, it produces no berrylike cones. 'Columnaris' (kol-um-*nay*-riss) is a dark green columnar form. 'Hetzii' (hetz-*ee*-eye) grows to 15 ft. tall and as wide. It has blue foliage and is a female with attractive "berries." 'Iowa' is similar to 'Ames'. 'Keteleeri' (ke-*tel*-ear-eye) becomes treelike and has bright green foliage. 'Mint Julep,' a compact variety to about 5 ft. high and wide, has mint-green foliage on arching branches and produces the effect of a green fountain; it is good for foundation planting. 'Mountbatten,' a narrow columnar tree with gray-green foliage, produces only juvenile leaves. 'Obelisk' is slow-growing, a pyramidal variety with steel-blue, juvenile foliage. 'Pfitzeriana' (fit-zer-ee-*ay*-nuh), Pfitzer juniper, is one of the most popular of the spreading junipers; it can become a very large shrub, 12 ft. high and 15 ft. wide if unpruned. 'Pfitzeriana Aurea' (*aw*-ree-uh), a sport of *J. chinensis*

'Pfitzeriana', is distinctive for its golden-shaded foliage. 'Kaizuka' (kye-*zoo*-kuh), or 'Torulosa' (tor-yew-*loose*-uh), is an upright female form with bright green, tufted foliage to 15 ft. tall and 15 ft. wide. Zones 4 to 9, with some cultivars a bit hardier.

J. communis (kom-*mew*-nis).
COMMON JUNIPER.
Varies in habit from a ground cover 2 ft. in height to a large shrub 10 ft. tall. Native to Asia, Eur., and N. Amer. Its fruit-like cones are used to flavor gin. The foliage is juvenile, distinctly white above and green below. 'Compressa' (kom-*press*-uh) is very slow growing, tightly columnar, becoming about 3 ft. tall and 10 in. wide. Variety *depressa* (dee-*press*-uh) is a low-growing shrub to about 5 ft. in height and spreads 8 ft. This variety is native to N. Amer. 'Gold Beach' is a flat form that is golden yellow in early spring. 'Hibernica', known as the Irish juniper, is a narrow upright column. Zones 3 to 8.

J. scopulorum (skop-yew-*loh*-rum).
WESTERN RED CEDAR.
ROCKY MOUNTAIN JUNIPER.
A small tree to 30 ft. tall and 12 ft. wide. It is distributed over the Rocky Mt. area of N. Amer. from British Columbia to Ariz. The trunk is short, often divided near the ground, with red-brown bark. Its fruit is blue, and ripens during the second year. Leaves are scalelike, green to silver blue. The tree withstands dry and difficult conditions, but tends to have foliar diseases in regions of high humidity (most of the eastern U.S.). 'Blue Heaven' is a silvery-blue pyramidal form. It does better in the East than most of this species. 'Skyrocket' (often listed as a form of *J. virginiana*), is extremely narrow, a blue plant to 8 ft. tall and 1 ft. wide. It is susceptible to snow damage and has many foliar disease problems in

the East. 'Silver King' has a spreading shrub form with bright silver foliage; it grows to 4 ft. tall by 6 ft. wide. Zones 3 to 6.

J. virginiana (vir-jin-ee-*ay*-nuh).
EASTERN RED CEDAR.

One of the hardiest tree junipers. Native to the eastern half of N. America, these trees vary greatly in form from narrow columnar to spreading pyramidal. Usually they grow to heights of 40 to 50 ft. tall and up to 20 ft. wide. Their red-brown to gray bark exfoliates, or peels away in long strips. Their berrylike cones are small and light to dark blue. The foliage is usually dark green in summer and on exposed sites becomes purplish in winter. 'Burkii' (burk-*ee*-eye), a cultivar with blue foliage—both needle-like and scale-like—becomes purplish in winter. A male, it produces no cones. 'Canaertii' (cah-*nah*-air-tee-eye) is a pyramidal plant with tufted foliage that remains dark green both summer and winter; it is female, and has attractive "berries". 'Glauca' (*glaw*-kuh) is a pyramidal tree to 20 ft. tall by 18 ft. wide. It has silvery blue foliage and is female. 'Kosterii' (kos-*tur*-ee-eye) is a low shrub to 4 ft. tall and 6 ft. wide. 'Skyrocket', often listed under this species, is actually a cultivar of *J. scopulorum*. Zones 3 to 8.

Kalmia (*kal*-mee-uh).
Heath Family (*Ericaceae*).

Mostly evergreen shrubs of N. Amer. With simple leaves that may be alternate, opposite or whorled. Produces showy clusters of flowers. These ornamental plants thrive in well drained soil in full sun or in partial shade. May be propagated by seeds, or, with difficulty, by cuttings. Cultivars are often propagated in a laboratory by tissue culture.

Kalmia latifolia
MOUNTAIN LAUREL

Kerria japonica

Kalmia

K. latifolia (lat-i-*foh*-lee-uh).

MOUNTAIN LAUREL.

Round-topped shrub to 10 ft. tall and as wide. Leaves are evergreen, to 5 in. long. White to rose flowers have purple inside markings, and expand to 1 in. across. The flowers bloom in large clusters, late in the spring. Native to eastern U.S. The flowers show considerable color variation and many cultivars of various colors have been selected. Zones 5 to 9.

Kalopanax (kal-oh-*pan*-ax).

Aralia Family (*Araliaceae*).

Bold textured, deciduous, Asian tree to 80 ft. tall and 60 ft. wide. Propagate by seeds.

K. pictus (*pik*-tus).

CASTOR ARALIA.

Leaves are large, simple, and look like huge maple leaves. Green in summer, they turn yellow in autumn. The flowers are small but in large, white clusters held above the foliage in mid-summer; they are followed by small blue-black fruits. Twigs are very stout; they are thorny on young plants but become almost thornless with age. Old trunks have a distinctive brown bark. Propagate by seeds. Zones 5 to 8.

Kerria (*kehr*-ee-uh).

Rose Family (*Rosaceae*).

This deciduous shrub is from China and is valued for its yellow flowers and green stems in winter. It thrives in ordinary garden soil under sun or in the shade. Propagate by cuttings or by division.

K. japonica (ja-*pon*-ik-uh).

A deciduous, spreading shrub to 6 ft. tall and 8 ft. wide. It is conspicuous in winter for its bright green, slender stems. Produces simple, alternate, bright green leaves to 4 in. long and yellow flowers, to 2 in. across, in spring; it blooms again

occasionally in the summer. 'Pleniflora' (plen-if-*floh*-ruh) has large double flowers that last longer than the single flowers of the species. 'Picta' (*pick*-tuh) has white-edged leaves and is slower growing than the species. It tends to mutate back to the species (any green-leaved shoots should be pruned away). Zones 5 to 8.

Koelreuteria (kohl-roo-*tee*-ree-uh).

Soapberry Family (*Sapindaceae*).

Ornamental, deciduous, Asiatic trees, with alternate, pinnately compound leaves and showy clusters of flowers that bloom in the summer. Requires well-drained soil and blooms best in full sun. Propagate by seeds or root cuttings.

K. paniculata (pan-ik-yew-*lay*-tuh).

GOLDEN-RAIN TREE.

A round-headed tree about 30 ft. high and 25 ft. wide. Leaves to 14 in. long, each with 7 to 15 coarsely toothed leaflets. Its chief virtue, is its small golden yellow flowers, which occur in showy clusters. Its early-summer blooms are followed by bright green, later tan, papery seed pods. 'September' blooms a month later than the species, significantly extending the bloom season. Zones 5 to 8.

Kolkwitzia (kol-wit-*zee*-uh).

BEAUTYBUSH.

Honeysuckle Family (*Caprifoliaceae*).

A showy, deciduous shrub from China introduced in this country early in the century by E. H. Wilson. It is especially lovely in bloom during the spring. Later interest is slight, primarily a flaky, exfoliating, tan bark. Plant in well-drained soil and full sun. Propagate by cuttings or seeds.

K. amabilis (a-*mab*-il-iss).

A large shrub growing to 10 ft. high and 8 ft.

Koelreuteria paniculata
GOLDEN-RAIN TREE

Laburnum × watereri
BEAN TREE

Kolkwitzia amabilis
BEAUTYBUSH

Lagerstroemia indica
CRAPE MYRTLE

wide. Arching branches and opposite leaves to 3 in. long stay green late into the fall season. Beautiful bell-shaped flowers, ½ in. long, are pink with yellow throats; the flower stalks are distinctive with white bristly hairs. Flowers are followed by dry capsules covered with soft bristles. Zones 5 to 8.

Laburnum (la-*burn*-um).
BEAN TREE.
Pea Family (*Leguminosae*).
Deciduous small trees from Eur., mainly grown for their ornamental flowers. Produces alternate, trifoliate leaves and long, showy drooping clusters of yellow flowers in mid-spring, followed by narrow pods. The seeds are poisonous. Does best in well-drained soil and light shade or full sun. Propagate by seeds, cuttings, or root cuttings.

L. anagyroides (an-aj-er-*roy*-deez).
GOLDEN-CHAIN TREE.
Small tree to 25 ft. high and wide. Leaves and flower clusters are hairy. Flowers hang in clusters to 8 in. long, but are not as showy as the following hybrid. Zones 6 to 7.

L. × watereri (*wat*-er-er-eye).
Also called *L. vossii* (vos-*see*-eye), this is a hybrid between *L. alpinum* (al-*pin*-um) and *L. anagyroides*. A small tree of dense, stiff habit, to 15 ft. tall and 12 ft. wide. Produces showy clusters of flowers. Zones 6 to 7.

Lagerstroemia (lay-gur-*stree*-mee-uh).
Loosestrife Family (*Lythraceae*).
Ornamental shrubs and trees of warm regions of Asia. Mostly opposite leaves and showy clusters of pink, purple or white flowers. Propagate by seeds or cuttings.

L. indica (*inn*-di-kuh).
CRAPE MYRTLE.
Densely branching, deciduous shrub or small tree to 20 ft. tall and 15 ft. wide. Attractive reddish-brown bark. Leaves to 2 in. long are green in the summer and bright orange-red in autumn. Crinkled, pink to red flowers to 1½ in. across in clusters to 9 in. long, bloom from midsummer till autumn. Blooms occur on new wood. Grow in full sun with good drainage. Sometimes grown in tubs to stand out in summer but brought in to winter in a cool place indoors. There are a number of cultivars, most selected by color. The U.S. National Arboretum has introduced some that are resistant to mildew, a major problem with this species. 'Catawba', 'Cherokee', 'Conestoga', 'Muskogee', 'Natchez', 'Potomac', 'Powhatan', and 'Seminole' are all National Arboretum, mildew-resistant cultivars. Dwarf cultivars are useful further north (to Zone 5) where they can be grown like herbaceous perennials (cutting to the ground each spring). Dwarfs include: 'Petite Orchid' with purple flowers, 'Petite Pinkie' with pink flowers, 'Petite Red Imp' with dark red flowers, 'Petite Embers' with rose-red flowers, and 'Petite Snow' with white flowers. Zones 7 to 9.

Larix (*lar*-iks).
LARCH.
Pine Family (*Pinaceae*).
Deciduous, coniferous trees. They produce green to bluish green needles during the summer that are borne in whorls on short, spur-like shoots. The needles turn bright yellow in autumn. Small cones, borne on the upper side of the branches, are a lovely violet color in the spring.

L. decidua (deh-*sid*-yew-uh).
EUROPEAN LARCH.
Grows to 75 ft. tall and 25 ft. wide. It is native to

Larix decidua
EUROPEAN LARCH

Laurus nobilis
BAY LAUREL

Europe, especially mountainous regions. Zones 4 to 6.

L. kaempferi (*kem*-fur-eye).
JAPANESE LARCH.
Grows 75 ft. tall by 40 ft. wide. Native to Japan. Zones 4 to 6.

L. laricina (*lar*-i-see-nuh).
TAMARACK.
AMERICAN LARCH.
Grows to 60 ft. high by 15 ft. wide. Native to eastern N. Amer. Zones 2 to 6.

Laurus (*law*-rus).
LAUREL.
SWEET BAY.
Laurel Family (*Lauraceae*).
The only cultivated species is an evergreen tree from the Mediterranean region, the historic laurel used by the ancient Greeks to crown victors. Bay leaves are among the oldest of European condiments and are widely used today for flavoring many dishes. Propagate by seeds or cuttings.

L. nobilis (noh-*bil*-iss).
BAY.
BAY LAUREL.
A fragrant shrub that can grow to 30 ft. tall. It shears well and is an important plant in Italian gardens. Often grown in pots and other containers in warm regions, or brought inside for the winter. It has stiff, dark green leaves to 4 in. long; the greenish yellow flowers are followed by black berries. Zones 9 to 10.

Leiophyllum (lye-oh-*fill*-um).
SAND MYRTLE.
Heath Family (*Ericaceae*).
Low, evergreen shrubs of N. Amer., with small,

alternate or opposite, glossy dark green leaves. Attractive clusters of small white or pinkish flowers bloom in the spring. Thrives in sandy, peaty soil. Requires excellent drainage. Propagate by seeds, cuttings, root cuttings, or layers.

L. buxifolium (buks-ih-*foh*-lee-uhm).
BOX SAND MYRTLE.

This plant is native to eastern N. Amer. It can grow up to 2 ft. high and spread to 3 ft. wide. The foliage is fine-textured. In late spring, the small pink flower buds open to a white star-shaped flower, edged in pink. In fall, the leaves take on a bronze coloration with cold weather. Plant in full sun to part shade in an acid, moist soil. Zones 6 to 8.

Lespedeza (les-peh-*dee*-zuh).
BUSH CLOVER.
Pea Family (*Leguminosae*).

Herbaceous perennials or shrubs of N. Amer., Asia and Australia. They have trifoliate alternate leaves. Their flowers are valuable for their late-season bloom, which is purple to white in color. Fruits are small, non-showy pods. Requires good drainage and full sun. Propagate by cuttings, seeds and division.

L. bicolor (*bye*-kol-lore).
SHRUB BUSH CLOVER.

The flowers are rosy-purple, pea-like, and are borne in 2- to 5-in. long racemes or clusters. These racemes arise from the leaf axils of the upper 2 ft. of each stem. Can grow to be 8 ft. tall and 8 ft. wide. Flowers are produced on the present season's growth, so it can be cut down to the ground each year in early spring. Zones 5 to 7.

L. thunbergii (thun-*bur*-gee-eye).
THUNBERG BUSH CLOVER.
Very similar to *L. bicolor*. Leaves are bluish green,

and it produces rosy purple flowers in late summer. Grows 6 ft. tall and 6 ft. wide. 'Alba' has white flowers. Zones 5 to 7.

Leucothoe (lew-*koth*-oh-ee).
Heath Family (*Ericaceae*).

Handsome, evergreen and deciduous shrubs of N. and S. Amer., Asia and Madagascar with good foliage and attractive flowers. The leaves are alternate and the small white or pinkish flowers bloom in the spring. They thrive in well-drained, moist, peaty soils in partial shade or full sun. With their graceful habit, they look good year-round. Propagate by seeds, cuttings or divisions.

L. fontanesiana (fon-tuh-neez-ee-*ay*-nuh).
DROOPING LEUCOTHOE.

Previously known as *L. catesbaei*. Evergreen shrub to 6 ft. tall and as wide with slender, arching branches and shiny leaves to 7 in. long. It assumes a bronzy color in the fall. The sprays make attractive winter bouquets. Waxy, showy, white, urn-shaped flowers in small clusters bloom early in the summer. 'Nana' (*nay*-nuh) spreads to 6 ft., but attains a height of only 2 ft. 'Rainbow' has variegated leaves with yellow, pink and white variegations. Zones 5 to 9.

Ligustrum (li-*gus*-trum).
PRIVET.
Olive Family (*Oleaceae*).

These ornamental, deciduous or evergreen shrubs are native to all continents except the Americas and the Antarctic. Vigorous and quick-growing, they have opposite leaves, small white flowers in clusters, often with a strong odor, and black or bluish, berrylike fruit. They are very useful and popular shrubs in hedges partly because they are very tough and tolerant of shade, sun, city and seaside conditions. Seedlings of many species can become troublesome weeds in natural areas. Propagate by seeds or cuttings.

Leucothoe fontanesiana
DROOPING LEUCOTHOE

L. amurense (am-moor-*ren*-see).
AMUR PRIVET.
A deciduous or half-evergreen erect shrub to 12 ft. high and 8 ft. wide with lustrous green leaves to 2 in. long; it has no fall color. Flowers in clusters to 2 in. long; bloom in late spring. One of the hardiest privets, it makes a neat hedge when pruned. Untrimmed, it forms a natural dense screen. Zones 4 to 7.

L. japonicum (ja-*pon*-ik-um).
JAPANESE PRIVET.
An evergreen shrub from Japan that grows to 10 ft. tall by 8 ft. wide, and produces shiny, leathery dark green leaves to 4 in. long. Flower clusters to 6 in. long are produced in summer. It is widely used in the South as a hedge and an ornamental plant. Zones 7 to 9.

L. lucidum (lew-*sid*-um).
GLOSSY PRIVET.
An evergreen shrub or small tree to 25 ft. tall, with very shiny leaves growing to 6 in. long. Its creamy white flower clusters, to about 10 in. long, bloom in summer. The large clusters of purple-black fruits, with contrasting orange stems, are effective in autumn and early winter. Zones 8 to 10.

L. obtusifolium (ob-tew-si-*foh*-lee-um).
BORDER PRIVET.
Deciduous shrub growing to 10 ft. high and 12 ft. wide. Leaves to 2 in. long occur on spreading, horizontal branches. Flower clusters to 4 in. long are borne in late spring. Its blue-black berries are somewhat showy and last into winter. The variety *regelianum* (ree-gel-ee-*ay*-num), known as regel privet, grows only half as high as the species. Its horizontal branches are handsome when unsheared. Zones 4 to 8.

Ligustrum vulgare
COMMON PRIVET

L. vulgare (vul-*gay*-ree).
COMMON PRIVET.
A half-evergreen shrub to 15 ft. tall and as wide. Naturalized in parts of the U.S. Produces narrow leaves to 2½ in. long, and flowers in small clusters, in early summer. The shiny black autumn berries are moderately showy. Makes a tall screen. 'Cheyenne' is more cold and drought resistant than the species. Zones 4 to 7.

Lindera (lin-*deer*-uh).

Laurel Family (*Lauraceae*).

Aromatic, deciduous or evergreen shrubs and trees of Asia and N. Amer. Flowers of separate sexes occur in small dense clusters; the leaves are alternate. The fruit is a fleshy berry. Lindera can be propagated by seeds, or by softwood cuttings.

L. benzoin (*ben*-zoh-in).

SPICEBUSH.

Also known as *Benzoin aestivale*. This deciduous shrub grows to 10 ft. tall and 10 ft. wide. It is native to the woods from Me. to Fla. and Tex. It tolerates sun or shade and poor drainage. Its leaves, to 5 in. long, turn a clear yellow in autumn. The tiny, greenish-yellow flowers in dense clusters make an attractive display in early spring before the leaves unfold. Scarlet, oblong berries, borne on female plants, are colorful into late autumn. Zones 5 to 9.

Liquidambar (lik-wid-*am*-bar).

Witch hazel Family (*Hamamelidaceae*).

Attractive deciduous trees of America and Asia, with alternate, maple-like leaves and inconspicuous flowers borne in dense heads. The fruit is a hanging, prickly, ball-like head, 1 in. in diameter. Propagate by seeds or grafts.

L. styraciflua (stye-ruh-si-*flew*-uh).

SWEET GUM.

Pyramidal tree to 75 ft. tall and 50 ft. wide. Branchlets are often corky. Shiny, dark green leaves to 7 in. long have five to seven lobes, which give them a starlike appearance. The foliage turns a dark crimson to purple to orange in the fall. Tolerates sun and shade, poor drainage as well as dry soils. 'Gumball' is a multi-stemmed shrub. 'Corky' has extremely corky twigs and consistently red fall color. 'Rotundiloba' (roh-tun-di-*loh*-buh) has rounded leaf lobes and is fruitless. Zones 5 to 9.

Liquidambar styraciflua
SWEET GUM

Liriodendron tulipifera
TULIP TREE

Liriodendron (lihr-ee-oh-*den*-dron).

TULIP TREE.

Magnolia Family (*Magnoliaceae*).

Deciduous trees of N. Amer. and China, with alternate leaves that usually are lobed. Produces tuliplike flowers, borne singly, and conelike fruit. Handsome trees of noble appearance that thrive best in rich, rather moist soil. Propagate by seeds or by grafting.

✳L. tulipifera (too-li-*piff*-er-uh).

The tallest native tree east of the Mississippi. It grows to 100 ft. or more in height and spreads to 50 ft., often with a long stretch of clean trunk. Leaves are of a distinct shape, with a deeply notched apex, and are more or less lobed. About 5 in. long, they are bluish-green, pale beneath, and turn clear yellow in the fall. Greenish-yellow flowers have an orange band at the base of the petals; they bloom in mid- to late spring, after the leaves have emerged. Zones 5 to 9.

Lonicera (lon-*iss*-er-uh).

HONEYSUCKLE.

Honeysuckle Family (*Caprifoliaceae*).

A very large group of shrubs and vines. Grown for their fragrant, attractive flowers. Blooms are white, pink, yellow or red. Fruits are berries, often loved by birds. This can actually be a problem with some, in that the resulting seedlings can become terrible weeds in natural areas. Plants generally thrive in any good garden soil and tolerate full sun or shade. Propagate by seeds or by cuttings.

L. fragrantissima (fray-gran-*tis*-i-muh).

FRAGRANT HONEYSUCKLE.

This plant is native to China. The best asset of this shrub is the early flowering period in late winter. The flowers are small, white and highly fragrant (lemon scented). It flowers on the pre-vious season's growth. Grows to 10 ft. high and 8 ft. wide. The leaves are 1 to 3 in. long, deciduous in the north and semi-evergreen in the south. The flowering period lasts for 3 to 4 weeks. Pairs of these fragrant flowers are borne in the leaf axils before the leaves open. The red fruit, if produced, appears in May but is eaten quickly by birds. Zones 5 to 9.

L. nitida (nit-*ee*-dah).

BOX HONEYSUCKLE.

This evergreen shrub gets its common name from its small, 1-in. leaves and dense growth habit, which are similar to box. It is often used as a hedge. The small white flowers appear in late spring and are followed by small purple fruits. Grows to 5 ft. tall and 5 ft. wide, but can be kept pruned to any size. Zones 6 to 9.

Lonicera fragrantisssima
FRAGRANT HONEYSUCKLE

L. tatarica (tuh-*tar*-ih-kah).
TATARIAN HONEYSUCKLE.
This extremely tough shrub, native to Russia, should be avoided because its seedlings become very weedy. The flowers appear in late spring and early summer. They are pinkish white, although red and white varieties are also available. In mid-to-late summer, the red fruit appears. Both flowers and fruit are moderately showy. The leaves are 1 to 2½ in. long, dull green, and produce no fall color. A multi-stemmed shrub, it grows to 10 ft. in height and width. Zones 3 to 7.

Loropetalum (lor-oh-*pet*-uh-lum).
Witch hazel Family (*Hamamelidaceae*).
A single species genus native to Asia. Propagate by seeds, grafts and cuttings.

L. chinense (chi-*nen*-seh).
A multi-stemmed evergreen shrub that grows to 8 ft. tall and wide. Attractive, creamy white flowers with narrow petals, much like a witch hazel, appear in early to mid-spring. Fruits are dry, green to brown, in non-showy capsules. Leaves are about 2 in. long. Zones 7 to 9.

Maclura (muh-*kloo*-ruh).
OSAGE ORANGE.
Mulberry Family (*Moraceae*).
A deciduous, spiny, American tree, native from Ark. to Kan. It grows well in dry and difficult places and has frequently been used as a hedge or windbreak in the past. Propagate by cuttings or by seeds.

M. pomifera (pom-*iff*-er-uh).
Tree to 40 ft. tall and wide, with bright green leaves, to 3 in. long, that turn yellow in the fall. Very small, greenish flowers bloom in May and June, with the sexes separate, occurring on different plants. These are followed on the female

plants by round, green, orangelike balls to 6 in. in diameter. The fruit is as interesting as it is messy, but it is not edible. Zones 5 to 9.

✱✱Magnolia (mag-*noh*-lee-uh).
Magnolia Family (*Magnoliaceae*).
Notably attractive and bold-textured deciduous and evergreen shrubs and trees of Asia and America. Large alternate leaves and buds. Twigs are usually thick, with a distinctive odor. All have large flowers. The American species usually bloom after the leaves appear, somewhat diminishing the floral effect. Many of the Asian species bloom before the leaves and are among the most showy species. Some species have handsome glossy leaves. Deciduous species tend to have yellow to yellow-brown autumn color. All have colorful—but usually not very showy—aggregate fruits during late summer and early fall. Most have smooth gray bark when young. The early blooming species are often damaged while in bloom by late frosts that turn the flowers a disgusting brown. Most species grow best with ample moisture but well-drained soil; they are tolerant of sun or shade, but bloom best in full sun. Because of the very fragile, fleshy roots, they must be transplanted with extra care, preferably in spring and with a firm earth ball. Propagate by seeds, cuttings, layers or grafts.

M. acuminata (uh-kew-min-*nay*-tuh).
CUCUMBER TREE.
A native tree to 80 ft. tall and 60 ft. wide. Its oval leaves grow to 8 in. long. Greenish-yellow flowers, to 3 in. wide, are pretty but generally masked by the leaves. The flowers bloom with the leaves in late spring. Fruits, green during summer and resembling small cucumbers, become pinkish in autumn. The variety *subcordata* (sub-cor-*da*-tuh), the yellow cucumber tree, has clear yellow flowers that are significantly more

showy than the species. 'Elizabeth' is a hybrid cultivar, selected from a cross between *M. acuminata* var. *subcordata* and *M. heptapeta* (hep-tuh-*pet*-uh). Flowers are yellow in bud and fade almost to white before dropping. Zones 4 to 8.

Magnolia grandiflora
SOUTHERN MAGNOLIA

✴**M. grandiflora** (gran-di-*floh*-ruh).
SOUTHERN MAGNOLIA.
BULL BAY.
A magnificent evergreen to 80 ft. tall and 50 ft. wide. Stiff lustrous leaves, green, to 9 in. long, are rusty-hairy beneath. Large, waxy, white, cup-shaped fragrant flowers to 8 in. across, bloom in late spring and through the summer. Heavy aggregate fruit, to 5 in. long, becomes cone-like during the winter. This is the magnolia of the Southern plantations and one of America's most valued additions to the world's gardens. It may be trained on a sheltered wall where it is not hardy enough to stand in the open. There are a number of cultivars. 'Edith Bogue' is thought to

be one of the hardiest. Zones 7 to 9.

M. heptapeta (hep-*tap*-eh-tah).
YULAN MAGNOLIA.
A showy deciduous tree to 30 ft. tall and wide, with oval leaves to 6 in. long. Large, very showy, white, fragrant, cup-shaped flowers envelop the tree in early to mid-spring before the leaves appear. Zones 6 to 9.

M. kobus (*koh*-bus).
A Japanese tree to 40 ft. in height, with single or multiple trunks. Leaves are somewhat narrow, to 4 in. long. Quantities of white blossoms to 5 in. across with narrow tepals (petals) bloom in April before the leaves appear. Tree does not bear flowers when it is young. Slow to come to bloom. Zones 5 to 8. The variety *borealis* can reach 70 ft. in height and is hardy to Zone 4.

Magnolia × *soulangiana*
SAUCER MAGNOLIA

Magnolia

M. × loebneri (*leb*-nair-eye)
LOEBNER MAGNOLIA.
This is a cross between *M. kobus* and *M. stellata*. The former is a fast grower that frequently does not come into bloom until it is 20 years old; the latter, which is small in size, blooms at a rather young age. The flowers are fragrant, white (sometimes with a tinge of pink) and occur in early spring before the leaves. It tends to start blooming at a young age. It is only a small tree, to 30 ft. tall and as wide. 'Merrill' blooms in five years; its big white flowers are similar to *M. stellata* but the tepals are wider. Propagate by cuttings. Zones 5 to 9.

M. macrophylla (mac-roh-*fill*-uh).
BIGLEAF MAGNOLIA.
A deciduous, American tree to 40 ft. high and as wide. Its huge leaves have a papery texture, grow to 30 in. long, and are silvery below. Its large pointed buds are covered with silvery hairs. Flowers are white, occurring after the leaves appear, and grow to 10 in. across. Fall color is yellowish brown. Zones 5 to 9.

M. × soulangiana (soo-lan-jee-*ay*-nuh).
SAUCER MAGNOLIA.
Incorrectly called "tulip tree" by some because the showy flowers resemble tulips. It is a hybrid between *M. heptapeta* (hep-*tap*-pet-uh) and *M. quinquepeta* (quin-kwe-*pee*-tuh). This small tree grows to 25 ft. tall and as wide. Its smooth gray bark and green oval leaves grow to 6 in. across. Its chief feature is its dramatic cup-shaped flowers, which are rosy purplish outside, whitish inside, and cover the branches in mid-spring before the leaves appear. One of the most familiar magnolias; there are several cultivars selected for color, ranging from white tinged with purple or pink, to dark rose and dark purple. 'Alba Superba' (*al*-buh soo-*pur*-buh) has white flowers; 'Alex-andrina' (al-ex-an-*dree*-nuh) purple outside and white inside; 'Lennei' (*len*-nee-eye) has deep purple flowers, 'Speciosa' (spee-*see*-oh-suh) white, blooming late and 'Rustica Rubra' (*russ*-ti-cuh *roo*-bruh) has large rosy red flowers with white centers. Zones 5 to 9.

Magnolia stellata
STAR MAGNOLIA

M. stellata (steh-*lay*-tuh).
STAR MAGNOLIA.
Much branched, this large spreading Japanese shrub has a dense habit and grows to 15 ft. tall and as wide. Its dark green narrow leaves, to 5 in. long, turn bronze in the fall. It produces fragrant white flowers with many narrow petals. One of the earliest Magnolias, it blooms in early spring before the leaves appear. It begins to flower when it is as small as 3 ft. 'Rosea' (*rohs*-ee-uh) has pink flowers. 'Royal Star' has larger flowers. 'Water-lily' begins pink and fades to white. Zones 5 to 8.

✱**M. virginiana** (vir-jin-ee-*ay*-nuh).
Sweet-bay.
Also known as *M. glauca* (*glau*-cuh). This tree, to 40 ft. tall and 20 ft. wide, is evergreen in its southern range; generally it is deciduous (but late to drop its leaves) farther north. Its leaves are shiny green above and bluish beneath. It produces creamy-white, wonderfully fragrant flowers to 3 in. across late in the spring and continues to

Magnolia virginiana
Sweet-bay

Mahonia aquifolium
Oregon-grape

bloom through most of the summer. Native to eastern U.S., it tolerates wet and dry soils. The variety *australis* tends to be evergreen. Zones 5 to 9.

Mahonia (muh-*hoh*-nee-uh).
Barberry Family (*Berberidaceae*).
Handsome, low-growing, thornless evergreen shrubs of Asia, N. and Cent. Amer. Alternate, pinnately compound leaves have leaflets that are mostly spiny toothed. The fragrant, bright yellow flowers emerge in dense erect clusters. The fruit is usually a dark blue berry with a silvery bloom. They thrive in sun or shade, as long as there is ample moisture. Leaves on some species turn reddish in winter if exposed to the sun. Propagate by seeds, cuttings, division, or suckers.

M. aquifolium (ah-kwi-*foh*-lee-um).
Oregon-grape.
Shrub to 3 or 4 ft. tall and wide. Produces dark green, often shiny leaflets to 3 in. long and compound leaves to 8 in. long. Showy flowers occur in mid-spring. Small bluish-black berries. Native to the Pacific Northwest. Zones 5 to 9.

M. bealei (*bell*-ee-eye).
Leatherleaf Mahonia.
Grows to 7 ft. high and 6 ft. wide, with stout erect stems. Bold, stiff leaves to 16 in. long (leaflets to 4 in. long) are held horizontally. Yellow, fragrant flowers, in showy clusters to 6 in. high, bloom in mid-spring. Blue-black berries. Tends to be leggy with age. Zones 6 to 9.

✱✱**Malus** (*mahl*-us).
Crabapples.
Apples.
Rose Family (*Rosaceae*).
This genus encompasses both orchard-type ap-

Malus

ples and strictly ornamental crabapples. All are edible, but crabs have small fruit, generally under 2 in. in diameter. There are many species and a large number of cultivars, varying in flower color from white to deep pink, in fruit size and color from red to yellow to green to fruitless, and in disease susceptibility.

Most people select crabapples on the basis of the flowers. Since almost all of them have attractive flowers, it is more important to select on disease resistance for your area (not all diseases are severe in all areas) and on fruit display. The fruit display can last through autumn and winter and be as showy as the flowers.

Native to North America, Europe and Asia, plants are usually trees but some are shrublike. The leaves of apples are larger than those of crab-

Malus floribunda
JAPANESE FLOWERING CRABAPPLE

apples, about 2 to 4 in. long, and are hairy. Crabapples generally have smaller, usually hairless (or slightly hairy) leaves (The leaves of *Malus ioensis*,

a Midwestern native, has quite pubescent leaves).

Much of the hybridizing in this genus has been done naturally, as these species cross-pollinate readily. The horticultural industry has often just performed the job of selection. Many of the parents of crosses are unknown. The species native to this country have very little resistance to the diseases and insects which pester this genus. The fruit of our native crabs is generally not very ornamental, and often remains green. The oriental species and their hybrids are generally the showiest landscape plants. Many are resistant to one or more of the disease and insect problems and they have many attractive ornamental characteristics.

A general description can be applied to this diverse genus. These trees are deciduous, with alternate, toothed leaves. The leaves may or may not be lobed. Heights vary from 8 to 40 ft. with the average being 15 to 25 ft. with a similar spread. There are five different characteristic growth habits. They are upright, round, spreading (wider than it is tall), columnar, weeping and shrub (dwarf). Crabapples flower in early to mid spring and the fruit ripens in late summer and early fall. The flowers are either single or double and are borne in showy clusters. They appear before or just with the leaves. Some cultivars and species bloom and fruit only every other year.

The genus is adaptable as to soil, but the optimum is a well-drained, acidic to slightly alkaline soil. Full sun is necessary for good flowers. Most crabapples produce watersprouts and many produce suckers. Pruning may be necessary to remove watersprouts, suckers and crossing branches or to develop the natural form. It can be done anytime, but is often done in late winter, when the tree's structure is clearly seen and there is often extra time. A goal with fruiting apples is to keep the center of the tree open to the sun and not overcrowded. This helps make the tree less susceptible to fungal attacks. Spraying for insects and diseases is not necessary with crabapples if disease resistant trees are chosen originally. Spraying is considered essential for apples if "perfect" fruits are desired. There is a whole range of pest and disease problems. If proper care is given to choosing trees that are resistant to the particular problems of your area of the country, you can avoid having to deal with many of them. Consult your local Cooperative Extension service for help in identifying your local problems. The most common of these problems are listed below:

FIRE BLIGHT
A bacterial disease, which causes the leaves to wilt and the stems and leaves to look charred, can be fatal. It is spread by rain, insects and pruning equipment that has not been disinfected. It can be controlled by winter pruning—eliminating infected limbs during dry weather—and timely spraying with bactericides.

CEDAR APPLE RUST
A fungal disease which has alternate hosts. On the Eastern red-cedar (*Juniperus virginiana*) a gall about the size of a golf ball appears, which gives rise to orange, spikey growths that release spores in the damp conditions of spring. The spores infect the leaves of susceptible apples and crabapples. Yellow-orange spots appear on the leaves and these spots grow until autumn. Spores are then released that infect the red-cedar. The disease is not fatal to crabapples, but the premature defoliation it causes is very stressful. Native crabapples and their hybrids are susceptible, but Asian crabs are resistant.

APPLE SCAB
The most common disease attacking crabs, this produces a dark leathery spot on the fruit and leaves, resulting in premature defoliation. While not fatal, the disease may result in repeated premature defoliation, which causes stress. The native species and many apples of commerce are very susceptible to this particular disease.

POWDERY MILDEW
A white, fungal disease of the leaves, while not fatal, is a serious problem in areas of warm spring temperatures.

APHIDS
These are generally found on the tender tips of branches where there is lush growth, such as occurs on suckers.

EASTERN TENT CATERPILLAR
This common pest forms silken tents in branches as leaves appear. Defoliated trees usually produce new leaves by midsummer with no ill effects, but three years of defoliation can be fatal. These insects are easily controlled by pruning, hand removal or insecticidal soaps.

OTHER INSECTS
Various insects can damage eating apples and are usually controlled by insecticides.

A guide to landscape considerations and a chart of recommended *Malus* species and varieties for the garden appear on pages 22–25.

Malus floribunda
JAPANESE FLOWERING CRABAPPLE

Metasequoia glyptostroboides
DAWN REDWOOD

Metasequoia (met-uh-seh-*kwoy*-uh).

DAWN REDWOOD.

Bald-cypress Family (*Taxodiaceae*).

This single species genus contains a remarkably handsome tree that had been known only as a fossil before the 1940s. It was discovered in remote, western China and introduced into the U.S. after World War II by the Arnold Arboretum. This fast-growing, stately tree grows most quickly in soils with ample moisture. Propagate by seeds or cuttings.

✶**M. glyptostroboides** (glip-toh-stroh-*boy*-deez).

Deciduous tree to 100 ft. or more and 25 ft. wide. Pyramidal, symmetrical form is very distinctive. The leaves are feathery, green during the summer, turning an attractive rusty-orange in mid- to late autumn before dropping. Cones are small and round. The bark is a showy reddish-brown and the trunk becomes deeply fluted and but-

tressed with age. Zones 5 to 9.

Morus (*moh*-rus).

MULBERRY.

Mulberry Family (*Moraceae*).

Deciduous trees of the Northern Hemisphere. Simple or lobed, alternate leaves and inconspicuous greenish flowers in catkins, male and female on separate trees. Cultivated for the edible, berrylike fruit, and in the Far East for the foliage, which is used to feed silkworms. Not particular as to soil. Propagate by seeds, cuttings. Fruit on all species is particularly messy.

Morus alba 'Pendula'
WEEPING WHITE MULBERRY

M. alba (*al*-buh).

WHITE MULBERRY.

Spreading, round-headed tree from China. Grows to 40 ft. tall and wide. Bright green leaves to 5 in. long, often variously lobed, expecially on young plants. Sweet, whitish to purplish-black fruit, to 1 in. long. Can become a serious weed problem in gardens and natural areas. Females should not be planted unless fruit for eating is desired. 'Kingan' and 'Striblingii' are male, non-fruiting cultivars. 'Pendula' is a weeping form, usually grafted onto a straight trunk. Zones 4 to 9.

M. rubra (*roo*-bruh).
RED MULBERRY.
AMERICAN MULBERRY.
This native American, broad-headed tree grows to 60 ft. tall and 40 ft. wide. Leaves to 8 in. long; purple fruits, about 1 in. long, are attractive to birds. Zones 4 to 8.

Myrica (mye-*ree*-kuh).
Sweet-gale Family (*Myricaceae*).
Evergreen or deciduous shrubs and trees of temperate and warmer regions. The alternate, simple leaves are pleasantly aromatic. Inconspicuous flowers of separate sexes appear on the same or different plants. Round, purplish or grayish berries, usually with a waxy covering, add a pretty touch in the fall. Propagate by seeds, layers, cuttings, division or suckers.

M. cerifera (see-*rif*-er-uh).
WAX MYRTLE.
Ornamental evergreen shrub or tree to 15 ft. high and wide, with leaves to 3 in. long and clusters of

Myrica pensylvanica
BAYBERRY

gray, waxy berries, which are aromatic. Zones 6 to 9.

M. pensylvanica (pen-sil-*van*-ik-uh).
BAYBERRY.
Semi-evergreen shrub to 8 ft. tall and 8 ft. wide, with dull green, aromatic leaves to 4 in. long. The ornamental gray berries are used to make bayberry candles. This shrub will thrive in poor, sandy soil. It is tolerant of salt and is one of the staples of seashore plantings in the North Atlantic states. Zones 4 to 9.

Nandina domestica
HEAVENLY BAMBOO

Nandina (nan-*dee*-nuh).
HEAVENLY BAMBOO.
Barberry Family (*Berberidaceae*).
An attractive, evergreen shrub (not a true bamboo) of China and Japan. An airy and graceful landscape plant grown for foliage, flowers, and fruits. Propagate by seeds, cuttings, and division. Does not reliably fruit in the north.

N. domestica (doh-*mess*-tik-uh).
Grows to 8 ft. high and wide, with reedlike stems. Leaves are compound, to 18 in. long, alternate, and turn a handsome red in autumn. The narrow, young leaflets, about ½ in. long, are bronze-pink in winter, green in summer. Small white flowers in large showy clusters in the spring, followed by long-lasting, bright red berries. Will grow in sun or shade (leaf color does not change as much in shade) and does best in a moist, well-drained soil. 'Alba' has white berries. 'Compacta' is shorter than the species. Zones 6 to 9.

Nerium (*neer*-ee-um).

Dogbane Family (*Apocynaceae*).
These are graceful and distinctive evergreen shrubs or small trees with opposite leaves, sometimes in whorls of threes or fours. They produce clusters of showy flowers. These are familiar pot or tub plants in the North, and are widely planted as hedge and specimen plants in the South and Southwest. Require a well-drained soil and full sun. They shear readily. Propagate by cuttings, seeds or division.

N. oleander (oh-lee-*an*-der).
OLEANDER.
Widely grown shrub or tree from the Mediterranean region. Grows to 20 ft. tall and 15 ft. wide, but is usually smaller. Narrow, leathery leaves to 5 in. long. White, pink or red flowers, 1½ in. across, often double, bloom throughout the summer. The sap is poisonous. Zones 9 to 10.

Nyssa (*niss*-uh).

TUPELO.
Nyssa Family (*Nyssaceae*).
Notable deciduous trees of N. Amer. and Asia with alternate, simple leaves and clusters of tiny, insignificant, greenish-white flowers. Male and female flowers, usually on different plants, and small, dark blue fruit on female trees. Brilliant autumnal foliage. Difficult to transplant from the wild because of its taproot. Tolerates sun or shade, although best fall color in sun. Tolerates poor drainage and dry soils. Propagate by seeds or suckers.

N. sylvatica (sil-*vat*-i-kuh).
BLACK GUM.
PEPPERIDGE.
SOUR GUM.
A picturesque, eastern N. American tree, to 60 ft. tall by 35 ft. wide. The branch effect is conspicuously horizontal. The shiny leaves, to 4 in. long, turn a brilliant scarlet in the fall, giving one of the finest foliage displays of any hardy plant. Zones 5 to 9.

Olea (oh-*lee*-uh).

OLIVE.
Olive Family (*Oleaceae*).
Attractive evergreen shrubs and trees of the Eastern Hemisphere. The opposite leaves are often silvery. Small, whitish flowers in clusters, and fleshy, one-seeded fruits. Propagate by seeds, cuttings, suckers, or grafting.

O. europaea (yew-*roh*-pee-uh).
COMMON OLIVE.
Native to the Mediterranean region, this tree grows to 25 ft. high and wide. Distinctive, gray-green leaves to 3 in. long are silvery beneath. Fragrant flowers are produced in short clusters. Oblong fruit, to 1½ in. long, is shiny black when ripe. A long-lived, picturesque tree, it has been cultivated for centuries for olive oil and for processed olives. Grown commercially in Calif. and, both there and in other Southwestern areas, for ornament. Zones 8 to 10.

Nerium oleander
OLEANDER

Olea europaea
COMMON OLIVE

Nyssa sylvatica
BLACK GUM

Ostrya virginiana
IRONWOOD

Osmanthus (oz-*man*-thus).

Olive Family (*Oleaceae*).

Many species of evergreen shrubs, from E. Asia, N. Amer., Hawaii and New Caledonia make up this genus. All have opposite leaves and fragrant flowers that are usually white, but sometimes yellow or orange. Flowers occur in short, axillary panicles. Fruit is fleshy, enclosing a stony seed.

O. heterophyllus (het-ur-oh-*fill*-us).

HOLLY OSMANTHUS.

Similar in effect to an evergreen holly, but has opposite leaves and blooms in late summer and autumn. Leaves usually spiny and toothed. Shrubs to 12 ft. high and wide. Small white flowers, very fragrant. Fruits are blue-black in color but not showy. Zones 6 to 9.

Ostrya (*oss*-tree-uh).

HOP HORNBEAM.

Birch Family (*Betulaceae*).

Deciduous trees of the Northern Hemisphere, with alternate, toothed leaves, and inconspicuous male and female flowers in separate catkins on the same tree. They are reminiscent of a small elm in appearance. The fruit consists of clustered nutlets enclosed in light green, bladderlike (hoplike) bracts. Propagate by seeds.

O. virginiana (vir-jin-ee-*ay*-nuh).

IRONWOOD.

AMERICAN HOP HORNBEAM.

This species is native to eastern N. America. It grows to 40 ft. tall and 25 ft. wide. Its brown bark is finely divided. Medium green, toothed, oval leaves grow to 4 in. long and turn an attractive yellow or orange in autumn. Fruit clusters 2½ in. long. Tolerates sun and shade and dry soil. Zones 3 to 8.

Oxydendrum (ox-si-*den*-drum).

SOURWOOD.

SORREL TREE.

Heath Family (*Ericaceae*).

This is a handsome deciduous tree native to eastern N. Amer. with a graceful pyramidal habit, fragrant white flowers and brilliant red autumn color. It requires good drainage. Tolerates sun or shade, but blooms and colors best in sun. Propagate by seeds.

Oxydendrum arboreum
SOURWOOD

Paeonia suffruticosa 'Joseph Rock'
TREE PEONY

O. arboreum (ar-*boh*-ree-um).

A slow-growing tree, 30 ft. by 20 ft. wide. Its small flowers in showy drooping panicles appear in mid-summer. The lustrous foliage turns scarlet in the fall, and dry tannish capsules remain decorative in winter. Zones 5 to 9.

Paeonia (pay-*oh*-nee-uh).

PEONY.

Buttercup Family (*Ranunculaceae*).

A group of shrubby and herbaceous plants with very showy flowers. The common peony is a herbaceous perennial, dying back to the ground each winter. Propagate by grafting.

In this country, the term "peony" typically brings to mind the May-flowering herbaceous plants, but the shrubby tree peonies are becoming more widely known.

P. suffruticosa (suf-frew-*tik*-koh-suh).

TREE PEONY.

From China. A shrubby peony with woody stems that live through the winter. Spectacular flowers to 10 in. across with crinkled, satiny petals appear in mid-spring; there are single and double forms in varying shades of white, cream, pink, rose, burgundy, maroon and recent hybrids with yellow are also available.

Like the herbaceous cultivars, it should be planted in Sept. and Oct., in a hole 3 by 2 ft., in well-prepared humusy soil. Mix in damp peat, humus or compost, and bone meal but do not use manure. The pH of the soil should be slightly alkaline so add lime if necessary. Plant with the graft 4 in. below the soil surface. Water it in well. In order to promote good foliage growth, do not permit flower buds to set the first year. Protect it with an upturned basket or some other airy covering the first winter and mulch well. Do not plant tree peonies facing east or the buds will suffer winter damage. Also avoid windswept

spots. These plants may be pruned for shape and to keep their size in hand, but don't cut them back. Work a well-balanced fertilizer into the soil in subsequent years.

Paeonia suffruticosa 'Hakuo-Jishi'
TREE PEONY

P. lutea has been crossed with *P. sufruticosa* to bring the qualities of its yellow-toned flowers into the tree-peony class. Many outstanding hybrids are available. A few examples include: 'Age of Gold', camellia-shaped flowers in creamy yellow deepening at the center to rich gold; 'Artemis', large single blossoms of pure light yellow, a crimson flare on each petal; 'Banquet', strawberry-red, semi-double blossoms with undersides of gold; 'Black Pirate', very dark mahogany-red with black flares on inner petals; 'Chinese Dragon' fine cut foliage and crimson-mauve, semi-double blossoms; 'Ezra Pound', mauve-pink, single to semi-double with purple flairs; 'Harvest', golden-yellow, semi-double blossoms held nicely above foliage; 'Mystery',

Paeonia

pearled-lavender, single blossoms, raspberry-red; 'Joseph Rock', pure white blossoms with purple inner flares, semi-double; 'Shintenchi', pure cameo-pink, semi-double; 'Vesuvian', maroon-red, semi-double, full rounded plant form when mature; and 'Zephyrus', pearly-pink with highlights of peach cream, ruby-red flares, semi-double. Zones 5 to 8.

Parrotia (par-*roh*-tee-uh).
Witch hazel Family (*Hammamelidaceae*).
A small deciduous tree native to Iran. Propagate by seeds or cuttings. Zones 6 to 9.

P. persica (*per*-sik-uh).
PERSIAN PARROTIA.
Notable for its brilliant orange and yellow autumn foliage. Grows to 25 ft. tall and wide. Coarsely toothed leaves to 4 in. long, very similar to witch hazels. Its reddish flowers, which are not very showy, appear in early spring before the leaves open. Bark exfoliates with age and becomes very attractive.

Paulownia (paw-*loh*-nee-uh).
Figwort Family (*Scrophulariaceae*).
Ornamental, deciduous trees of Asia, with large, opposite, dull green leaves and erect, showy clusters of tubular flowers in mid-spring, just before the leaves emerge. Propagate by seeds.

P. tomentosa (toh-men-*toh*-suh).
EMPRESS TREE.
PRINCESS TREE.
From China, this messy tree grows to 50 ft. tall by 40 ft. wide. Its pale violet flowers are about 2 in. long in large, bold clusters. Flower buds are produced on the previous season's wood, and may be killed by severe winters. Plants pruned (or killed) to the ground in the spring will grow shoots to 12 ft. or more. The leaves are 18 in. or

more across. Zones 6 to 9 (to Zone 4 for foliage only).

Paulownia tomentosa
EMPRESS TREE

Phellodendron (fel-lo-*den*-dron).
CORK TREE.
Rue Family (*Rutaceae*).
Deciduous trees of Asia, with opposite, pinnately compound, aromatic leaves that are green in summer and produce yellow autumn color. Clusters of small, inconspicuous flowers, male and female, occur on separate trees; and small, black, berrylike fruits develop on female trees and hang all winter. Seedlings can become weedy and escape to natural areas. Bark gray, thick and corky. (This is not the cork of commerce, which is *Quercus suber*, the cork oak.) They require well-drained soil and tolerate sun or shade. Fast growing. Propagate by seed or grafts.

P. amurense (uh-moor-*ren*-see).
AMUR CORK TREE.

Shapely, widespreading tree to 40 ft. tall and wide. Attractive, gray, corky bark. Decorative, dark green compound leaves to 15 in. long. 'Macho' is a male, fruitless cultivar. Zones 4 to 7.

Philadelphus (fil-ad-*del*-fus).

MOCK ORANGE.

Saxifrage Family (*Saxifragaceae*).

These are deciduous shrubs of the Northern Hemisphere, grown for their lovely white blossoms (occuring in late spring after the leaves appear), some of which are deliciously fragrant. Simple, opposite leaves are dull green with no fall color. They thrive in any good, well-drained soil and flower best in full sun. They lack distinction when out of flower. Propagate by seeds or cuttings.

P. coronarius (kor-oh-*nay*-ree-us).

SWEET MOCK ORANGE.

A tall shrub to 12 ft. tall and wide. Produces fragrant flowers to 1½ in. across. Tolerant of dry soils. 'Aureus' has yellow foliage that tends to turn green by the end of the summer. Zones 4 to 7.

P. × lemoinei (lee-*moy*-nee-eye).

Hybrid of *P. microphyllus* × *P. coronarius*. Upright shrub grows to 6 ft. high and wide. Fragrant flowers are 2 in. across. There are many cultivars. 'Avalanche' is very fragrant, has single flowers, and is low-growing; 'Boule d'Argent' has large, double flowers; 'Erectus' (ee-*rek*-tus) produces single flowers and has a compact, upright habit; 'Mont Blanc', with a moundlike habit to 4 ft. tall, produces single flowers; 'Belle Etoile' has very large, fragrant single flowers on 6-ft. plants; and 'Innocence,' one of the most fragrant cultivars, grows to 6 ft. tall. Zones 5 to 8.

P. × virginalis (vir-jin-*nay*-liss).

A hybrid between *P.* × *lemoinei* and (perhaps)

Philadelphus coronarius
SWEET MOCK ORANGE

Philadelphus × *virginalis* 'Minnesota Snowflake'
MOCK ORANGE

Philadelphus

P. × *nivalis.* Mainly grown for its cultivars. 'Argentine', 'Minnesota Snowflake' and 'Glacier', all have double flowers and reach about 5 ft. heights. 'Virginal' is a vigorous, leggy shrub to 8 ft. Zones 5 to 8. 'Minnesota Snowflake' and 'Virginal' are hardy to Zone 4.

Photinia (foh-*tin*-ee-uh).
Rose Family (*Rosaceae*).

Attractive shrubs or small trees from Asia with handsome foliage. Characterized by alternate leaves, small white flowers in showy clusters and berrylike fruit. Perform best in well-drained soil in either full sun or shade. Propagate by seeds or cuttings.

P. × **fraseri** (*frays*-er-eye).
A hybrid between *P. serrulata* and *P. glabra*. This evergreen shrub or tree grows to 15 ft. high and 8 ft. wide. Its new foliage is glossy and flame-red, turning green with age. 'Red Robin' and 'Birmingham' are two of its named cultivars noted for their new red foliage. Zones 7 to 9.

P. villosa (vil-*loh*-suh).
A hardy, deciduous, wide-spreading shrub to 15 ft. tall and 10 ft. wide. The leaves, to 3 in. long, turn a colorful yellow to orange in the fall. Bright red berries. Zones 5 to 7.

Physocarpus (fye-soh-*karp*-us).
NINEBARK.
Rose Family (*Rosaceae*).

Attractive, deciduous shrubs of N. America and Asia, they have shreddy bark and alternate, toothed, often three-lobed leaves. Their small, white or pinkish flowers occur in profuse clusters in the spring. The small, inflated fruit capsules are brown or reddish. They tolerate dry soil, sun or shade. Propagate by seeds or cuttings.

Photinia × *fraseri* 'Red Robin'

Physocarpus opulifolius 'Luteus'
YELLOW NINEBARK

P. opulifolius (op-yew-lee-*foh*-lee-us).
Arching, American shrub to 9 ft. tall and 6 ft. wide. Three-lobed leaves grow to 3 in. long. White flowers occur in dense clusters to 2 in. across. Pinkish tan seed capsules appear in the fall. 'Luteus' (lew-*tee*-us) has yellow foliage in spring, fading to green. 'Nanus' (*nay*-nus) is a dwarf, growing to 3 ft. tall and wide. Zones 3 to 6.

Picea (*pye*-see-uh).

SPRUCE.

Pine Family (*Pinaceae*).

Evergreen trees of cool and temperate regions of the Northern Hemisphere that are similar in appearance to firs. They are generally pyramidal in form, with whorled branches, narrow needlelike leaves that drop quickly when dry, and long-lasting, drooping cones. Male and female cones are borne separately but on the same tree. The needles differ from those of the fir because they end in a woody, peglike base. Because of their dense habit, spruces are excellent for visual and wind screens. Also very ornamental as single specimens. They thrive in moist, well-drained soil and full sun, in regions where the summers are not too hot and humid. Propagate by seeds, cuttings or grafts.

P. abies (*ay*-beez).

NORWAY SPRUCE.

A wide-spreading tree to 90 ft. tall and 40 ft. wide with graceful, drooping branchlets and dark green leaves to ¾ in. long. Its light brown cones, to 7 in. long, resemble cigars. Highly wind resistant, it is a valuable windbreak in cold regions. 'Clanbrassiliana' (klan-bruh-sil-ee-*ay*-nuh), is a dwarf ball to 3 ft. across; 'Inversa' has drooping branches, usually on a somewhat upright plant; 'Nidiformis', also called the Bird's Nest Spruce, is a dwarf, growing 3 ft. tall and 5 ft. wide. Zones 3 to 7.

Picea glauca 'Conica'
DWARF ALBERTA SPRUCE

Picea pungens forma *glauca*
BLUE COLORADO SPRUCE

P. glauca (*glaw*-kuh).
WHITE SPRUCE.
Grows to 60 ft. tall and 20 ft. wide and produces gray bark and horizontal branches in a dense habit. Bluish-green leaves, to ¾ in. long, are somewhat prickly. Light brown, shiny cones are 2 in. long. It does not tolerate hot summers well. 'Conica' (kon-*i*-kuh) also called the dwarf Alberta spruce, is a compact conical shrub of slow growth. Its new growth is a bright, light green. It is very susceptible to spider mite attack. The variety *densata* (den-*say*-tuh), the Black Hills spruce, is slower growing than the species, but does become treelike. Zones 2 to 5 (Zones 4 to 6 for 'Conica').

P. omorika (oh-mor-ee-kuh).
SERBIAN SPRUCE.
A graceful tree to 60 ft. tall and 20 ft. wide with a pyramidal form, and drooping branches that turn up at the ends. Leaves, to 1 in. long, are marked with two white bands above and are shiny, dark green beneath, giving the plant an overall two-tone (green and blue) effect. Brown cones grow to 2½ in. long. One of the healthiest spruces for regions with hot summers. 'Nana' (*nay*-nuh) is a dwarf, growing about 4 ft. tall and as wide. 'Pendula' is similar to the species, but grows more slowly and its branches droop more prominently. Zones 4 to 7.

P. orientalis (or-ee-en-*ta*-lis).
ORIENTAL SPRUCE.
A narrow, dark green spruce that grows to 60 ft. tall but only about 20 ft. wide. Its leaves, to ½ in. long, are appressed to the stem. Cones 2 to 3 in. long. One of the best spruces for areas of hot, humid summers. 'Skylands', slower growing than the species but reaching almost the same size, has bright golden needles. Zones 5 to 7.

P. pungens (*pun*-jenz).
COLORADO SPRUCE.
A beautiful, western N. Amer. forest tree growing to 60 ft. tall and 20 ft. wide. It has stiff, horizontal branches and sharp-pointed, bluish-green leaves to 1 in. long. Its shiny, tan cones grow to 4 in. long. It tends to have a relatively short ornamental life (30 years) in warm, humid regions. The form *glauca*, the Blue Colorado Spruce, is bluer than the species; the cultivars 'Koster', 'Argentea', 'Hoopsii', and 'Moerheimii' are all bright silver in color. 'Montgomery' (also known as 'R. H. Montgomery') is a blue dwarf, to 5 ft. tall and wide. Zones 3 to 6.

Pieris (*pie*-er-iss).
Heath Family (*Ericaceae*).
Broadleaved evergreen shrubs of N. Amer. and Asia. Produces alternate leaves and clusters of white, urn-shaped flowers in spring. The flower buds are conspicuous all winter. Fruits are small, roundish capsules that are not very showy. Generally grow best in partial shade. Requires good drainage, acid soil and ample moisture. Propagate by seeds, cuttings or layers.

P. floribunda (floh-ri-*bun*-duh).
MOUNTAIN ANDROMEDA.
This dense, erect, eastern N. Amer. shrub grows to 6 ft. tall and as wide with glossy green leaves to 3 in. long. Erect 4 in. flower clusters have ¼ in. long flowers. They appear in early spring. Zones 5 to 7.

P. japonica (ja-*pon*-ik-uh).
JAPANESE ANDROMEDA.
An Asian shrub that grows to 10 ft. tall and 7 ft. wide. Shiny leaves, to 3 in. long, are bronze colored in the spring. Creamy-white flowers occur in drooping clusters to 5 in. long. 'Dorothy Wycoff' has reddish-green leaves in the fall and

dark red buds in the winter, which turn slightly pink when they open. 'White Cascade' blooms are pure white; it is an especially heavy bloomer. 'Variegata' (vay-ree-uh-*gah*-tuh) has white margins on the leaves, and is slower growing than the species. 'Forest Flame' (actually a hybrid) has bright red new foliage that then turns green. Zones 6 to 8.

Pieris japonica
JAPANESE ANDROMEDA

✳✳ **Pinus** (pye-nuss).

PINE.

Pine Family (*Pinaceae*).

These trees and shrubs are evergreen and widely distributed throughout the N. Hemisphere. They are important timber trees and rugged landscape plants. The genus is easily distinguished from other conifers as the long, needlelike leaves are sheathed in bundles, each with a specific number (usually in 2s and 3s, or 4s and 5s). Male and female flowers occur separately but are found on the same tree. The male, cylin-

drical cones or catkins are found at the base of young shoots. When the pollen is ripe, great clouds of yellow can be seen blowing from the trees. The young female cones appear as miniature cones at the end of shoots. They grow into the large cones for which pines are well known. The size of the cones varies with the species. New shoots appear in mid-spring. These shoots, called candles, elongate to full length before the needles emerge. Pines require full sun; most need good drainage and tolerate dry soils. Propagate by seeds or grafts.

P. aristata (a-*ris*-tah-tuh).
BRISTLECONE PINE.
This shrub or small tree is native to the mountains of the southwestern U.S. Its needles are in bundles of five; they are short and have white resin dots. Sometimes growing horizontally, they can range from 5 ft. to 20 ft. high and equally wide. The cones, to 4 in. long, have sharp bristles on the scales. Zones 4 to 7.

Pinus bungeana
LACEBARK PINE

P. bungeana (bun-gee-*ay*-nah).
LACEBARK PINE.
This pine is grown for its bark, which exfoliates, exposing smooth white to green patches. Can be multi- or single stemmed, the overall shape is pyramidal to rounded. Typically reaches 30 to 50 ft. in height and spreads to 35 ft. The stiff, dark

green needles are 2 to 4 in. long and are borne in bundles of 3. The cones are rounded, about 2 to 3 in. long. Plant in full sun in well-drained soil. Zones 5 to 8.

Pinus cembra
SWISS STONE PINE

✱**P. cembra** (*sem*-bruh).
SWISS STONE PINE.
This narrow tree is native to central Eur. It grows to 40 ft. high by 12 ft. wide. Leaves are in bundles of five, to 4 in. long, and tend to point towards the tip. Leaves remain on the tree for four or five years, resulting in a very dense appearance. Slow in growth rate. Twigs are thick and covered with dense brown hairs. Zones 3 to 6.

P. densiflora (den-sih-*floh*-rah).
JAPANESE RED PINE.
With its irregular branching and flat top, this pine lends an exotic form to the landscape. This plant is native to Japan and Korea and is tolerant of salt spray. It grows to about 60 ft. high and 50 ft.

wide. The bark is orange-red and can be very showy. Each bundle of 2 green needles is 3 to 5 in. long, with only a slight twist to the needles. The cones are 2 in. long. It requires well-drained soil. 'Pendula' (pen-*dew*-luh) has drooping branches. 'Umbraculifera' (um-bray-coo-*lif*-ur-uh), the Tanyosho pine, is slow growing, multi-stemmed, with wonderful reddish burrs. Zones 5 to 7.

P. flexilis (*flek*-sil-iss).
LIMBER PINE.
Native to western U.S., this tree grows to 50 ft. high and 35 ft. wide, producing five bluish-green needles to the bundle. Can be single- or multi-stemmed. The cones are about 5 inches long. 'Pendula' has drooping branches and makes an interesting, low-spreading mound. Zones 4 to 7.

P. koraiensis (kor-ay-eye-*en*-sis).
KOREAN PINE.
The bundles of five bluish-green needles remain on the tree 3 to 4 years. Needles are long and somewhat drooping and the tree has a very full appearance. Twigs are thick and covered with brown hairs. It grows to 60 ft. high and 35 ft. wide. Zones 4 to 7.

P. mugo (*mew*-go).
SWISS MOUNTAIN PINE.
The straight species is a large shrub or small tree. It can grow to 30 ft. tall and as wide. Generally this is not what is used in landscapes. The most popular forms are shrubby and propagated vegetatively, not from seed. The dark green, curved needles are carried in pairs and are 1 to 2 in. long and twisted. The cones are round and about 1 in. across. These plants require good drainage. Variety *mugo*, Mugho Pine, grows to about 15 ft. high and is multi-stemmed. Several low-growing cultivars, such as 'Gnom' and 'Mops', have been selected and named. Zones 3 to 6.

P. nigra (*nigh*-grah).
AUSTRIAN PINE.
This rugged, coarse-textured tree grows to about 60 ft. in height and 30 ft. wide. Young trees are pyramidal but at maturity the trees have a flat top and usually lose their lower limbs. Widespread across Eur., the diversity of the gene pool results in variability in size, shape, and growth rate, depending upon geographical origin. The needles are dark, shiny green, and they are held in pairs. They are stiff, sharply pointed and are 4 to 6 in. long. The cones are short, 2 to 3 in. long. Tolerates city conditions but needs good drainage. Diplodia tip blight can be a serious problem in humid areas. Zones 4 to 6.

P. palustris (pah-*lus*-tris)
LONGLEAF PINE.
Southeastern U.S. native that is an important timber tree. It is known for its extremely long needles in clusters of three. It has large white buds and grows to about 90 ft. tall and 30 ft. wide. Zones 7 to 9.

P. parviflora (par-vi-*floh*-ruh).
JAPANESE WHITE PINE.
Native to Japan and Korea. This tree grows naturally along the seashore and is tolerant of salt spray. It produces five short, bluish-green needles to the bundle. Its cones are short, attractive, and tend to remain on the tree for a number of years. It has an irregular growth habit, to 50 ft. high and 35 ft. wide, and can become flat-topped with age. 'Glauca' has bluer, more twisted needles. Zones 5 to 8.

P. ponderosa (pon-dur-*oh*-suh).
PONDEROSA PINE.
This western U.S. native grows to 70 ft. tall and 25 ft. wide. It has rugged, coarse texture and needles in threes that are long and stiff. Zones 3 to 6.

P. resinosa (rez-ih-*no*-sah).
RED PINE.
NORWAY PINE.
This tree, native to eastern Amer., is noted for its cold hardiness, its tolerance of poor, dry soils, and its slightly reddish bark. It grows to 60 ft. tall and 25 ft. wide. The stiff, dark green needles are borne in pairs, are 5 to 6 in. long, and snap when bent in half. The cones are 2 to 3 in. long. In youth, the tree is pyramidal; it maintains that overall shape at maturity, but loses its lower limbs. Needs well-drained soil and good air circulation. Zones 3 to 6.

P. strobus (*stroh*-bus).
EASTERN WHITE PINE.
Native throughout eastern N. Amer. While some specimens in the wild may reach 150 ft. tall, the average mature tree size is usually no taller than 80 ft. It spreads to 40 ft. In youth they are pyramidal in shape, but as they grow older, the top flattens out, lower branches are lost, and the tree becomes open and picturesque. Soft blue-green needles are in bundles of 5 and are 3 to 5 in. long. The cones are 6 in. long and extremely resinous. They require well-drained soil and ample moisture. 'Fastigiata' (fas-tij-ee-*ah*-tuh) is columnar when young, but becomes wider with age. Branches come off the trunk at a 45 degree angle. 'Nana' (*nay*-nuh) is shrubby, slowly becoming about 8 ft. high and wide. 'Pendula' (pen-dew-luh) is a very weeping clone that must be staked in order to have upright growth. Zones 3 to 7.

P. sylvestris (sil-*ves*-tris).
SCOTS PINE.
Native of northern and central Eur., this pine grows to 60 ft. high and 30 ft. wide. Becomes open, flat-topped, and picturesque with age. Its attractive orange bark eventually becomes charcoal gray with orange blotches, and its blue-

green, twisted needles are borne in pairs. Needles are from 1 to 4 in. long. The cones are 1½ to 2 in. long. Plant in well-drained soil. 'Beuvronensis' (bow-vron-*nen*-sis) is a dwarf form, growing to almost 3 ft. 'Fastigiata' (fas-tij-ee-*ah*-tuh) is a narrow, columnar form. Zones 3 to 6.

Pinus strobus 'Nana'
— EASTERN WHITE PINE

Pinus taeda
LOBLOLLY PINE

✱ **P. taeda** (*tee*-duh).
LOBLOLLY PINE.
Native to southeastern U.S., the Loblolly grows to 80 ft. tall and 40 ft. wide. Its three needles to the bundle grow to about 8 in. long. It will grow in dry as well as poorly-drained soils. Zones 6 to 9.

P. thunbergiana (thun-*bur*-gee-*aye*-nah).
JAPANESE BLACK PINE.
Native to Japan. This wonderful accent plant has a contorted growth habit and tolerates salt spray. It has escaped and become naturalized along much of the Atlantic coast of the U.S. It can reach heights as high as 50 ft. and its spread varies greatly. The growth habit is irregular, which results in the desirable contorted look of the mature trees. The shiny, dark green needles are 5 in. long and are held in pairs. The cones are 2½ in. long. Plant in well-drained soil. 'Oculus-draconis' (oh-*cul*-us druh-*cohn*-us), Dragon's Eye Black Pine, has yellow-banded needles. 'Thunderhead' is a dwarf form, growing to 3 ft. tall by 4 ft. wide. Zones 5 to 8.

P. wallichiana (wal-lik-ee-*ay*-nuh).
HIMALAYAN PINE.
Native to northern India and Pakistan, this pine has five needles to the bundle and bluish-green needles to 7 in. long that are pendulous. The cones are long, to 9 in. An elegant tree, it grows to 80 ft. tall and 50 ft. wide. 'Zebrina' has yellow bands on the needles. Zones 6 to 8.

Pittosporum (pit-oh-*spoh*-um).
Pittosporum Family (*Pittosporaceae*).
These attractive, tender evergreen shrubs and trees have alternate or somewhat whorled leaves, clusters of small fragrant flowers, and capsule-like fruit with sticky seeds. The foliage is foul-smelling when bruised. Some are used for sheared hedges. Propagate by seeds or cuttings.

P. tobira (toh-*bye*-ruh).
JAPANESE PITTOSPORUM.
A shrub to 10 ft. tall and 15 ft. wide whose leaves are 4 in. long. The greenish-white flowers are fragrant. Good for hedges and massing. Tolerant of sun or shade. 'Variegata' (vay-ree-uh-*gay*-tuh) has creamy-white variegations. Zones 8 to 10.

Pittosporum tobira
JAPANESE PITTOSPORUM

Platanus (plat-*an*-us).
PLANETREE.
Planetree Family (*Platanaceae*).
These deciduous trees of N. Amer., Eur. and Asia attain great size. They are distinguished by pale bark, which shreds off in places to give a pleasing mottled effect. They have long-stalked, palmately lobed leaves similar to maples, which are borne in an alternate arrangement on the branches. Inconspicuous flowers occur in dense, round, drooping heads, with male and female flowers separate but on the same tree. In rich, moist soil and ample space, they develop into massive specimens, but are tolerant of less favorable conditions. They tolerate poor drainage, sun or partial shade, and city conditions. Propagate by seeds or cuttings.

P. × acerifolia (ah-sur-uh-*foh*-lee-uh).
LONDON PLANETREE.
Also called P. × hybrida. A hybrid between *P. occidentalis* and *P. orientalis* (or-ee-en-*tal*-iss), it grows to 90 ft. tall and 70 ft. wide. Maple-like leaves grow to 10 in. across and are moderately lobed. Fruit heads occur in pairs. Its exfoliating bark tends to have a yellowish cast. This is a widely grown street tree, especially in cities. It may or may not be anthracnose resistant, depending on the individual plant. It is susceptible to canker stain disease. Zones 6 to 9.

Platanus occidentalis
AMERICAN PLANETREE

P. occidentalis (ok-si-den-*tay*-liss).
AMERICAN PLANETREE.
SYCAMORE.
BUTTONWOOD.
A dramatically striking species native to eastern N. Amer. that grows to 100 ft. tall and 80 ft. wide. Its leaves, to 10 in. across, are less deeply lobed than the above species. Fruit heads, to 1 in. across, are usually solitary. It is susceptible to anthracnose, which causes dieback of new growth following wet springs. Zones 7 to 8.

Poncirus (pon-*sye*-rus).
Rue Family (*Rutaceae*).
A very spiny, deciduous, thorny shrub or small tree of China and the hardiest of the citrus group. Its fruit is very sour, edible, but not commercially used. Valuable commercially as a rootstock on which to graft more tender citrus fruits. Also useful as a specimen for its fragrant, white flowers, green winter stems and thorns, ornamental, yellow to orange fruit, and as an impenetrable hedge plant. Propagate by seeds or cuttings. Zones 6 to 9.

P. trifoliata (trye-foh-lee-*ay*-tuh).
HARDY-ORANGE.
A dense shrub or small tree to 15 ft. high and wide. Its stiff branchlets have dark green, alternate, compound, leathery leaves with three leaflets, to 3 in. long, on winged stalks. Very sharp thorns occur on branches. Fragrant, showy white flowers to 2 in. across appear in advance of the leaves in mid-spring. The fruit is yellow, furry, orangelike, fragrant, acidy and about 2 in. across. Zones 5 to 9.

Populus (*pop*-yew-lus).
POPLAR.
ASPEN.
Willow Family (*Salicaceae*).
Deciduous trees of the Northern Hemisphere. In some species their alternate leaves shiver in the slightest breeze. Male and female flowers occur on separate trees, both in catkins, opening in early spring before the leaves appear. Fast-growing, vigorous trees, they are not particular as to soil, but tend to be short-lived. The wood is soft and brittle, easily broken during storms. Propagate by seeds or by cuttings.

P. nigra (*nye*-gruh).
BLACK POPLAR.
Grows to 80 ft., with a wide-spreading head. Triangular leaves grow to 4 in. long. Best known for its cultivar 'Italica' (i-*tal*-i-kuh), the Lombardy poplar, a male tree of narrow, upright form. It seems to do best in regions of low humidity. Zones 3 to 9.

Potentilla (poh-ten-*till*-uh).
CINQUEFOIL.
Rose Family (*Rosaceae*).
This large genus is composed of herbaceous and woody plants of cool regions. They range from 6 in. to 3 ft. in height and are rugged, requiring little care once established in sunny, well-drained sites. They have compound, small, alternate leaves and five-petaled strawberrylike flowers, mostly yellow, but some white, rose or red. Propagate by seed or cuttings.

P. fruticosa (frew-ti-*koh*-suh).
SHRUBBY CINQUEFOIL.
This is the most widely grown species for garden display. It is a hardy, rugged shrub, 2 to 3 ft. high and wide. Its showy white, yellow or red-orange flowers, 1 to 1½ in. across, begin their display in late spring and continue it well into fall. There are many cultivars, selected primarily for flower color: 'Beesii' (*bee*-zee-eye), buttercup yellow; 'Abbotswood', white; 'Goldfinger', bright yellow; 'Katherine Dykes', lemon yellow; 'Princess', pink; 'Tangerine', orangish yellow. Zones 2 to 7.

Poncirus trifoliata
HARDY-ORANGE

Potentilla fruticosa 'Abbotswood'
SHRUBBY CINQUEFOIL

Populus nigra 'Italica'
LOMBARDY POPLAR

Prunus cerasifera 'Atropurpurea'
CHERRY PLUM

✶✶**Prunus** (*proo*-nus).

Rose Family (*Rosaceae*).

This is a large and horticulturally very important group of flowering and fruit-bearing deciduous and evergreen shrubs and trees of the North Temperate Zone. The genus includes almonds, apricots, cherries, peaches, plums and nectarines in fruit-bearing and ornamental varieties. They have alternate, simple, toothed leaves. The majority have showy flowers, double in some forms, which bloom early in the spring. While the orchard species are important both commercially and in many home gardens, the ornamental forms are of landscape value. Their bark typically is reddish-brown, with prominent corky pores called lenticels. The foliage and twigs have a distinctive odor. They thrive in well-drained sandy loam and sunny situations, although most will tolerate some shade at the expense of bloom and fruit. They are subject to many pest problems. Many of these need to be controlled on the fruit-bearing *Prunus*. Ornamentals can be chosen on the basis of health (there is no reason to plant a *Prunus* in a landscape if it will need spraying). Propagate by seeds, grafts or cuttings. Many of the fruit-bearing species are available in dwarf and semidwarf cultivars, which will produce fruit in one to three years, while standard varieties take longer to mature. They require full sun and well-drained locations.

P. armeniaca (are-men-ee-*uh*-kuh).
APRICOT.

Tree native to China, to 25 ft. tall and wide, has attractive bark and is grown for its tasty fruit and occasionally for its showy pink flowers. The flowers, about 1 in. across, are borne singly before the leaves appear. Often they are hit by late frosts, which ruin fruit production. The yellow-red fruit, 1 in. or more across, has firm, sweet flesh. As ornamental trees for the lawn and landscape, apricots are very suitable both when in bloom and when the fruit is ripening. Apricots grow best in full sun on dryish, well-drained soils. They are best planted in the open, away from shelter that would encourage frost-vulnerable early blooms. Most apricots set fruit without cross pollination. Plants are hardy to Zone 4, but best fruit production is in Zones 6 to 9.

P. avium (*ay*-vee-um).
SWEET CHERRY.

This large tree from Eurasia, naturalized in N. Amer., grows to 40 ft. wide and tall, producing leaves to 6 in. long. Clusters of fragrant, white flowers bloom in mid-spring. It is grown for ornament as well as for its fruits. There are many cultivars, most selected for fruit. Choices include hardiness, ripening dates, and color (red or yellow). Sweet cherries are not self-pollinating, so plant two cultivars that can cross-pollinate each other. 'Plena' (*plen*-uh) has double flowers, is very attractive in bloom, and is sterile. As is typical, the sterile flowers last at least a week longer than fertile ones. 'Scanlon' also has sterile, double flowers, but only reaches about 20 ft. in height. Zones 6 to 8.

P. besseyi (*bess*-see-eye).
WESTERN SAND CHERRY.

A low shrub to 5 ft. high and wide. Native in the Northwest. The leaves are 2 in. long and whitish beneath. Small white flowers bloom with the leaves. Produces sweet, edible, purple-black fruit, about ½ in. across. Improved and exceptionally hardy forms are available for their sweet fruit. Zones 3 to 6.

P. cerasifera (sur-as-*if*-ur-uh).
CHERRY PLUM.
MYROBALAN PLUM.

This slender, twiggy tree grows to 25 ft. tall and

20 ft. wide. Its thin, light green leaves are 2 in. long. Produces pinkish flowers, to ¾ in across, and sweet, juicy red fruit, about 1 in. across. Generally this species is only grown for its purple-leaved cultivars. 'Atropurpurea' (at-roh-pur-*poo*-ree-uh), has purple leaves, pink flowers and wine-red fruit. The cultivar 'Pissardii' is the same plant. 'Newport' and 'Thundercloud' have purple leaves and hold their purple throughout the season. All purple-leaved forms require sun for best color. Zones 5 to 8.

P. cerasus (ser-*ay*-sus).
SOUR CHERRY.
This round-headed tree, to 30 ft. high, has leaves to 3½ in. long and clusters of white flowers, about 1 in. across, and soft, sour red fruit. Numerous varieties are cultivated for the fruit, and others for the ornamental double flowers. Fruit of the sour cherry is not generally preferred for eating fresh, but makes very fine preserves and pies. They are the easiest cherries to grow, and are hardier than the sweet cherries. They are generally self-pollinating. 'Montmorency' is a popular cultivar. Zones 5 to 8.

P. domestica (doh-*mess*-tik-uh).
PLUM.
A small tree to 25 ft. tall and wide with leaves to 4 in. long. The showy blossoms are white, blooming just before the leaves. Usually not grown for ornament, only for the sweet, blue or purple, round or oval fruit. Most of our cultivated plums are derived from this species, which is also called the European plum. 'Green Gage' and 'Italian' are two good European cultivars, but it is best to consult local nurseries for the best cultivars to suit your climate. *P. domestica* is self-pollinating, so a solitary plant will produce fruit. Zones 5 to 8.

P. dulcis (*dulk*-iss).
ALMOND.
This is one of the smallest and loveliest of the nut plants. It is grown both as an ornamental and as a nut producing plant. It produces showy pink-white blooms and usually grows no taller or wider than 20 or 25 ft. It blooms early and its blossoms are often hit by frost, ruining both the flowers and the nut crop. The center of the fruit (the pit) is where the edible, tasty almond nut is found. Calif. exports almonds and they grow well in Utah, parts of Texas, Idaho, Ariz. and N. Mex. Almonds require cross-pollination, so two different cultivars are needed for nut production. Zones 7 to 9.

Prunus laurocerasus
CHERRY LAUREL

P. laurocerasus (*lar*-oh-ser-*ay*-sus).
CHERRY LAUREL.
Vigorous, large evergreen shrubs or small trees native to southeastern Eur. and Asia, they have shiny leaves to 6 in. long. Their fountain-like form, reaching 6 ft. in height and about 10 ft. in width, is covered by small white flowers in showy elongated clusters that are about 4 in. long. The small, dark purple fruit is not showy. Zones 6 to 9. 'Schipkaensis' (ship-kah-*en*-siss) is hardier than the species. 'Otto Luyken' is lower and slower growing than the species. Zones 6 to 9.

Prunus

P. maackii (*mack*-ee-eye).
AMUR CHOKECHERRY.
A deciduous tree that grows to 40 ft. high and about 30 ft. wide. One of the hardiest ornamental cherries, it is known for its showy coppery-orange bark. Flowers are white, in elongated clusters, but are often hidden by the foliage. It grows in full sun or light shade. Zones 3 to 6.

P. persica (*per*-si-kuh).
PEACH.
An attractive tree from China that grows to 25 ft. It has shiny, drooping leaves to 6 in. long, and showy pink flowers that bloom before the leaves appear. This species includes all the orchard peaches and is sometimes grown as an ornament. Delicious yellow or white fruit is sometimes suffused with red. Many cultivars have been selected for fruit (tree and fruit size, color, ripening date and hardiness); a few have been selected for ornament (often for double flowers or especially attractive foliage). Early spring frosts often damage flowers and may reduce or ruin the fruit crop. Variety *nucipersica* (new-seh-*per*-seh-kuh) is the nectarine, which has fruits without fuzz. Zones 6 to 9.

P. sargentii (sar-*jen*-tee-eye).
SARGENT CHERRY.
A deciduous, ornamental tree to 35 ft. high and wide. Native to eastern Asia. Its flowers are showy, pink, occurring just before the leaves appear. New foliage is reddish, summer leaves are green, and it is an attractive orange in the autumn. Fruits are small and inconspicuous. Zones 5 to 9, it is the hardiest of the flowering Japanese cherries.

P. serotina (ser-*oht*-i-nuh).
BLACK CHERRY.
An eastern N. Amer. native. This common woodland tree grows to 60 ft. tall and 30 ft. wide. White flowers that are moderately showy, in elongated clusters, appear after the leaves have expanded. Blue-black fruits, enjoyed by birds, ripen in late summer and are edible but not very tasty. The bark is dark gray, and exfoliates slightly in round chips. Zones 3 to 8.

Prunus serrulata forma *grandiflora*
SNOWY JAPANESE CHERRY

P. serrulata (sehr-yew-*lay*-tuh).
JAPANESE CHERRY.
An upright tree to 30 ft. high and wide, with leaves to 6 in. long. Its clusters of white or pink flowers, 1½ in. across, bloom just as the leaves are expanding; they are followed by black, inconspicuous fruit. Spectacular when in bloom. Among the numerous cultivars are flowers in white or pink as well as double or single forms. Most of the cultivars are propagated by grafts or, less commonly, cuttings. 'Amanogawa' (ah-man-o-*gah*-wuh) is a columnar form with pink, semi-double flowers. 'Kwanzan' (*kwan*-zan) has

pink, double flowers and is probably the most commonly-grown form of this species. 'Ukon' has semidouble, fragrant, pale yellow flowers. It is also known as *P. serrulata* forma *grandiflora*. Zones 6 to 8.

P. subhirtella (sub-her-*tell*-uh).

HIGAN CHERRY.

A very showy, fine-textured Japanese tree that grows to 30 ft. high and wide. The leaves, to 3 in. long, occur after the light pink flowers bloom, in early spring. The flowers are followed by small black, inconspicuous fruit. The bark is light reddish-brown in color. 'Pendula' (pen-*dew*-luh), the Weeping Higan Cherry, has pendulous branches. 'Autumnalis' (aw-tum-*nal*-is) often opens some of its flowers in autumn and during warm periods in the winter. Usually it also produces a good show in early spring. Zones 6 to 8.

P. triloba var. **multiplex** (trye-*loh*-buh *mul*-ti-plex).

FLOWERING ALMOND.

Also sold as flowering plum. This deciduous shrub, which can grow to 10 ft. tall and wide, has very showy double pink flowers opening before the leaves. The plant is not very interesting the rest of the year. Zones 4 to 8.

P. yedoensis (yed-oh-*en*-sis).

YOSHINO CHERRY.

Sometimes listed as a hybrid of unknown origin. It is a very showy deciduous Japanese tree that was made famous by the planting at the Tidal Basin in Washington DC. To 40 ft. tall and wide, it has smooth, pale gray bark. The leaves are up to 4 in. long and it produces clusters of pale pink to white, fragrant flowers before the leaves. The fruit is black and inconspicuous. Zones 6 to 8.

Prunus subhirtella 'Pendula'
WEEPING HIGAN CHERRY

Pseudolarix

Pseudolarix (soo-doh-*lar*-ix).
GOLDEN LARCH.
Pine Family (*Pinaceae*).
There is only one species, a large ornamental, deciduous tree of China. Its whorled branches and light green, feathery leaves turn rusty orange in the fall. It thrives in well-drained soil and a sunny situation and tolerates heat better than the true larches (*Larix*). Propagate by seeds.

P. kaempferi (*kem*-fer-eye).
A broad, pyramidal tree to 70 ft. tall and 40 ft. wide. It has a strong central leader, but its branches are produced irregularly, resulting in a more informal effect than *Larix*. Spur shoots are conspicuously longer and leaves wider than *Larix*, varying in length within the whorl from 1 in. to 2½ in. long. Male and female cones occur separately on the same tree: the male catkinlike. Its very attractive female cones, to about 3 in. long, turn reddish-brown and shatter in autumn when mature. Zones 5 to 7.

Pseudotsuga (soo-doh-*soo*-guh).
Pine Family (*Pinaceae*).
Evergreen trees of western N. Amer. and Asia. These gigantic firlike trees have hanging cones with conspicuous exserted bracts. They are valuable timber trees, popular Christmas trees and popular ornamentals. They require good drainage, but do best with ample moisture; they tolerate some shade, but are most attractive in full sun. Propagate by seeds and grafts.

P. menziesii (men-*zee*-zee-eye).
DOUGLAS FIR.
Sometimes called *P. taxifolia*. A densely pyramidal tree to 250 ft. tall in the wild, it is more likely to be 80 ft. tall and 35 ft. wide in landscapes. Needles grow to 1 in. long, are dark green to bluish-green above and have white bands beneath. The cones are to 4½ in. long, with bracts protruding beyond the scales. Very attractive as a young tree, it tends to lose lower branches and become less ornamental with age, especially in areas with hot summers. The variety *glauca* (*glaw*-kuh), a Rocky Mountain native with bluish needles, is more hardy to cold and drought. 'Fletcheri' (*fletch*-er-eye) is a dwarf, horizontal form. Zones 3 to 7.

Pterostyrax (tehr-oh-*stye*-rax).
Storax Family (*Styracaceae*).
Deciduous shrubs or trees of Asia with fairly coarse, alternate, toothed leaves and large clusters of fragrant white flowers. Plant in full sun with good drainage. Propagate by seeds or cuttings.

P. hispidus (*hiss*-pid-us).
EPAULETTE TREE.
An interesting but somewhat coarse tree, growing to 40 ft. high and wide. Produces oblong

Pseudotsuga menziesii
DOUGLAS FIR

leaves to 7 in. long and flowers in bold drooping clusters, with individual flowers born horizontally, looking like epaulettes on a military uniform. The fruit is a ribbed, dry and bristly drupe. Zones 6 to 8.

Punica (*pew*-nik-uh).

Pomegranate Family (*Punicaceae*).

Shrubs or small trees of southern Eur. and Asia. One species has been grown for centuries in warm regions for its edible fruit. It is a much prized and adaptable ornamental deciduous shrub in the South and Southwest. Propagate by seeds and cuttings.

Punica granatum 'Nana'
DWARF POMEGRANATE

P. granatum (gran-*nay*-tum).

POMEGRANATE.

A deciduous shrub or tree to 15 ft. high and wide. Shiny leaves to 3 in. long. Its orange-red flowers, 1 in. or more across, are showy. The dark yellow to red fruit, 2½ in. across, has a very hard rind

and juicy, edible red seeds. 'Nana' (*nay*-nuh) is a dwarf to 4 ft. tall. Zones 7 to 10.

Pyracantha (pye-ruh-*kan*-thuh).

FIRETHORN.

Rose Family (*Rosaceae*).

Evergreen or semi-evergreen, thorny shrubs of Eur. and Asia with fine foliage, white flowers, and decorative fruit. Produces alternate, simple leaves and clusters of small white flowers in late spring. Showy, brilliant red, orange or golden fruit. These plants need well-drained soil and sun for best effect, but will tolerate shade. They may be grown as specimen shrubs or may be trained against a wall or fence as an espalier. Fire blight can be a serious disease. Disinfect pruning shears (dip in a dilute solution of household bleach or rubbing alcohol) after each cut to avoid spreading the disease.

Pyracantha coccinea
SCARLET FIRETHORN

P. coccinea (kok-*sin*-ee-uh).
SCARLET FIRETHORN.
The species grows to 10 ft. or more, with leaves to 1½ in. long. Flowers occur in showy clusters and profuse orange, yellow or red berries follow. 'Lalandei' (lay-*land*-ee-eye) has deep orange fruits. 'Monrovia' is upright in growth, with orange-red fruits. 'Kasan' with orange-red berries, is more compact in growth and is hardier than the species. Zones 6 to 9.

Pyrus (*pye*-rus).
PEAR.
Rose Family (*Rosaceae*).
Trees of the Northern Hemisphere with mostly deciduous, alternate leaves, some species providing fruit, and some grown as ornamentals. Clusters of showy flowers bloom before or with the leaves. The juicy, edible fruit and slow-growing nature of some species make them popular subjects for espalier. They thrive in any

good, well-drained soil and in full sun. They are susceptible to many of the same pests as apples, especially fire blight. Propagate by seeds, cuttings or grafting.

P. calleryana (kal-ler-ee-*ay*-nuh).
CALLERY PEAR.
Pyramidal tree to 40 ft. tall with a variable spread. Shiny leaves, about 3 in. long, usually turn a very attractive wine- to orange-red in the autumn. The clustered white flowers are very showy, appearing in mid-spring before the leaves. The tree bears round, inedible, non-showy brown fruit about ½ in. It is relatively resistant to fire blight. 'Bradford', one of the first cultivars named, still extremely popular, was selected for uniformly symmetrical growth. Tends to produce clustered branches with weak, narrow crotch angles. Branches then break off from middle-aged trees during winter storms. Withstands city conditions. Because of the branching

Pyrus calleryana 'Bradford'
BRADFORD CALLERY PEAR

problems, 'Bradford' is generally not recommended. Newer cultivars offer greater promise of structural strength and a variety of forms. These include: 'Capital', a narrow, upright tree, and 'Whitehouse', a pyramidal form. 'Autumn Blaze' is attractive but reportedly susceptible to fire blight, as is 'Red Spire'. Zones 5 to 9.

★★Quercus (*kwur*-kus).

OAK.

Beech Family (*Fagaceae*).

These evergreen and deciduous trees and shrubs are found throughout the northern hemisphere. N. America is particularly rich in oak species. They are important timber trees and ornamentals. Their leaves are alternate, heavy textured, and usually are lobed. The flowers, not conspicuous, consist of a long male catkin and a separate, tiny, spiky female flower. The seed is an acorn, carried in a hatlike cup, a characteristic of all oaks. Closely related species of oaks, when planted or growing near each other, tend to cross-pollinate and natural hybrids are often found. Propagate by seeds or grafts. Tolerant of light shade, most grow to best effect in full sun, and most require good drainage. Most have a strong tap root, making transplanting difficult. Nursery-grown trees, however, generally move easily. Although oaks have a reputation of being slow in growth, once established most grow rapidly if the soil is fertile and there is ample moisture. For simpler identification, the oaks can be divided into two groups, the evergreen and the deciduous. The evergreen species are found in the warmer climates, as they are not winter-hardy species. Of these evergreen species, the most notable are the California live oak *Q. agrifolia* (agri-*foh*-lee-uh), canyon oak *Q. chrysolepis* (chry-so-*lep*-is), holly oak *Q. ilex* (*eye*-lix), cork oak *Q. suber* (*soo*-ber) and live oak *Q. virginiana* (ver-jin-ee-*ay*-nuh). The deciduous species can be

further divided into two groups, the black oaks and the white oaks. Black oaks have leaves with bristle-tipped lobes. White oaks have rounded lobes. Black oaks include the following: scarlet, scrub, shingle, laurel, blackjack, water, pin, willow, northern red and black oak. The white oaks include the following: swamp white, Oregon, valley, overcup, bur, chestnut, chinquapin, post and white oak.

Q. acutissima (a-kew-*tis*-i-mah).

SAWTOOTH OAK.

A native of eastern Asia, this oak grows to about 45 ft. high with a similar spread. Leaves are toothed with many soft bristles on the margins. Leaf resembles a chestnut leaf, and is deep green and very shiny. The foliage turns golden tan in autumn and the dry leaves tend to remain on all winter. Zones 6 to 9.

★Q. alba (*al*-buh).

WHITE OAK.

A valuable hardwood timber tree and beautiful, wide-spreading ornamental shade tree that is native to eastern N. Amer. Grows to 80 ft. tall, and when open-grown, trees can spread equally wide (trees in wooded areas are much narrower). It is deciduous, with large, deeply rounded lobed leaves that turn red in the fall. Many impressive old specimens are still around. Deserves to be planted more often, so future generations can enjoy its majesty. Zones 4 to 8.

Q. coccinea (kok-*sin*-ee-uh).

SCARLET OAK.

Native to the eastern and central U.S., it grows to 75 ft. tall and 40 ft. wide. Leaves, to 6 in. long, are bristle-tipped and deeply lobed, somewhat intermediate between red and pin oak leaves. The fall foliage is a brilliant scarlet. Zones 5 to 8.

Quercus alba
WHITE OAK

Q. imbricaria (im-bri-*kay*-ree-uh).
SHINGLE OAK.

Native to the eastern part of N. Amer. Its leaves are unlike most oaks in that they are unlobed and untoothed. Instead, they are long, fairly narrow, dark green, shiny, and deciduous. Tree grows to 60 ft. tall and 50 ft. wide. It has tan autumn color. Zones 5 to 9.

Q. macrocarpa (mak-roh-*kar*-puh).
BUR OAK.

A picturesque tree with an open spread that grows to 80 ft. tall and wide. Native to the eastern and central U.S., it is an important tree in prairie regions. Leaves are large and coarse with rounded lobes. Deep green during the summer, it has no autumn color. Bark is gray, very rugged and deeply furrowed. Zones 3 to 8.

Q. palustris (pa-*lus*-tris).
PIN OAK.

This deciduous tree of pyramidal habit has characteristic drooping branches. Native to eastern N. Amer., it grows to 70 ft. tall and 40 ft. wide. Widely planted as a street and shade tree, although the drooping branches can be a problem when it is used along streets. Tolerates dry and wet soils but does not tolerate alkaline soils and can become severely chlorotic (yellow leaves) and eventually will die unless the soil is acid. Autumn foliage is showy red-bronze. Zones 5 to 9.

✳**Q. phellos** (*fel*-ose).
WILLOW OAK.

Tree to 70 ft. tall and 40 ft. wide. Native to eastern N. Amer. Leaves 2 to 5 in. long are narrow and willowlike; they turn an attractive yellow in autumn. The bark is finely divided and the tree is fine-textured. Zones 6 to 9.

Quercus phellos
WILLOW OAK

Quercus robur
ENGLISH OAK

Q. robur (*roh*-ber).
ENGLISH OAK.
Native to Eur. and northern Africa. Leaves, to 5 in. long, are rounded shallow lobes with an ear-lobe-like leaf base, which helps distinguish it from White Oak. No autumn color. May be bothered by mildew, which turns the deciduous leaves whitish during the summer. 'Fastigiata' (fas-tij-ee-*ay*-tuh) has a columnar growth habit. Zones 5 to 9.

Q. rubra (*roo*-bruh).
RED OAK.
Sometimes listed as *Q. borealis* (bow-ree-*al*-iss). It is native to the eastern and central states. Fast growing, this spreading, round-headed tree reaches 90 ft. in height and spreads to 75 ft. The new leaves are bristle-tipped, shallowly lobed, greenish-red in spring and turn dark red in fall. Valuable as a timber tree, it is an excellent ornamental as well. Zones 3 to 8.

Q. velutina (vel-yew-*tye*-nuh).
BLACK OAK.
Deciduous tree, native to eastern N. Amer., that grows to 80 ft. tall and 50 ft. wide. The leaves are shiny dark green, similar to red oak's but they are more deeply lobed and turn reddish in the fall. Zones 4 to 8.

Q. virginiana (vir-jin-ee-*ay*-nuh).
LIVE OAK.
An evergreen oak that is native from Va. to Fla. and Mexico; it is one of the most beautiful trees of the Deep South, where it is often draped with Spanish moss. It grows to a height of 70 ft. and width of up to 100 ft. Its leaves are unlobed, to about 4 in. long, and shiny dark green. Zones 8 to 10.

Rhamnus (*ram*-nus).
BUCKTHORN.
Buckthorn Family (*Rhamnaceae*).
Deciduous or evergreen shrubs or small trees mostly of the North Temperate Zone, a few from the tropics. They are more or less spiny, with greenish, inconspicuous flowers and berrylike fruits. They grow in almost any soil and tolerate sun or shade. Propagate by seeds and cuttings.

R. frangula (*fran*-jew-luh).
ALDER BUCKTHORN.
A deciduous shrub to 15 ft. high and wide with dark green, shiny leaves to 2½ in. long, turning yellowish late in the fall. The berries change from red to black. The best species for ornamental purposes because of its attractive foliage and dense habit of growth. However, birds love the fruit and spread the seeds widely. It easily becomes weedy in gardens and natural areas, and therefore should not be planted. Zones 4 to 8.

✶✶Rhododendron (roh-doh-*den*-dron).

RHODODENDRON.

AZALEA.

Heath Family (*Ericaceae*).

A large genus of evergreen and deciduous flower-ing plants. In size the rhododendrons range from small bushes to trees. At one time, rhodo-dendrons and azaleas were separated into two genera. Now they are considered to be in one genus that is divided into two major parts. Rho-dodendrons tend to have ten stamens while aza-leas mostly have five; rhododendrons are usually evergreen (with exceptions) while azaleas are pri-marily deciduous (also with exceptions); rhodo-dendron leaves may have scales on the undersides while azalea leaves do not have scales and are often hairy on the undersides.

For detailed information on cultivating rhodo-dendrons, see the essay on pages 32–33.

The large, often confusing genus is tax-onomically broken into series, with each series having one or more species which are similar. Series with extremely numerous species are fur-ther divided into sub-series. Much breeding work has been done by individuals to develop hybrids with special characteristics such as hardi-ness and time, color and size of bloom. As a result, distinct hybrid groups have been devel-oped. Some of the best known are:

GABLE HYBRID AZALEAS.

The breed was developed by Joseph Gable in Pennsylvania. The objective was to obtain an evergreen hardy azalea. They may not be fully evergreen in the northern part of the range. Shrubs grow to 4 ft. high and wide. The flowers are to 2 in. across and mostly purplish, pink or red. These are hardy in Zones 5 to 8.

GHENT AZALEAS.

(Properly *R.* × *gandavense*.) These are large (8 ft.

tall and 6 ft. wide) deciduous shrubs that were originally developed in Ghent, Belgium, using crosses including *R. calendulaceum*, *R. viscosum*, *R. luteum*, *R. molle* and *R. periclymenoides*. Colors include white and yellow, oranges, pinks and scarlets. Among the single-flowered ones are: 'Charlemagne', pale orange; 'Coccinea Speciosa', orange; 'Daviesii', pale yellow fading to white; 'Flamboyant', orange; 'Gloria Mundi', orange. 'Narcissiflora' is a double yellow. They are hardy from Zones 5 to 7.

GLENN DALE HYBRID AZALEAS.

This series is named after Glenn Dale, Md., where Mr. B. Y. Morrison, first director of the National Arboretum in Washington, D.C., worked to produce an evergreen azalea hardy for the Middle Atlantic States. A number of species and hybrids were used including the Indian hy-brids, *R. kaempferi*, *R. mucronatum*, *R. obtusum* and *R. yedoense* var. *poukhanense*. They vary in height by cultivar, but most grow 4 to 6 ft. tall and wide. Zones 7 to 8.

BELGIAN INDIAN HYBRID AZALEAS.

Known for their large flowers, these were se-lected for greenhouse forcing. Parentage includes *R. simsii*, *R. pulchrum* var. *phoeniceum* and *R. mu-cronatum*. They are single- or double-flowered. Hardy in Zones 8 to 9.

KNAP HILL HYBRID AZALEAS.

A complex, deciduous group, it includes the Slocock, Ilam and Exbury hybrids. Several spe-cies were involved in their creation, among them *R. calendulaceum*. Mostly late-spring-blooming with large flowers ranging from cream, pink and rose to yellow, oranges and reds. 'Balzac', fra-grant, orange-red; 'Cecile', pink buds turning salmon-pink with yellow; 'Gibraltar', bright or-ange; 'Golden Eagle', orange; 'Satan', flame-red;

'Seville', orange-copper. Many of the cultivars are reliably hardy in zones 5 to 8.

KURUME AZALEAS.
Created from the parents *R. obtusum*, *R. kiusianum* and *R. kaempferi*. They have small, semi-evergreen leaves, dense twiggy growth and bloom extravagantly. Grow about 6 ft. tall and wide. Extremely popular where winters are not too severe. There are dozens of cultivars. 'Hinodegiri', maroon red; 'Coral Bells', shell pink; 'Hino-crimson', red; 'Hinomayo', deep rose-pink; 'Pink Pearl', double, deep salmon-pink and 'Snow', large white. Zones 6 to 9.

MOLLE HYBRID AZALEAS.
(Properly *R. × kosterianum*.) These hybrids are a reliably hardy, deciduous group resulting from a cross of *R. molle* and *R. japonicum*. The flowers are yellow to red, bloom in mid- to late spring. Grow 5 ft. tall and wide. Zones 5 to 8.

NORTHERN LIGHTS HYBRID AZALEAS.
Similar to the above hybrid, but include *R. prinophyllum* in their parentage. Fragrant. To 6 ft. tall and wide. Generally pink in color. Zones 3 to 6.

CATAWBA HYBRID RHODODENDRONS.
Some of the hardiest evergreen cultivars. *R. catawbiense*, the parent for whom the group was named, is native to the southern Appalachians. The colors are mainly in the mauve to purple range, but also white and crimson. 'Catawbiense Album', a white; 'Charles Dickens', purple with red markings; 'Lady Armstrong', cyclamen-pink; 'Mrs. Charles S. Sargent', rose with greenish markings; 'Roseum Elegans', lavender-pink. *R. × russellianum* is a cross between *R. catawbiense* and *R. arboreum*. Zones 5 to 8.

FORTUNE HYBRIDS.
A fairly hardy, evergreen group. Much work in this group was done by Charles O. Dexter at Sandwich on Cape Cod, using *R. fortunei* and other species. 'Ben Mosley', pink; 'Scintillation', pink; 'Westbury', pink. Zones 6 to 7.

R. arborescens (ar-boh-*ress*-enz).
SWEET AZALEA.
This deciduous species is native to the mountains from Pa. to Ga. The bright green leaves are 1 in. long and turn bright red in the fall. It grows to 8 ft. tall and 6 ft. wide. Fragrant white flowers appear in late spring to early summer. Zones 5 to 9.

R. bakeri (*bay*-ker-eye).
CUMBERLAND AZALEA.
Deciduous native of the Appalachians. Red, orange-red, to yellow flowers bloom in early summer. Not much autumn coloration. To 6 ft. high and 4 ft. wide. Zones 5 to 8.

R. calendulaceum (ka-len-dew-*lay*-see-um).
FLAME AZALEA.
The most colorful of the native N. Amer. azaleas, found from Pa. to Ga., this puts on a two week show in late spring. A blaze of yellow, orange and reddish flowers envelops the plants. The deciduous, slightly shiny leaves turn slightly yellow in autumn. Plants grow to 9 ft. high and wide. Zones 5 to 8.

R. californicum. See *R. macrophyllum*

R. carolinianum (ka-roh-lin-ee-*ay*-num).
CAROLINA RHODODENDRON.
This evergreen shrub grows to 6 ft. high and wide, with small leaves to 3 in. The latter are brownish on the underside and curl up when it is cold. The rose-purple flowers bloom in mid-spring. The variety *album* (*al*-bum) has white blooms. This species and variety are native to N. Car. Zones 5 to 7.

Rhododendron

Rhododendron carolinianum
CAROLINA RHODODENDRON

Rhododendron catawbiense 'Blue Ensign'

R. catawbiense (kuh-taw-bee-*en*-see).
CATAWBA RHODODENDRON.
This is the native American species from which the Catawba Hybrids are derived. The species is native from Va. to Ga. It has passed along its hardiness to countless cultivars. It grows to 10 ft. tall and 8 ft. wide; its bold evergreen leaves grow to 5 in. The flowers are lilac-purple spotted with olive-green. The variety *album* (*al*-bum) has white flowers with yellow spots. 'Blue Ensign' has lavender flowers with a dark blotch in the upper petal. Zones 4 to 7.

R. kaempferi (*kem*-fur-eye).
This was once labeled *R. obtusum* var. *kaempferi* but is now considered its own species. It is native to Japan. It grows to 10 ft. high and 6 ft. wide. This azalea is semi-evergreen to deciduous. The leaves, which are small, turn reddish in the presence of cold weather before dropping. The

Rhododendron kaempferi

flowers open in spring in a range of colors from white through pinks and rose to salmon red, They are held in groups of up to four flowers. Each funnel-shaped flower is about 1½ to 2½ in. long. They can be grown in full sun, but the colors of the flowers last better in part shade. 'Mary' has reddish-violet flowers. Zones 5 to 8.

R. macrophyllum (mak-roh-*fill*-um).
CALIFORNIA ROSEBAY.
Also called *R. californicum* (cal-i-*for*-ni-kum). It is native along the Pacific Coast. Produces rose-purple flowers and evergreen leaves. Plants grow to 10 ft. in height, leaves to 8 in. long. Zones 7 to 9.

R. maximum (*max*-i-mum).
ROSEBAY RHODODENDRON.
The hardiest of the large rhododendrons, this has leaves to 8 in. long. Evergreen shrubs grow to 15 ft. high and wide. The large clusters of rose-purple flowers bloom after the new growth and

may be obscured by it. It is valuable for its foliage, which makes a fine background for other shrubs. It is also a fine specimen to grow in the shade. The form *album* (*al*-bum) has white flowers and the form *purpureum* (per-*pu*-ree-um) is deep rose-pink to purple. Zones 5 to 6.

R. mucronulatum (mew-kron-yew-*lay*-tum). KOREAN RHODODENDRON.
A deciduous rhododendron, this species grows to 8 ft. tall and 6 ft. wide. It is native to China, Manchuria, Korea and Japan. The rosy-purple flowers bloom before the leaves in early to mid-spring. The 3-in. leaves turn yellow to bronze in the fall. 'Cornell Pink' has soft pink flowers. Zones 5 to 7.

R. nudiflorum. See *R. periclymenoides*

R. obtusum (ob-*toos*-um). HIRYU AZALEA.
These evergreen to semi-evergreen shrubs have 1-in. leaves. They grow to 5 ft. tall and wide. Native to Japan. Their orange-red to red to magenta flowers bloom in mid-May. Known primarily for several cultivars and as one of the parents of the Kurume and Kaempferi (*kem*-fer-eye) Hybrids. 'Amoenum' has double, magenta flowers that are almost iridescent in their color intensity. Zones 6 to 9.

R. obtusum var. **kaempferi.** See *R. kaempferi*

R. periclymenoides (per-i-di-men-*oy*-dez). PINXTERBLOOM.
Also known as *R. nudiflorum* (new-dee-*floh*-rum). This deciduous azalea grows to 6 ft. tall and wide and is a familiar sight in open woodlands from Mass. to N. Car. and inland to Ohio. It blooms in mid-spring, just before the leaves, with showy pink flowers. Zone 5 to 8.

Rhododendron 'P.J.M. Hybrids'
P.J.M. HYBRID RHODODENDRON

✴R. 'P. J. M.' Hybrids
P.J.M. HYBRID RHODODENDRON.
A very hardy, small-leaved, evergreen, early-blooming group. These were obtained by hybridizing *R. dauricum* var. *sempervirens* (daw-*ree*-cum var. sem-per-*vye*-rens) and *R. carolinianum* (ca-row-li-nee-*ay*-num). Pink to lavender flowers smother these plants in mid-spring. They grow to 5 ft. tall and wide, with 3 in. leaves, which turn purple in the fall and winter. 'Elite' has pink-lavender flowers and is a bit later in bloom. 'Victor' is earlier than the rest of this group. Zones 4 to 7.

Rhododendron schlippenbachii
ROYAL AZALEA

✴R. schlippenbachii (shlip-en-*bak*-ee-eye). ROYAL AZALEA.
A deciduous, eastern Asian azalea with bold, 4-in. rounded leaves and large, fragrant, pink flowers before the leaves appear. Grows to 8 ft. tall and

wide. Autumn color an attractive yellow to bronze. Zones 5 to 8.

R. vaseyi (*va*-zeh-eye).
PINKSHELL AZALEA.
This deciduous shrub is native to the mountains of N. Car. Fragrant, light pink flowers occur before the foliage. The leaves are narrow, to 4 in. long, and produce reddish autumn color. Grows 8 ft. tall by 6 ft. wide. Zones 5 to 8.

R. viscosum (viss-*koh*-sum).
SWAMP AZALEA.
SWAMP HONEYSUCKLE.
This deciduous species is native in boggy soil from Maine to S. Car. The very fragrant white to pinkish-white flowers occur in early summer. The leaves turn bronze in the fall. Zones 4 to 9.

R. yakusimanum (yah-koo-sih-*may*-num).
YAK RHODODENDRON.
This Japanese native is a compact, dense, evergreen shrub that grows slowly to about 3 ft. tall with a spread of up to 4 ft. The dark green leaves are up to 3½ in. long, curled at the edges; the undersides are covered thickly with tannish hairs. The pink buds open in spring into apple-blossom pink flowers that fade to white. All three of these colors can be present in a truss of flowers at the same time, which is quite a handsome effect. Each truss may include as many as 10 bell-shaped flowers. Zones 5 to 7.

Rhodotypos (ro-do-*tye*-pus).
Rose Family (*Rosaceae*).
A deciduous shrub, native to E. Asia, that is especially useful in shaded areas. Propagate by seeds and cuttings.

R. scandens (*scan*-denz).
JETBEAD.
Showy, single white flowers over an inch in

diameter after the leaves emerge, in late spring. Fruits are borne in groups of three to four; small, they are blue-black in color. Leaves are opposite and turn slightly yellow in autumn. Zones 5 to 8.

Rhus (russ).
SUMAC.
Cashew Family (*Anacardiaceae*).
A large group of deciduous or evergreen shrubs or small trees that is widely distributed in subtropical and temperate regions of both hemispheres. The species described below are all deciduous. They produce alternate, usually compound leaves and small yellowish flowers in clusters with male and female flowers usually on separate plants. Attractive, red, hairy fruits occur on the non-poisonous, ornamental species. This genus includes Poison Ivy, Poison Sumac, and Poison Oak, all of which have white fruits. Sumacs can be used as specimens but are most effective when massed to show off the brilliant scarlet fall foliage. Very tolerant of dry conditions. Propagate by seeds, root cuttings or divisions.

R. aromatica (ar-roh-*mat*-ik-uh).
FRAGRANT SUMAC.
This is a fast-spreading, deciduous, dense shrub that grows to about 6 ft. high and spreads to 10 ft. Leaves of three leaflets, to 3 in. long, are coarsely toothed and aromatic. Yellowish flowers in short clusters appear in early to mid-spring before the leaves. Red, berrylike fruit appearing in late summer may last into winter. A good shrub for bank plantings due to its brilliant red to orange fall coloring. 'Gro-Low' is lower growing than the species, usually staying below 3 to 4 ft. tall. Zones 3 to 8.

R. chinensis (chin-*nen*-sis).

CHINESE SUMAC.

Native to China and Japan, this species is the most showy of the sumacs for flowers. Produces large clusters of white flowers in mid-summer. It grows to 20 ft. and suckers widely. Leaves 12-in. or longer have seven to thirteen leaflets. Leaf rachis (leaf stalk) is winged. Orange-red foliage in autumn. Showy reddish-orange berries follow the blooms. 'September Beauty' has larger clusters of flowers and is more showy than the species. Zones 6 to 9.

Rhus typhina
STAGHORN SUMAC

R. typhina (tye-*fye*-nuh).

STAGHORN SUMAC.

This suckering shrub or tree grows to 20 ft. tall and spreads widely due to its suckers. It produces velvety, fuzzy branchlets and leaves to 24 in. long, with numerous leaflets. Greenish-yellow flowers occur in dense clusters to 8 in. long in late June. They are borne above the foliage and are some-

what showy. Attractive, long-lasting crimson fruit is produced on female plants. It thrives in full sun and provides a wonderful show of fall color. 'Laciniata' (la-sin-ee-*ah*-tuh), the cut-leaf staghorn sumac, has finely cut leaves and a more spreading, irregular growth habit. Zones 3 to 7.

Ribes (*rye*-beez).

CURRANT.

GOOSEBERRY.

Saxifrage Family (*Saxifragaceae*).

These deciduous shrubs of cool and temperate regions of the world have alternate, usually palmately lobed leaves. Produce clusters of small flowers in spring. The fruit is tasty and juicy. Several species are valued for their edible fruit, a few for ornament. They thrive in moist, well-drained soil, in full sun or partial shade. Cultivation, especially that of black currants and gooseberries, is restricted in some areas since they are host to white pine blister rust, which can kill Eastern White Pines (*Pinus strobus*) (*pi*-nus *stroh*-bus). Propagate by seeds, cuttings or layers. Currants and gooseberries are considered two separate groups within this genus. Currants generally have no thorns and bear flowers in clusters. Gooseberries are prickly and have solitary or only a few flowers in a cluster.

R. alpinum (al-*pye*-num).

MOUNTAIN CURRANT.

An ornamental, European, upright shrub to 6 ft. high and wide. Three-lobed leaves grow to 2 in. across and produce pale yellow fall color or none at all. The small, greenish-yellow flowers are in small, insignificant, erect clusters, with males and females on separate plants. Scarlet berries occur on female plants. This is a popular hedge plant in northern areas. Sun or shade. Immune to white pine blister rust. Zones 3 to 6.

R. odoratum (oh-dor-*ah*-tum).
CLOVE CURRANT.
Showy yellow flowers that are wonderfully fragrant, appear just as the leaves come out. The black-blue fruit is not always produced. Zones 3 to 7.

Ribes sanguineum
WINTER CURRANT

R. sanguineum (san-gwi-*nee*-um).
WINTER CURRANT.
A western Amer. shrub to 8 ft. high and 6 ft. wide. Leaves to 4 in. across with three to five lobes. Grown for its clusters of red flowers, which bloom in mid-spring. Has blue-black berries. Popular ornamental shrub on the Pacific Coast. Zones 5 to 7.

R. sativum (sah-*tiv*-um).
RED CURRANT.
Grown for fruit. Native to W. Eur. Grows to 5 ft. high and as wide. The flowers are green or pur-

plish in drooping clusters. Fruits are red or white. Zones 5 to 7.

R. uva-crispa (*you*-vah-cris-puh).
ENGLISH GOOSEBERRY.
A spiny shrub, native to Eur., that grows to 4 ft. high and as wide. Flowers are greenish, sometimes tinged with pink. It is grown for its red, yellow, or green fruits. Zones 5 to 7.

Robinia (roh-*bin*-ee-uh).
LOCUST.
Pea Family (*Leguminosae*).
A small genus of deciduous shrubs and trees of N. Amer. with alternate, pinnately compound leaves, drooping clusters of white, pink, or purple flowers and flat pods. Locusts have graceful foliage and showy flowers. They thrive in any well-drained soil and, since at least some of the species produce their own nitrogen, they thrive even on poor soil. Tolerant of dry conditions. They grow rapidly from seed, grafts, or root cuttings.

R. hispida (*hiss*-pid-uh).
ROSE ACACIA.
A southeastern U.S. suckering shrub that grows to 6 ft. high and wide. The leaves grow to 1½ in. long, each with seven to thirteen leaflets. Showy, rose-colored or pale purple flowers grow about 1 in. long, in late spring. Densely hairy pods to 3 in. long. It is handsome in bloom, but can become a nuisance because of suckering habit. Obtainable as grafted plants in small tree form. Can be used to stabilize steep banks. Zones 4 to 8.

R. pseudoacacia (soo-doh-ah-*kay*-see-uh).
BLACK LOCUST.
A tree native to the central part of the U.S., it has escaped cultivation and has become weedy in much of N. Amer., Eur., and Asia. It grows to 60

Robinia pseudoacacia 'Frisia'
BLACK LOCUST

ft. high and 30 ft. wide. Has deeply furrowed, dark brown bark and brittle, prickly branches (due to paired thorns at the leaf bases). The leaves grow to 10 in. long, with seven to nine leaflets on each leaf. Slightly bluish-green during the summer, the leaves have almost no autumnal coloration. White, very fragrant, showy flowers are in drooping clusters to 8 in. long. Flowers occur in late spring after the leaves have emerged. The smooth pods, to 4 in., stay on the tree all winter. Old trees are susceptible to borer attack. 'Frisia' (*free*-see-uh) has yellow foliage that holds fairly well during the summer. 'Umbraculifera' (um-brak-yew-*lif*-er-uh) forms a round head. Zones 4 to 9.

Salix (*say*-lix).
WILLOW.
OSIER.
Willow Family (*Salicaceae*).
Deciduous shrubs and trees of primarily the N.

Hemisphere. The leaves are alternate; the flowers, in catkins, with males and females on separate plants, appear before or with the leaves. On some plants, the male flowers are very showy; on some species the stems are very colorful during the winter. Willows vary greatly in size and form, from prostrate shrubs to large trees. All are fast-growing and likely to be brittle. Lawns are littered by falling twigs and leaves during the growing season. Most thrive in wet soil but are tolerant of ordinary garden soil. Willows tend to be short-lived, and are subject to insect and storm damage. Propagate by cuttings or seeds.

Salix alba var. *tristis*
GOLDEN WEEPING WILLOW

S. alba (*al*-buh).
WHITE WILLOW.
A tree of Eur. and Asia, the willow grows to 75 ft. high and wide. Narrow, finely-toothed leaves, to 4 in. long, are whitish beneath. Yellow-green catkins are somewhat showy, as are the bright yellow twigs in early spring. Zones 3 to 8. Var.

tristis (*triss*-tiss), is a golden willow with a weeping form. It is grown much more often than the
species. Hardy north to Zone 4. It is hardier than
S. babylonica, and similar to it but has yellow
bark. Var. *vitellina* (vye-teh-*lye*-nuh) has brighter
yellow stems than the species. Var. *chermesina*
(cher-may-*sye*-nuh) is red-stemmed during the
winter. Var. *sericea* (sir-uh-*see*-uh) has gray leaves.

S. babylonica (bab-il-*lon*-i-kuh).
WEEPING WILLOW.
Probably the most weeping of the willows. This
willow has been cultivated so long its origin is
unknown but it is thought to be Chinese. It
grows to 40 ft. tall and as wide. Its narrow, finely-
toothed leaves grow to 6 in. long. Produces green
catkins and stems. Zones 6 to 9.

Salix caprea 'Pendula'
WEEPING GOAT WILLOW

S. caprea (*kap*-ree-uh).
GOAT WILLOW.
FRENCH PUSSY WILLOW.
One of the showiest of the pussy willows, which
are grown for their late winter flowers. The male
catkins are the showiest. This small tree grows to
25 ft. high and 15 ft. wide. Its leaves are dark
green all summer. 'Pendula' is a weeping form.
Zones 4 to 9.

S. discolor (*dis*-kol-er).
PUSSY WILLOW.
An eastern Amer. shrub or tree to 20 ft. tall and 12
ft. wide. Its leaves are whitish beneath and its silky
catkins are smaller than *S. caprea*. Zones 3 to 8.

S. pentandra (pen-*tan*-druh).
LAUREL WILLOW.
A rounded, European tree that grows to 40 ft.
with broad, shiny green leaves to 5 in. long. Its
yellow catkins are showy. Zones 3 to 8.

Sambucus (sam-*bew*-kus).
ELDER.
ELDERBERRY.
Honeysuckle Family (*Caprifoliaceae*).
Deciduous shrubs and small trees of the temperate and subtropical regions of both hemispheres.
They have a coarse rather than rampant habit;
compound, opposite, toothed leaves; showy clusters of small, white flowers; and red or black
berrylike fruit. Propagate by seeds, cuttings or
suckers.

S. canadensis (ka-na-*den*-sis).
AMERICAN ELDERBERRY.
A vigorous, fast-growing shrubby native eastern
Amer. tree that grows to 10 ft. high and 8 ft.
wide. Its bright green leaves are 8 in. long. The
white flowers are showy, occurring in flat clusters
to 8 in. across in late June. The blue-black berries

Sambucus canadensis
AMERICAN ELDERBERRY

are shiny, valued for preserves and homemade wines. Zones 3 to 9.

Sassafras (*sas*-uh-frass).
Laurel Family (*Lauraceae*).
These deciduous, aromatic trees of N. Amer. and Asia have alternate, entire or lobed leaves and clusters of yellowish-green flowers that bloom in mid-spring before the leaves appear. The male and female flowers are on the same or different trees. All parts of the plants are fragrant. Produces plumlike, ½-in. bluish-black fruit. Propagate by seeds or suckers.

S. albidum (al-*bid*-um).
SASSAFRAS.
A native of eastern N. Amer. that can grow to 60 ft. tall and 40 ft. wide, but is often shorter. It has a pyramidal form with distinctly horizontal branches that turn upward at the tips. The deeply furrowed bark is divided into squares. Leaves

take three forms, usually all found on the same individual plant. They can be oval without lobes, elliptical with two lobes, looking like a mitten, or they may have three lobes. They turn brilliant yellow, orange and scarlet in the fall. Fragrant yellow, moderately showy flowers occur in clusters about 2 in. long. The fruit is ½ in. across, on fleshy, bright red stalks. The tree suckers freely from the roots. Zones 5 to 9.

Sciadopitys (sy-uh-*dop*-it-iss).
Bald-cypress Family (*Taxodiaceae*).
The only species is considered by many to be the finest of conifers. The needles are evergreen, thick and a glossy dark green with a yellow, indented stripe on the lower side. They are borne in whorls, with several inches of bare stems between whorls. Cones, produced only on old trees, grow to 5 in. long with very thick cone scales.

Sciadopitys verticillata
JAPANESE UMBRELLA PINE

✱S. verticillata (ver-ti-si-*lay*-tuh).
JAPANESE UMBRELLA PINE.
Grows best in full sun, but will tolerate some shade. Can grow to 100 ft. but usually less in cultivation. Propagate by seed or cuttings. Zones 5 to 8.

Sequoia (see-*kwoy*-uh).
REDWOOD.
Bald-cypress Family (*Taxodiaceae*).
There is only one species, a magnificent, long-lived, evergreen tree that is native to coastal regions of Calif. and Oregon. It is considered the tallest tree in the world and thrives under cool, moist conditions. Propagate by seeds or cuttings.

Sequoia sempervirens 'Adpressa'
COASTAL REDWOOD

S. sempervirens (sem-per-*vye*-rens).
COASTAL REDWOOD.
Grows to 300 ft. or more in the wild; its maximum height in cultivation is closer to 80 ft. Produces fibrous, thick red bark and narrow, dark green, sharp-pointed leaves about 1 in. long. Its natural habitat is limited to Calif. and Ore. Zone 7. 'Adpressus' has white shoot tips and shorter needles. It is smaller than the species, but does become a tree. Zones 7 to 9.

Sequoiadendron (see-kwoy-uh-*den*-dron).
GIANT SEQUOIA.
Bald-cypress Family (*Taxodiaceae*).
There is only one species, a massive evergreen tree of Calif., considered to be the largest tree in volume in the world. It is not as tall as the redwood but has a much larger trunk. Propagate by seeds or grafts.

Sequoiadendron giganteum
GIANT SEQUOIA

S. giganteum (jye-gan-*tee*-um).

BIG TREE.

Sometimes listed as *Sequoia washingtonia* or *Wellingtonia*. Its natural habitat today is a few groves in central Calif. It grows to 300 ft. tall in the wild with trunks large enough to cut a tunnel through, but rarely grows over 80 ft. tall in gardens. Its trunk is covered with a very thick, fire-resistant reddish-brown bark. The bluish-green, prickly leaves to ½ in. long resemble a juniper or *Cryptomeria* (krip-toh-*meh*-ree-uh). Zones 6 to 9.

Skimmia (*skim*-ee-uh).

Rue Family (*Rutaceae*).

These handsome, evergreen shrubs from Asia have alternate, entire leaves. They produce clusters of small, fragrant flowers and showy, berrylike, inedible fruit. They require good soil drainage and do best with protection from the sun in winter. Propagate by seeds or cuttings.

Skimmia japonica

S. japonica (ja-*pon*-ik-uh).

A low, densely branched, Japanese shrub, it grows to 4 ft. high and wide. Its dark green leaves grow to 5 in. long. Creamy-white flowers, male and female on separate plants, occur in upright clusters in mid-spring. The male flowers are larger and very fragrant. Bright red berries occur on female plants and remain showy most of the winter. Zones 6 to 8.

S. reevesiana (ree-ves-ee-*ay*-nuh).

A Chinese species that is very similar to *S. japonica* (ja-*pon*-i-kuh) but lower growing, slightly finer textured, and, most importantly, each plant bears fruit (because the flower clusters are bisexual). Zones 6 to 8.

Sophora (sof-*foh*-ruh).

Pea Family (*Leguminosae*).

These handsome flowering shrubs and trees of Asia and N. Amer. have pinnately compound, alternate leaves and showy clusters of pealike flowers followed by rounded or four-winged pods that are tightened between seeds. They are evergreen or deciduous, but only the deciduous species are hardy in the North. They need a well-drained soil and full sun. Propagate by seeds, cuttings or grafts.

Sophora japonica
JAPANESE PAGODA TREE

Sophora

S. japonica (ja-*pon*-i-kuh).
JAPANESE PAGODA TREE.
CHINESE SCHOLAR TREE.
Spreading, round-headed and deciduous, these Chinese and Korean trees grow to 60 ft. tall and spread to about the same distance. The leaves grow to 9 in. long, each with seven to seventeen medium green leaflets to 2 in. long. Yellowish-white flowers occur in large, loose clusters to 15 in. long. They bloom in mid- to late summer, when almost no other tree is blooming, making a striking effect. Pods to 3 in. long. Pods are attractive on the tree in autumn and early winter. The seeds are hard and round and can be a slipping hazard if the tree is in a paved area. Withstands city conditions well. Zones 5 to 8.

Sorbaria (sor-*bay*-ree-uh).
FALSE SPIREA.
Rose Family (*Rosaceae*).
Deciduous shrubs of Asia. False spirea has alternate, compound leaves and large branching clusters of white flowers in early to mid-summer. They grow best in rich, moist soil and sun, and spread rapidly. Propagate by seeds, cuttings or division.

S. sorbifolia (soar-bih-*foe*-lee-ah).
URAL FALSE SPIREA.
Grows to 6 to 10 ft. tall and spreads 10 ft. wide. It forms large clumps by suckering. The large, pinnately compound leaves have leaflets that are 2 to 4 in. long, with sharply toothed edges. A terminal cluster of tiny white flowers opens in early summer. It is 4 to 10 in. long, pyramidal in shape, with a soft appearance. Prune in early spring before the leaves emerge as the flowers are produced on the present year's growth. Zones 3 to 7.

Sorbaria sorbifolia
URAL FALSE SPIREA

Sorbus (*sor*-bus).
MOUNTAIN ASH.
Rose Family (*Rosaceae*).
Deciduous shrubs or trees of the N. Hemisphere. They bear simple or compound, sharply toothed leaves, borne in an alternate arrangement. Flat clusters of small white flowers appear in late spring, followed by showy fruit clusters, and attractive autumn foliage. Requires well-drained soil. Propagate by seeds, cuttings, or grafts.

S. alnifolia (al-ni-*foh*-lee-uh).
KOREAN MOUNTAIN ASH.
This tree grows to 50 ft. tall and 30 ft. wide. Its simple, bright green leaves, to 4 in. long, turn a brilliant orange and red in the fall. The flowers are small, in showy white clusters, late in the spring after the leaves have emerged. Pinkish orange fruits are about 1/3 in. across. One of the least susceptible to borer attack, but it is susceptible to fireblight. Zones 4 to 7.

Sorbus aucuparia
EUROPEAN MOUNTAIN ASH

S. aucuparia (aw-kew-*pay*-ree-uh).
EUROPEAN MOUNTAIN ASH.
ROWAN TREE.
A spreading tree to 35 ft. tall and 25 ft. wide. Native to Eur. and Asia Minor. Its pinnately compound leaves grow to 8 in. long; the leaflets, to 2 in. long, are bluish beneath and turn reddish in the fall. Showy clusters of white flowers, to 5 in. across, are followed by bright red berries. Where healthy (areas with cool summers), it is an attractive plant throughout the year. Planting it on the north side of buildings, where the soil is shaded (and cooler), can help prolong the lifespan. Very susceptible to borers and foliar diseases. Zones 3 to 5.

S. rufoferruginea 'Longwood Sunset'
(roo-foh-fur-rug-ah-*nee*-ah).
LONGWOOD SUNSET MOUNTAIN ASH.
Very similar to European Mountain Ash, but this new cultivar of a Japanese species appears to be much healthier. Attractive white flowers appear in mid-spring, followed by excellent maroon autumn foliage, with showy orange fruit remaining on the tree into early winter. Zones 4 to 7.

Spiraea (spye-*ree*-uh).
SPIREA.
Rose Family (*Rosaceae*).
This is a large and important group of ornamental deciduous shrubs from the Northern Hemisphere, with simple, alternate leaves and showy, freely produced clusters of small flowers in spring or summer. They grow best in good moist soil and sun. The early-flowering species all have white blooms; the later group includes some with pink and reddish flowers, as well as white. Prune spring bloomers (S. × *arguta*, S. *nipponica*, S. *prunifolia*, S. *thunbergii*, S. × *vanhouttei*) after flowering, summer bloomers (S. × *bumalda*, S. *japonica*) in the spring. Fruits are dry capsules, not showy. Propagate by seeds, cuttings or division.

Spiraea × arguta
GARLAND SPIREA

Spiraea

S. × **arguta** (are-*goo*-tah).
GARLAND SPIREA.
BRIDAL WREATH SPIREA.
This early blooming species of spirea generally reaches a height of 5 to 6 ft. and achieves an equal spread. It is the product of crossing *S. thunbergii* with *S. multiflora* (multi-*floh*-ruh). The twiggy branches are long and arching. In early to mid-spring, the branches are covered with flat clusters of small, white, five-petaled flowers. The leaves are small and narrow. Prune after the flowers are finished. Zones 4 to 8.

S. × **bumalda** (bew-*mald*-uh).
Hybrid of *S. japonica* and *S. albiflora* (al-buh-*floh*-ruh). A bushy shrub to 3 ft. high and wide. Leaves to 3 in. long. Flat clusters of dark pink flowers begin blooming in early summer and continue sporadically throughout the summer. Plants can be totally cut to the ground in the spring and will still bloom well. 'Anthony Waterer' is more compact, and blooms regularly throughout the summer. 'Froebelii' has dull rose flowers and is about the size of the species. 'Gold-flame' has bright, golden new leaves that are tinged with red. Zones 4 to 8.

S. nipponica (ni-*pon*-i-kuh).
Grows to 8 ft. in a stiff habit, with bluish-green leaves 1½ in. long. Produces numerous small, flat clusters of white flowers in late spring after the leaves emerge. 'Snowmound' grows to 5 ft. tall and wide, producing denser flower clusters. Zones 4 to 8.

S. prunifolia (prew-ni-*foh*-lee-uh).
BRIDAL WREATH.
A graceful shrub to 6 ft. high and wide with slender, arching branches. Its neat, glossy, oval leaves, to 2 in. long, turn orangish-red in autumn. Small clusters of showy, distinctly double,

white flowers bloom in April and May. Zones 5 to 8.

S. × **vanhouttei** (van-*hoot*-ee-eye).
Hybrid of *S. cantoniensis* (can-toh-nye-*en*-sis) and *S. trilobata* (tri-low-*bah*-tuh). Grows to 8 ft. tall, with arching branches reaching 8 ft. in width. Its bluish-green leaves are about 1½ in. long, pale beneath and slightly lobed. Profusions of flat clusters of white flowers give these shrubs fountainlike effects in late spring after the leaves appear. Zones 3 to 7.

Staphylea (staf-i-*lee*-uh).
BLADDER-NUT.
Bladdernut Family (*Staphyleaceae*).
These are ornamental, deciduous shrubs or small trees of North Temperate regions, with opposite, compound leaves, clusters of whitish flowers and bladderlike fruits. They tolerate full sun and par-

Staphylea colchica
CAUCASIAN BLADDERNUT

tial shade, and they need moist, rich soil. Propagate by seeds, cuttings or layers.

S. colchica (col-*cheek*-uh).
CAUCASIAN BLADDERNUT.
A large shrub growing 15 to 20 ft. tall with very showy, creamy-white flowers in mid-spring. Zones 6 to 8.

S. trifolia (trye-*foh*-lee-uh).
An eastern N. Amer. native to 15 ft. tall and 10 ft. wide. Suckers may cause it to spread further. Pendant clusters of white flowers appear in mid- to late spring, after the leaves expand. Seed pods, maturing in Oct., are attractive but not terribly showy. Zones 4 to 7.

Stewartia (stew-*ar*-tee-uh).
Tea Family (*Theaceae*).
These deciduous shrubs or trees of the southeastern U.S. and Asia have smooth flaky bark, alternate, simple, toothed leaves and showy white, camellialike flowers that are borne singly and appear in the summer. They grow best in a rich moist loam with peat, in partial shade. They tolerate full sun if there is ample moisture but require good drainage. Rich fall coloring of the foliage. Propagate by seeds, cuttings.

✶**S. koreana** (kor-ee-*ay*-nuh).
KOREAN STEWARTIA.
Also known as *S. pseudocamellia* var. *koreana*. Grows in a pyramidal form to 40 ft. high and 20 ft. wide. It has extremely showy, flaking bark and leaves to 4 in. long that turn orange-red in autumn. Its white flowers, to 3 in. across, open in July. Zones 6 to 8.

S. pseudocamellia (soo-doh-kah-*mell*-ee-uh).
A Japanese tree to 30 ft. tall and 20 ft. wide with

Stewartia koreana
KOREAN STEWARTIA

attractive, flaky bark. Its bright green leaves, to 3 in. long, turn deep maroon in the fall. Its summer flowers grow to 2 in. across. Zones 6 to 8.

S. pseudocamellia var. **koreana.** See
S. koreana

Styrax (*sti*-raks).
SNOWBELL.
Storax Family (*Styracaceae*).
Shrubs or small trees, these handsome plants have unlobed, alternate leaves, showy clusters of white, bell-shaped flowers in late spring or early summer and round, dry fruit. They thrive in well-drained soil in sun or shade. Bark smooth, dark gray. Propagate by seeds or cuttings.

S. japonicus (ja-*pon*-i-kus).
JAPANESE SNOWBELL.
A widespreading, deciduous small tree to 25 ft. high and wide, it occasionally grows to 30 ft. It

Styrax

Styrax japonicus
JAPANESE SNOWBELL

has twiggy, slender branches, pointed leaves to 3 in. long, and small, fragrant, drooping, bell-like flowers about 1½ in. across, in small clusters, in later spring after the leaves appear. The fruits are dry, rounded capsules that hang from the branches, looking a bit like flower buds. Zones 6 to 8.

S. obassia (oh-*bass*-ee-uh).
FRAGRANT SNOWBELL.

An erect, deciduous, Japanese and Korean small tree to 25 ft. tall and wide. Bold, broadly oval leaves can be 8 in. long. The fragrant flowers blooming in late spring in many-flowered clusters to 8 in. long, are somewhat hidden by the large leaves. The fall color is dull yellow at best. Zones 6 to 8.

Symphoricarpos (sim-foh-ri-*kar*-pos).
Honeysuckle Family (*Caprifoliaceae*).
Deciduous shrubs, both decorative and durable,

they come from Asia and N. Amer. They produce simple, opposite leaves, clusters of small, pink flowers and ornamental berrylike fruits. They will grow in sun or shade, and tolerate drought. Their fruit is showier than the flowers. Propagate by seeds, cuttings or division.

Symphoricarpos albus
SNOWBERRY

S. albus (*al*-bus).
SNOWBERRY.
WAXBERRY.

A northeastern N. Amer. shrub, growing to 5 ft. tall and wide, with erect, slender branches. The bluish-green, oval leaves grow to 2 in. long. The small, tubular, pinkish flowers appear in June, followed by soft, white berries, which turn brown with heavy frosts. Zones 3 to 6.

S. × chenaultii (she-*now*-tee-eye).
A hybrid of *S. microphyllus* and *S. orbiculatus*, this shrub grows to 4 ft. tall and 5 ft. wide. Its small, oval leaves hold their green color late. Produces

pinkish flowers and attractive, small, oval, coral-red berries. It is valued for its light and graceful effect and for its abundant berries. 'Hancock' is lower growing, staying under 2 ft. in height. Zones 5 to 7.

Symphoricarpos orbiculatus
CORALBERRY

S. orbiculatus (or-bik-yew-*lay*-tus).
INDIAN CURRANT.
CORALBERRY.
Grows to 5 ft. high and wide. Similar to *S. × chenaultii* but with smaller fruits. Produces oval leaves about 2 in. long, small, yellowish-white flowers in early summer and interesting maroon-red berries strung along stems. Unprepossessing during the summer, it is attractive in autumn and winter with its profusion of fruit. Zones 3 to 8.

S. vulgaris: S. orbiculatus.

Syringa (si-*rin*-guh).
LILAC.
Olive Family (*Oleaceae*).
Lilacs are deciduous shrubs or small trees of Eur. and Asia, with opposite, mostly simple leaves, showy clusters of tubular flowers, some of which are very fragrant, and almost all are strikingly beautiful for a brief period. Brown, oval capsules for the fruit. These plants need sun and well-drained soil. Cultivars are generally propagated by cuttings today, but in the past were grafted on seedling lilac roots or on privet. Care must be taken when pruning grafted plants to make sure the entire top of the plant is never removed. To rejuvenate old specimens, prune out one or two of the oldest stems on a yearly basis until rejuvenation is complete. This can be done any time of the year, but since flowers are produced on the previous season's growth, pruning right after bloom will avoid the loss of flowers the following year. Susceptible to scale and borer infestations. Regular renewal pruning generally will control borers, since they are most severe on old plants. Mildew often whitens the leaves on some types, but it is more unsightly than harmful. Hundreds of named cultivars are availible, primarily of *S. vulgaris*. Many of them are known as French lilacs because of the country where the early breeding work was done. Propagate by seeds, grafts or cuttings.

S. amurensis. See *S. reticulata.*

S. amurensis var. **japonica.** See *S. reticulata.*

S. × chinensis (chi-*nen*-sis).
A hybrid of *S. laciniata* and *S. vulgaris*. This shrub grows to 12 ft. high and wide, with somewhat slender branches and leaves to 3 in. long. Loose clusters of sweetly fragrant lilac, reddish or purple flowers bloom in mid-spring. 'Alba' has white flowers. Many other cultivars available. Zones 4 to 7.

S. × josiflexa. See *S. prestoniae.*

S. laciniata (la-sin-ee-*ay*-tuh).
CUTLEAF LILAC.
A graceful Chinese species to 6 ft. tall and wide. The leaves, about 2½ in. long, are deeply lobed. Small clusters of lavender flowers cover the branches in mid-spring. The entire plant is very fine textured. Zones 4 to 8.

Syringa

Syringa laciniata
CUTLEAF LILAC

S. meyeri (*mye*-er-eye).
A dense, compact Asian shrub to 6 ft. tall and 8 ft. wide with oval leaves about 1½ in. long that have wavy margins. Purple-violet flowers in dense, showy clusters, to 3 in. long, bloom in late spring. Zones 4 to 7.

S. microphylla (mye-kroh-*fill*-uh).
LITTLELEAF LILAC.
Widely spreading, slender-branched Chinese shrub, 6 ft. tall and 9 ft. wide. Ovate leaves to 1½. in. long, hairy beneath. Rosy-lilac, fragrant flowers in loose clusters to 3 in. long in mid-spring. Zones 5 to 7.

S. × persica (*per*-si-kuh).
PERSIAN LILAC.
A hybrid of *S. afghanica* (af-*gan*-i-kah) and *S. laciniata*, this shrub reaches 8 ft. tall and 10 ft. wide. Its leaves are somewhat narrow, to 2½ in. long. Very fragrant, pale lilac flowers in loose clusters to 3 in. long. 'Alba' has white flowers. Zones 4 to 7.

S. × prestoniae (pres-*toh*-nee-uh).
PRESTON HYBRID LILAC.
A hybrid of *S. reflexa* (re-*flex*-uh) and *S. villosa* (vil-*oh*-suh), this is an upright shrub to 9 ft. tall and wide. Its leaves grow to 7 in. long and it produces clusters of flowers of various colors in late spring. Hybridized in Canada, it is noted for

Syringa × persica 'Alba'
WHITE PERSIAN LILAC

its hardiness. *S. × josiflexa* 'Bellicent' is the result of a cross between *S. reflexa* and *S. joskaea* and has clean pink flowers in large fragrant clusters. Zones 2 to 7.

S. reticulata (ree-tic-u-*lay*-tuh).
JAPANESE TREE LILAC.
Also known as *S. amurensis* var. *japonica* (am-yew-*ren*-sis ja-*pon*-i-kuh). This is an upright shrub or tree to 25 ft. tall and 20 ft. wide. Its ovate leaves, to 5 in. long, are green during the summer and slightly yellow in autumn. Yellowish-white flowers in loose clusters, to 6 in. long, appear in late spring or early summer, at the end of the lilac season. Its shiny, cherrylike bark and clusters of yellowish-tan fruit capsules are somewhat showy in fall and early winter. Zones 3 to 7.

S. vulgaris (vul-*gay*-ris).
COMMON LILAC.
An upright, vigorous, suckering shrub that

grows to 15 ft. tall and 12 ft. wide. Native to S. Eur. It produces rounded leaves to 5 in. long and fragrant flowers, of various colors, in clusters to 10 in. long in mid-spring. There are many cultivars, with single or double flowers in many colors, including the French Hybrids. 'Mon Blanc' is an attractive white, 'President Lincoln' has blue flowers, 'Sensation' is purple. Zones 3 to 7.

Syringa vulgaris
COMMON LILAC

Tamarix *(tam-*uh-rix).
TAMARISK.
Tamarisk Family (*Tamaricaceae*).
These are deciduous, extremely fine-textured shrubs or small trees from Eur. and Asia, with small, alternate scale-like leaves, and small pretty flowers in clusters that have an attractive feathery appearance. These shrubs are unusual-looking with their long slender branches that appear almost leafless. They tolerate both very dry and very humid climates. Propagate by seeds or cuttings.

Tamarix tetrandra
TAMARISK

T. pentandra. See *T. ramosissima*.

T. ramosissima (ram-oh-*sis*-uh-ma).
A fine-textured tall shrub growing to 15 ft. tall and 8 ft. wide. Produces small bluish-green leaves. The pink flowers, in dense racemes, form large clusters on new growth in mid to late summer. Drastic pruning keeps this plant healthier and more attractive. Salt tolerant, thus useful at the seashore. Zones 4 to 8.

T. tetrandra (tet-*ran*-druh).
Very similar to T. ramosissima, but blooming on old wood.

Taxodium *(tax-*oh-dee-um).
Bald-cypress Family (*Taxodiaceae*).
Deciduous or evergreen trees of southern N. Amer., with light brown, scaly bark and graceful, feathery foliage. Male and female cones occur separately but on the same tree. The female cones

Taxodium

Taxodium distichum
BALD CYPRESS

are round and small and disintegrate when ripe. The male cones are catkinlike. These majestic and picturesque trees thrive in swampy places, but will tolerate ordinary garden soil. Propagate by seeds, cuttings and grafts.

T. ascendens (ah-*sen*-denz).
POND CYPRESS.
Also known as *T. distichum* var. *nutans* (*nue*-tans). Pond cypress is native to wet areas in the southeastern U.S. but is not as common as the following species. It grows 75 ft. tall and 18 ft. wide. It differs from bald cypress in bark color, more orange; branchlets, which are erect; the leaves, which are small, scalelike and result in string-like texture; and narrower form. Deciduous, its autumn color becomes an attractive rusty orange. Zones 5 to 9.

T. distichum (*dis*-ti-kum).
BALD CYPRESS.
A beautiful, deciduous tree to 70 ft. tall and 30 ft.

wide. The form varies; some trees are quite narrow, while others are wide-spreading. Its flat, needlelike, light green leaves grow to about ½ in. long and turn orange in the fall. Cones, about 1 in. across, disintegrate when ripe. Its bark is reddish brown and the trunk is sometimes buttressed. In swamps, woody projections called cypress knees arise from the roots. Zones 5 to 9.

Taxus (*tax*-us).
YEW.
Yew Family (*Taxaceae*).
Evergreen shrubs or trees with narrow, needlelike leaves, ranging in height from 2 to 30 ft. Native to the N. Hemisphere. The flowers are inconspicuous, with sexes on different plants; the red berrylike seeds occur on female plants. All parts of the plants are poisonous, except for the red flesh surrounding the seeds. They require well-drained soil; they tolerate full sun and shade, but require ample moisture if planted in full sun. Propagate by seeds or cuttings.

Taxus baccata
ENGLISH YEW

Taxus baccata 'Fastigiata'
IRISH YEW

Taxus is one of the most widely used landscape plants. Yew is amenable to extensive pruning and so is used for borders, screens, hedges, walls, doorways and for topiary work. New shoots will come from old wood, so plants can be pruned back severely. The species are very difficult to distinguish. Generally the plants are available as cultivars, rather than species. Cultivars are primarily selected for form; a few for color.

T. baccata (bah-*kay*-tuh).
ENGLISH YEW.
Shrubs and trees to 30 ft. high and wide. From Eur., N. Africa and W. Asia, they have dark green leaves, a lighter color beneath, which grow to 1¼ in. long. This common yew of England is widely cultivated in the U.S. Zones 5 to 7. 'Repandens' (ree-*pan*-denz) is one of the hardiest of the *T. baccata* cultivars. It is wide-spreading, eventually reaching 6 ft. in height and 12 ft. widths. 'Fastigiata' (fas-tij-ee-*ah*-tuh), Irish yew, is a tall growing, columnar plant. Very impressive, formal in appearance, it grows about 20 ft. tall and 6 ft. wide.

T. cuspidita (kuss-pi-*day*-tuh).
JAPANESE YEW.
This is the yew most commonly cultivated in the U.S., as it is hardier than *T. baccata*. An erect or spreading tree to 30 ft., it comes from Japan and Korea. 'Capitata' (kap-i-*tay*-tuh) is a pyramidal-shaped small tree with a central leader. This is actually the straight species and can be grown either from seed or from cuttings of upright shoots. If cuttings of side shoots are rooted, the plants become spreading, and never form a central leader. This form is sold in this country as Japanese yew. 'Nana' (*nay*-nuh) has a low, spreading, compact habit, with leaves that spiral around the stem. Zones 4 to 7.

T. × media (*mee*-dee-uh).

ANGLO-JAPANESE YEW.

A hybrid of *T. baccata* and *T. cuspidata* that has produced a number of forms combining the hardiness of Japanese yew and the ornamental values of English yew. 'Brownii' (*brow*-nee-eye) is a male clone and has a rounded, compact, slow growth habit to 4 to 8 ft., with diameter equaling, or exceeding, the height. It makes an excellent hedge. 'Hatfieldii' (hat-*feel*-dee-eye) makes a splendid, dense pyramid with upright branches. 'Hicksii' (*hix*-ee-eye), long popular for landscaping, is upright, in youth looking like Irish yew, but becoming much wider with age. 'Wardii' (*war*-dee-eye) is exceedingly wide-spreading to three times its height. A slow grower to 6 ft. Zones 5 to 7.

Thuja (*thew*-yah).

ARBORVITAE.

Cypress Family (*Cupressaceae*).

Distinctive, adaptable, evergreen trees and shrubs of N. Amer. and E. Asia, with fragrant, frondlike branchlets, opposite scale-like leaves, and small, erect cones. There are many cultivars, offering various sizes, shapes, and colors. Many are useful for hedge planting and stand shearing well. Because they will sprout new growth from old wood, they can be cut back severely. Arborvitae grow best in rich, moist soil in cool locations, either in sun or shade. Some tolerate poor drainage. Propagate by seeds or cuttings.

T. occidentalis (ok-si-den-*tay*-lis).

AMERICAN ARBORVITAE.

These pyramidal trees, to 50 ft. tall and 15 ft. wide, have reddish-brown bark. Their bright green leaves are yellowish-green beneath and tend to tan in winter if the tree grows in full sun, especially in dry areas. The cones are about ½ in. long. Scores of named cultivars are grown. They

Thuja occidentalis 'Rheingold'
AMERICAN ARBORVITAE

tolerate poor drainage, as well as regular garden soil. 'Douglasii Pyramidalis' (doug-*las*-ee-eye pyr-ah-mi-*dal*-is) is a dense, columnar tree; 'Fastigiata' (fas-tij-ee-*ay*-tuh) and 'Pyramidalis' are narrow upright plants, generally multi-stemmed and have a tendency to spread apart in ice and snow storms. 'Nigra' (*nye*-gra), a narrow, columnar form, holds a deep green color year round. 'Rheingold' is cone-shaped, to 5 ft. tall and 4 ft. wide, has yellow foliage that turns bronze in winter, and grows about a third as quickly as the species. 'Globosa' (glow-*boh*-sa) and 'Woodward' are broadly globe-shaped and very slow growing, eventually attaining their 8 ft. tall and 10 ft. wide size. Zones 3 to 6.

T. orientalis (or-ee-en-*tay*-lis).

ORIENTAL ARBORVITAE.

Also known as *Platycladus* (plah-tee-*clad*-us) *orientalis* and by its very old name, *Biota* (by-*oh*-ta) *orientalis*. Native to China and Korea. A graceful, widely pyramidal tree growing to 25 ft. tall and 15 ft. wide. Its branches and foliage are distinctly vertical and erect, finer textured than other *Thuja* species. It has bright green leaves and 1-in. cones that are bluish, eventually turning brown, with hornlike projections on the scales. 'Aurea Nana' (*aw*-ree-uh *nay*-nuh), to 5 ft. high and 3 ft. wide, has yellow foliage; 'Bakeri' (*bay*-ker-eye) is cone-shaped, green, and adaptable to hot, dry locations. Zones 6 to 8.

✴T. plicata (plye-*kay*-tuh).
GIANT ARBORVITAE.

This fast-growing, pyramidal, western Amer. tree attains heights of to 70 ft. and 20 ft. widths. It has grayish, reddish-brown bark. The shiny green scalelike leaves are larger and slightly coarser and darker than those of *T. occidentalis*, and have faint white marks beneath. Cones are about ½ in. long. They are less likely to be eaten by deer than *T. occidentalis* and seem better adapted to

Thuja plicata
GIANT ARBORVITAE

warmer areas. 'Zebrina' has foliage dotted with gold. Zones 4 to 7.

Tilia (*till*-ee-uh).
LINDEN.
BASSWOOD.
LIME TREE.
Linden Family (*Tiliaceae*).
Deciduous trees of the North Temperate Zone, Tilias have alternate, mostly heart-shaped, toothed leaves that are fairly symmetrical in their overall form. Their small, yellowish-white flowers occur in long-stalked, drooping clusters that are somewhat showy; they are attached to a thin oblong bract, a distinguishing feature. Bloom occurs after leaves appear, in early summer. Some species have very fragrant flowers. Their dry and hard fruits are the size of small peas. They need a rich, moist soil and cannot withstand prolonged drought. Propagate by seeds, cuttings and grafts.

T. americana (ah-mer-i-*kah*-nuh).
AMERICAN LINDEN.
BASSWOOD.
Grows 80 ft. tall and 50 ft. wide. Native to eastern N. Amer. Its leaves are large, to 8 in. long, a pale yellow in the autumn. The flowers are very fragrant. Seeds, bracts, and leaves are larger than most other species of linden. The stout, gray twigs have reddish buds. Zones 3 to 7.

T. cordata (kor-*day*-tuh).
LITTLELEAF LINDEN.
A shapely European tree of pyramidal form, 75 ft. tall and 50 ft. wide. Its dark green, shiny leaves, to 3 in. long, are pale beneath. Produces clusters of very fragrant flowers in early summer. Twigs, as well as the buds, are thin and brown; the seeds are small. Zones 3 to 7.

Tilia cordata
LITTLELEAF LINDEN

Tilia × europaea
COMMON LIME

T. × euchlora (yew-*cloh*-ruh).
CRIMEAN LINDEN.
Probably a hybrid of *T. cordata* and *T. dasystyla* (daisy-*sti*-lah). It grows to 70 ft. tall and 50 ft. wide. Its leaves, twigs, buds and seeds are larger than *T. cordata*. Dark green, glossy leaves, to 4 in. long, are pale beneath. Very fragrant yellowish flowers. Yellowish autumn color. 'Redmond' is more drought resistant than most lindens and is considered an improved plant. Zones 4 to 8.

T. × europaea (yew-*rope*-ee-uh).
COMMON LIME.
Similar to *T. cordata*, but faster growing and producing larger leaves. Probably a cross between *T. cordata* and *T. platyphyllos*. Zones 4 to 7.

T. petiolaris (pet-ee-oh-*lay*-ris).
WEEPING SILVER LINDEN.
This tree, from southeastern Eur., grows 60 to 80 ft. tall and about 50 ft. wide in a very symmetrical

shape. It has slender, drooping branches. This tree by no means weeps the way other pendulous trees do. The leaves are about 4 in. long, white beneath. Most parts of the tree are covered with whitish hairs. It has very fragrant flowers and yellow fall color. Zones 6 to 9.

Tsuga (*tsoo*-guh).
HEMLOCK.
Pine Family (*Pinaceae*).
This is not the poisonous hemlock, which is a white-flowering plant and not even closely related. Instead they are very graceful evergreens of the N. Hemisphere. Hemlocks have an informal, almost feathery appearance. Since they have shallow roots, they can be transplanted readily, and they all can be clipped to form hedges. They are pyramidal in form, have narrow leaves (needles), usually about ¾ in. long, that are dark green above with two white bands on the undersides, and small woody cones. They grow well where

there is plenty of moisture and do not thrive where the summers are dry and hot. They tolerate both sun and shade. Hemlocks can be divided into three groups—those that are native to eastern N. Amer., those native to western N. Amer. and the ones from Asia. The two best-known eastern species, *T. canadensis* and *T. caroliniana*, are the most likely to be used in landscaping. The western Amer. species, on the other hand, flourish in the high, moist areas of the Pacific Coast and do not grow well in the East. Several of the ones native to eastern Asia have been grown in the U.S. since the middle of the 19th century. In eastern N. Amer. gardens, all species seem to be very susceptible to attack by pests, including scale, aphids and spider mites. In many areas the infestations are severe enough to warrant avoidance of the plants. Hemlocks are propagated by seeds, grafting and cuttings.

T. canadensis (ka-na-*den*-sis).
CANADA HEMLOCK.
This is the hemlock that is grown most extensively in eastern N. Amer. areas, and is native from Nova Scotia to Alaska., west to Minnesota in areas with cool summers and moist, well-drained soils, very often on north-facing slopes. Unless such conditions are provided, the plants do not thrive. It grows to 70 ft. tall and 40 ft. wide. The leaves are about ½ in. long, and a series of upside-down leaves are found growing along the twigs. All foliage is borne essentially on a flat plane. The cones are ¾ in. long, barely open at maturity. It shears well to form evergreen hedges and is sometimes sheared to encourage more dense growth. There are many cultivars; perhaps the best known is 'Pendula' (pen-*dew*-luh). Called the Sargent hemlock, this weeping form in maturity is twice as broad as it is high. It is fast-growing. 'Bennett' is a dwarf, with slightly pendulous branches, to 4 ft. tall and 6 ft. wide.

Tsuga canadensis 'Pendula'
SARGENT HEMLOCK

'Albospica' (al-boss-*pi*-ka) is large growing, with foliage that is white when new. Zones 3 to 6.

T. caroliniana (ka-ro-lin-ee-*ay*-nuh).
CAROLINA HEMLOCK.
Native to the Smoky Mountains. Apparently, Carolina Hemlock is a bit more tolerant of heat and drought than Canada hemlocks. It grows to 50 ft. tall and 25 ft. wide. Its foliage is ¾ in. long and spreads all around the upper side of the twig. Cones, to 1½ in. long, open widely. Zones 5 to 7.

T. mertensiana (mer-ten-see-*ah*-nuh).
MOUNTAIN HEMLOCK.
Primarily useful only in its native range of the Pacific Northwest. The bluish-green leaves grow all around the branch, giving it a plump effect. Trees grow 50 to 90 ft. in the wild but less in the garden. 'Blue Star' is an attractive blue-foliaged tree that grows to 50 ft. tall. Zones 5 to 8 (but only regions with cool summers and in organically rich soil).

Ulmus

Ulmus (*ul*-mus).

ELM.

Elm Family (*Ulmaceae*).

These deciduous trees are native to the North Temperate Zone. They bear alternate, toothed leaves with short stalks and an uneven leaf base. Their inconspicuous flowers appear in insignificant clusters; most species bloom in very early spring, usually before the leaves. Fruits are small, flat nutlets with wings. Some species, most importantly the American Elm, are attacked by Dutch elm disease, which is first indicated by the yellowing of leaves. Twigs and branches soon die. The disease is spread by bark beetles and through naturally occurring root grafts. Most infected trees die and most treatment methods are only moderately successful. Propagate by seed, cuttings and grafts.

U. americana (a-mer-i-*kay*-nuh).

AMERICAN ELM.

The most extensively known of the elms, it is a favorite shade tree and once the primary street tree in the United States. The tree grows to 80 ft. tall and 60 ft. wide, with a distinctly beautiful vase-shape. Leaves are coarse, to 6 in. long, and turn golden-yellow in the fall. It flowers in early spring and wafer-like fruits ripen just as the leaves are emerging. It is tolerant of city conditions, poor drainage, light shade and sun, but is very susceptible to Dutch elm disease, which has killed most of the planted trees as well as the ones growing in their native habitat of eastern N. Amer. Many hybrids have been introduced with varying degrees of disease resistance. Their ultimate forms are yet to be determined. Zones 2 to 8.

U. campestris. See *U. procera*.

U. carpinifolia (kar-pin-ee-*foh*-lee-uh).

SMOOTH-LEAF ELM.

This native of Eur. and western Asia grows to 70 ft. tall and 30 ft. wide. Its leaves, 2 to 3 in. long, turn yellowish in the fall. A naturally narrow, fine-textured elm that is slightly resistant to Dutch elm disease. Zones 5 to 9.

Ulmus carpinifolia
SMOOTH-LEAF ELM

U. glabra (*glay*-bruh).

SCOTCH ELM.

WYCH ELM.

A native of Eur. and W. Asia. Growing to 80 ft. tall and 50 ft. wide., this tree has a wide-spreading habit. It is susceptible to Dutch Elm Disease. Zones 4 to 8. 'Camperdownii' (kam-per-*down*-ee-eye), Camperdown elm, has a rounded head and long, drooping branches.

U. parvifolia (par-vi-*foh*-lee-uh).

CHINESE ELM.

Native to China, Japan, and Korea. An open-headed, small tree with small leaves that turn reddish late in the fall. There are some evergreen forms that are not as hardy as the species. It grows to 50 ft. tall and 35 ft. wide with beautiful, exfoliating bark that becomes very mottled with age. Its flowers are very small, borne in late summer. Fruits ripen in the fall. It is resistant to Dutch elm disease, but in no way resembles the American Elm, so is not really a substitute. There is another elm sometimes sold as Chinese Elm. It is fast-growing and weak-wooded, in general a tree to avoid and is more correctly the Siberian elm, *U. pumila*. Zones 5 to 9.

U. procera (pro-*see*-ruh).
ENGLISH ELM.
A native of England and western Eur. It is a wide-spreading tree growing to 80 ft tall and 50 ft. wide. Form is very different than American Elm. Slightly resistant to Dutch elm disease. Shiny green leaves. Zones 6 to 9.

Vaccinium (vak-*sin*-ee-um).

BILBERRY.
BLUEBERRY.
CRANBERRY.
Heath Family (*Ericaceae*).
These deciduous or evergreen shrubs, mostly of the N. Hemisphere, are grown both for their decorative value and for the berries of several species and hybrids. They have alternate leaves, small, creamy-white or pinkish, urn-shaped flowers that are borne singly or in clusters, and many-seeded berries for fruits. Usually they have brilliant fall leaf coloring and bright reddish-brown bark and twigs. They grow best in a well-drained, acid, peaty soil, and they tolerate some shade. Propagate by seeds, cuttings, layers or division.

Vaccinium corymbosum
HIGHBUSH BLUEBERRY

V. corymbosum (kor-im-*boh*-sum).
HIGHBUSH BLUEBERRY.
A deciduous, bushy, American shrub, growing to 10 ft. high and wide, with leaves to 3 in. long. Its white or pinkish flowers, about ⅓ in. long, bloom in short clusters in late spring. Blue-black berries with a whitish wax coating follow. The leaves turn orange and scarlet in autumn. Winter bark and twigs are a warm reddish-brown. This is the best blueberry for landscape use, growing in shade or full sun. Fruiting is best in full sun. It is also the finest for edible berries. Cultivars are grown for specific timing of fruit and for larger fruits, although the largest berries do not necessarily have the finest flavor. The prime requirement for successful growing of the highbush blueberry is an acid soil and good drainage. Plant several cultivars to insure cross-fertilization. Many good ones are available, including early, midseason and late types. Birds are the chief pest as harvest time approaches and the berries show

color. Cloth nets or cages are the best means of insuring a crop. Zones 4 to 8.

✴✴ Viburnum (vye-*bur*-num).
Honeysuckle Family (*Caprifoliaceae*).
A large genus of deciduous and evergreen shrubs and small trees, native to the N. Hemisphere. The viburnums are among the most widely grown and most popular plants for both home landscaping and public planting. Their showy clusters of small flowers, mostly cream-colored, attractive fruit, some of which are edible, and good fall color make them attractive plants throughout the year.

Some viburnums have large snowball-like clusters. Some bear their flowers in flat clusters, and others have flat clusters of fertile flowers ringed with larger sterile flowers. Many are deliciously fragrant; however, several have a disagreeable odor. With careful selection it is possible to have viburnums blooming from late winter until summer. They also provide fall and winter interest since their fruits are popular with birds and they are attractive year-round. Viburnums are propagated by seeds, cuttings and grafts.

V. × bodnantense (bohd-nan-*ten*-see).
BODNANT VIBURNUM.
Hybrid of *V. farreri* (*far*-er-eye) and *V. grandiflorum* (gran-di-*floh*-rum). This viburnum is valued for its pink, very fragrant flowers which are produced in late winter. It grows to 12 ft. tall and 7 ft. wide, producing reddish leaves in the spring and again in autumn. 'Dawn' is the most commonly grown form, with large pink flowers. Fruits are usually not produced. Zones 6 to 9.

V. × burkwoodii (burk-*wood*-ee-eye).
A hybrid of *V. carlesii* and *V. utile* (*yew*-ti-lee), it grows to 10 ft. high and 8 ft. wide. It is partially

evergreen and has shiny green leaves during the summer that turn wine-red to orange in autumn. Pinkish white, very fragrant flowers bloom from early to mid-spring. Zones 5 to 8.

Viburnum × *burkwoodii*

V. × carlcephalum (karl-*sef*-uh-lum).
FRAGRANT SNOWBALL.
This deciduous hybrid, *V. carlesii* × *V. macrocephalum* (mac-roh-*cef*-a-lum), grows 8 ft. tall and wide. It has very large, white, fragrant, round flower heads. Flowers are pinkish in bud. Zones 5 to 8.

V. carlesii (kar-*lee*-see-eye).
KOREAN SPICE VIBURNUM.
Native of Korea. This is one of the old-fashioned favorites. Its very fragrant pinkish flowers bloom in early to mid-spring, just as the leaves appear. Its fruit is orange to blue-black in early summer, but is quickly eaten by birds and therefore has little landscape effect. To 8 ft. tall and wide.

'Compactum' grows to about 5 ft. high and wide. Zones 4 to 8.

Viburnum carlesii
KOREAN SPICE VIBURNUM

V. dentatum (den-*tay*-tum).
ARROWWOOD.
This native to the eastern U.S. grows to 8 ft. tall and 6 ft. wide. The white flowers appear in 3 in. clusters in late spring. Fruit is showy, dark blue, and the glossy, strongly toothed leaves turn red-dish-orange in autumn. Tolerates sun and shade, wet or dry soils. Zones 4 to 8.

V. dilatatum (dye-la-*tay*-tum).
LINDEN VIBURNUM.
A native of Japan. Growing to 8 ft. high and 6 ft. wide, this vase-shaped shrub tends to be open at the base. It is especially handsome in fall because of its profusion of red fruit and rust-red foliage. The flowers are white, in 5-in. clusters. All parts of the shrubs are quite hairy. 'Iroquois' is larger than the species in most features and is more showy. 'Xanthocarpum' (zan-thoh-*car*-pum) has yellow fruits. Zones 5 to 8.

V. × juddii (*jud*-ee-eye).
JUDD VIBURNUM.
This species is a product of crossing *V. carlesii* and *V. bitchiuense* (bitch-i-yew-*en*-see). The flowers are similar to *V. carlesii*—tubular, scented, with a pink blush—but they are not as strongly scented as

V. carlesii. The habit is taller than *V. carlesii* and it produces wine-red fall color. Full sun or shade in any well-drained soil. Zones 4 to 8.

✱**V. nudum** (*new*-dum).
SMOOTH WITHE-ROD.
Its shiny green leaves turn wine-red in autumn. The flowers are showy white, in late spring, after the leaves. Fruits ripen pink then turn blue and remain on the plant into winter. Zones 6 to 9.

Viburnum nudum 'Winterthur'
SMOOTH WITHE-ROD

V. opulus (*op*-yew-lus).
EUROPEAN CRANBERRY BUSH.
Native to Eur., N. Africa and northern Asia. It grows to 12 ft. tall and 8 ft. wide, producing flat clusters of white flowers with large marginal flowers, bright red fruit and orange fall foliage. Blooms after the leaves in late spring. Leaves are often disfigured due to aphid infestation. 'Compactum' (kom-*pak*-tum) grows 5 ft. high and 3 ft. wide and flowers and fruits like the species; 'Nanum' (*nay*-num), a dwarf form to 2 ft. high and 3 ft. wide, does not flower or fruit; 'Roseum' (roh-*zee*-um) produces white sterile flowers in round, snowball-like clusters; and 'Xanthocarpum' (zan-thoh-*kar*-pum) has yellow fruit. Zones 3 to 8.

Viburnum opulus 'Roseum'
EUROPEAN CRANBERRY BUSH

V. plicatum (pli-*kay*-tum).
JAPANESE SNOWBALL.
A deciduous shrub with sterile, round, white, snowball-like flower clusters in mid- to late spring. It reaches 12 ft. high and wide and is native to China and Japan. The form *tomentosum* (toh-men-*toh*-sum), doublefile viburnum, has showy clusters of fertile flowers ringed by sterile flowers and showy red fruits. 'Mariesii' (ma-*ree*-see-eye) has large clusters of fertile flowers ringed by sterile flowers. Fruit and fruit stalks are red and showy. 'Pink Beauty' and 'Roseum' (ro-*zee*-um) have petals that darken to an attractive pink. Zones 5 to 8.

V. prunifolium (prew-ni-*foh*-lee-um).
BLACK HAW.
This deciduous species can be grown as a small tree, for it reaches a height of 15 ft. and a spread of 12 ft. Native to eastern U.S. It has white flowers in flat clusters, shiny foliage that turns maroon-

red in the fall and blue-black fruit. Branches have small stiff twigs that are almost as prickly as thorns. Zones 3 to 8.

V. rhytidophyllum (rye-ti-doh-*fill*-um).
LEATHER-LEAF VIBURNUM.
This large evergreen shrub, native to China, grows to 12 ft. high and 9 ft. wide. The oblong, crinkled leaves are up to 7 in. long, with dense whitish or brownish hair underneath. Flowers are white, occuring in showy clusters in late spring. Zones 6 to 8.

✳**V. setigerum** (set-*tij*-er-um).
TEA VIBURNUM.
A deciduous, vase-shaped Chinese shrub that grows to 10 ft. tall and 6 ft. wide. It produces white, flat flower clusters and 5-in. pointed leaves. The fruit is orange-red, remaining showy well into winter, when it is eaten by birds. Zones 5 to 8.

Viburnum setigerum
TEA VIBURNUM

V. sieboldii (see-*bowl*-dee-eye).
SIEBOLD VIBURNUM.
This Japanese species could be considered a small tree and is often pruned as such. It usually reaches 15 to 20 ft. in height with a spread of 15 ft. Its leaves are bright green, wrinkled, bold, 5 in. long. In late spring, the creamy white flowers appear in 3- to 6-in. flat-headed clusters. In late summer, the fruits start to ripen, turning red first and then black. They last about two weeks and then fall, leaving behind red stems that give the plant an attractive red haze. The fruit will attract birds in great number and the plant can escape to natural areas and become a weed. Plant in full sun or shade; it tolerates poorly drained soil. Zones 5 to 8.

V. tinus (*tye*-nus).
LAURESTINUS VIBURNUM.
Evergreen shrub growing 10 ft. high and wide. Showy white or pinkish flowers in late winter or early spring. Zones 8 to 9.

V. tomentosum. See *V. plicatum.*

V. trilobum (try-*loh*-bum).
AMERICAN CRANBERRY BUSH.
Native to northern U.S. and southern Canada. This viburnum grows to 10 ft. high and 6 ft. wide, has bright red fruit that start to color in late summer, and fruits that are edible and are used in preserves. The flowers are white and showy, much like the flowers of *V. opulus.* These fruits taste better than those of *V. opulus.* Zones 2 to 7.

Vitex (*vye*-tex).
Verbena Family (*Verbenaceae*).
These are shrubs with opposite, palmately compound leaves and terminal clusters of flowers in late summer. Coarse-textured, they are chiefly valued for their late bloom. They require well-drained soil and full sun. In the North, stems are usually killed back in the winter, but new shoots come from the base to flower the same year. Propagate by seeds and cuttings.

Vitex agnus-castus
CHASTE TREE

V. agnus-castus (*ag*-nus-*kas*-tus).
CHASTE TREE.
A deciduous European shrub to 10 ft. tall and wide. It has long-stalked, dark green, aromatic, palmately compound leaves. Each leaflet grows to 4 in. long, gray beneath, with five to seven leaflets per leaf. Dense, showy, terminal clusters of small, lavender, fragrant flowers, to 7 in. long, bloom in late summer. Like *Buddleia*, this species may die back to the ground in severe winters. Even in areas where it is not set back in winter, it is best to cut back the stems to 12 in. from the ground. 'Alba' (*al*-buh) has white flowers. 'Rosea' (*roh*-zee-uh) has pink flowers. Zones 6 to 9.

Weigela (wye-*jee*-luh).
Honeysuckle Family (*Caprifoliaceae*).
Adaptable, deciduous flowering shrubs of Asia, with opposite leaves and clusters of showy flowers in late spring and early summer. Valued chiefly for the profuse, bright-colored flowers, since most lack outstanding foliage or showy fruits. Best in full sun with good drainage. Propagate by cuttings, seeds.

Weigela florida 'Variegata'

W. florida (*flor*-i-duh).
A wide-spreading shrub to 8 ft. tall and 10 ft. wide. Produces leaves to 4 in. long, and profuse rose-pink flowers 1 in. long. 'Foliis Purpuriis' (foh-lee-is pur-*pu*-ree-is) has purple leaves that turn green by late summer and purple flowers. 'Bristol Ruby' and 'Vanicekii' (va-ni-*see*-kee-eye) have bright red flowers and tend to produce a few flowers throughout the summer. 'Alba' (*al*-buh), 'Bristol Snowflake' and 'Candida' (can-*dee*-duh) have white flowers. 'Variegata' has leaves that are edged in white or yellow. Zones 5 to 8.

Zelkova (zel-*koh*-vuh).
Elm Family (*Ulmaceae*).
These deciduous trees of Asia have alternate, toothed leaves, inconspicuous flowers, and small, hard one-seeded fruits. They resemble elms and thrive under similar conditions. Propagate by seeds, cuttings or grafts.

Z. serrata (ser-*ray*-tuh).
JAPANESE ZELKOVA.
A round-topped tree growing to 75 ft. tall and 60 ft. wide. The main trunk typically divides at a fairly low height into several upright spreading stems to form a broad head. Early pruning to remove some of the upright, competing shoots results in better eventual form. Leaves grow to 4 in. long and are rough above. They turn yellow or rust-brown in the fall. The bark is attractive; it exfoliates and reveals an orangy-green inner bark. 'Village Green' is a rapidly growing selection. Zone 6.

Ziziphus (*zi*-zuh-fus).
Buckthorn Family (*Rhamnaceae*).
A small, deciduous tree that produces tasty fruits, which look like dates that can be eaten fresh or dried. Propagate by seeds or grafts.

Z. jujuba (joo-*joo*-bah).
JUJUBE.
CHINESE DATE.
Native to Asia. Produces brown fruits that are ½ in. to 1½ in. long. The leaves are shiny green, 2 in. long. Young stems are greenish, with paired thorns. Best fruit production is obtained with two or more trees. It grows to 20 ft. tall and 15 ft. wide. 'Li' has 2 in. long fruits. 'Lang' produces fruit at a young age, smaller than those of 'Li' but larger than those of the species. Zones 6 to 9.

UNDERSTANDING THE ZONE MAP

Gardening is an inexact science, but one unshakable truth is that plants grow, mature, bloom and produce seeds. The key to their success is location—the right plant in the right place will succeed. A plant provided with the right sunlight exposure in a setting where the native climate, moisture and soil conditions meet its needs, will flourish and largely take care of itself.

Climate comes first. The encyclopedic entries in the Hearst Garden Guides are zone-keyed to the United States Department of Agriculture Plant Hardiness Zone Map, which is reproduced on pages 194–195. The lower the number, the lower the winter minimum temperatures are in the zone. The zones identified in the entries describe the recommended range in which the plant will usually thrive. Thus, *Ilex opaca* (American holly), which is listed as zones 6 to 9, grows well in zones 6, 7, 8 and 9. North of zone 6 (zones 5 and lower), the winter low temperatures are too cold for it to survive. South of zone 9 (zone 10), the summers are too warm and the winters are not cold enough for it to succeed.

The boundaries of the zone map are oversimplifications, however; they are generalizations that ignore microclimates. For example, an L-shaped wall with a southern exposure or a windbreak to the north, can create pocket climates in which plants prove hardy north of their normal range. Conversely, an exposed or north-facing slope will jeopardize a plant that is marginally hardy in the region.

Plants have individual soil requirements as well as climate preferences. In fact, if the soil is ideal, a plant may stand up to adverse weather conditions. Most evergreens require well-drained, slightly acid soil. Evergreens can be grown in a region where soils are alkaline if the trouble is taken to create and maintain suitable soil conditions. But that plant won't really be in the right place, and it will demand higher maintenance and find the going tougher. Tender cacti and other succulents can be grown in the North—in the heated indoors in winter—and bog plants in the desert—if a bog is created for it. But the low-maintenance way to success is to select plants that thrive naturally in the region.

HARDINESS

Hardiness, commonly accepted as the ability of a plant to withstand low temperatures, should rather be considered a plant's ability to grow well in the presence of a complex variety of physical conditions, of which temperature may be only one factor. Other factors are high temperatures, drought and humidity (rainfall), altitude, soil characteristics, orientation and exposure (sun, shade, available light, prevailing winds), day length (latitude), air quality and ground drainage.

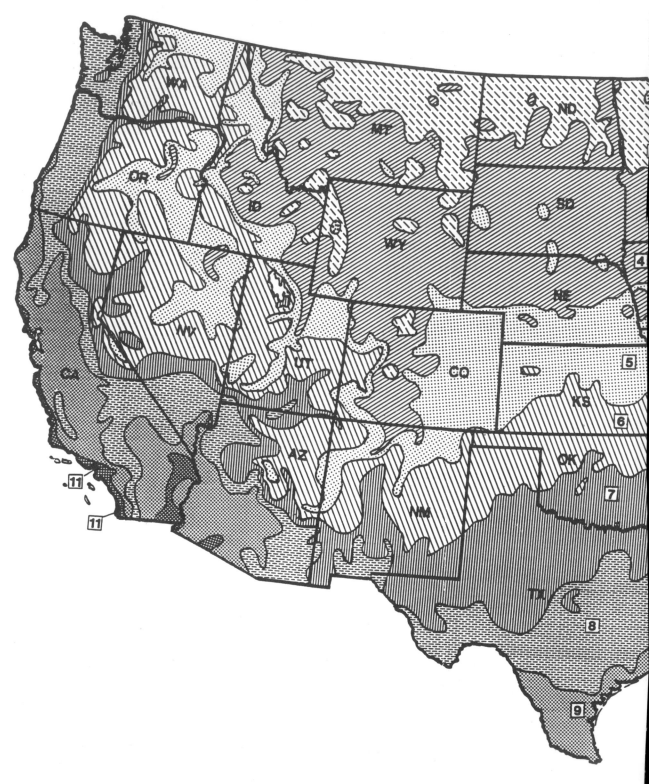

The zone map is reprinted courtesy of
the Agriculture Research Center, USDA.